Rainbows Among the Ruins

One man's epic journey.

By
Alexander Baron
(born Imre Balla)

INTRODUCTION

My Father, Alex, passed away less than one month prior to his 96th birthday.

During the last 2 years of his life, his health was starting to fail somewhat, but his mind and memory was as brilliant as ever.

As has become our custom during the last 2 decades, I was scheduled to visit him around his birthday on April 8 and in 1995 the ticket was set for an April 2nd arrival. Unfortunately I had to move the trip back to March when I was notified that after a night in the hospital, where he was having difficulties breathing, he passed away peacefully.

He was a great man, with an extremely brilliant mind. His character was hardened by the events of his life, his upbringing and his trial and tribulations while trying to stay alive and succeed as a professional.

He always remarked how life was a sequence of chance events, as during World War II, each time they stepped outside the door of their house, a decision to turn left or right, was frequently a life-or-death decision. He was fortunate, as each time he made that choice, he survived, while on many occasions people going in the other direction, turned a corner, some gun-shots were heard and they were never seen again.

As we say "Zichrono Le'Bracha" - May he rest in peace…

Robi, 2009

Alex would have celebrated his 100th Birthday this year.

FOREWORD

The motivation to write this book was a direct result of the interest expressed by my son Robi and my grandson Gil, who both wanted to learn about my eighty-six year's life, my background, upbringing and heritage.

That was the initial reason for recording the memories about my life during sixty years of professional activity, together with their overlaying agonies and ecstasies.

The second and more important reason was my personal commitment to pay off my moral debt, and erect symbolic memorials to two superhuman persons, to who I DEDICATED this book :

    my wife of 35 years – Evi (Picture 2) and
    my brother - Gyuri (Picture 3),

without whom I wouldn't have been able to accomplish the things I did.

Picture 1 - Alex arriving in India 1953

Picture 2 – Evi, Alex's wife of 35 years

Picture 3 – Gyuri, Alex's brother and mentor

TABLE OF CONTENTS

SECTION 1 - THE IMPACT OF WORLD WAR I 9

    CHILDHOOD - 1909 - 1919 9

    THE FORMATIVE YEARS - 1919 - 1927 35

    FORMAL EDUCATION - 1927 - 1932 50

SECTION 2 - THE RUMBLINGS OF WORLD WAR II 82

    JOB HUNTING UNDER PREJUDICE - 1932 - 1937 82

    FALLING IN LOVE - 1937 - 1938 118

SECTION 3 - WORLD WAR II 147

    THE GATHERING STORMCLOUDS - 1938 - 1940 147

    THE WORLD AS I KNEW IT DISAPPEARS - 1940 - 1945............... 167

SECTION 4 - FASCISM TO COMMUNISM 206

    HOPES OF RECOVERY AFTER THE WAR – 1945 - 1948................. 206

    RESCUERS TURN INTO SLAVE-MASTERS - 1948 - 1956 226

SECTION 5 – AFTER THE REVOLUTION 257

    ESCAPE FROM COMMUNISM - 1956 - 1957 257

    START LIFE ONCE AGAIN IN FREEDOM- 1957 - 1969................... 266

    NIGHTMARE ENDING TO HAPPINESS - 1969 - 1973 301

    CONTINUING LIFE ON MY OWN - 1973 – 1990 326

    GIVING UP MY LAST HOME - 1990 – 1995 341

EPILOGUE - 2007 346

SECTION 1 - THE IMPACT OF WORLD WAR I

CHILDHOOD - 1909 - 1919

I was born on April 8, 1909, in Budapest, Hungary; a late-comer (Picture 4): my brother was eight years older. My father was 42, my mother 33 years of age. I do not know very much about the previous life-story of my parents and of their families: these were subjects that were not discussed with children, mainly because of shyness and partly because in our middle and lower-middle class Jewish social strata people were rather reserved, taciturn, and laconic. What I know is rather a compilation of my memories of conversations, chats of family members that I overheard as a child.

I did not know personally the parents of my father, who lived somewhere in the north-east of Hungary, near the river Tisza, on the exclusively agricultural part of the country. My grandfather was a butcher, who must have lived the very simple and hard life of the surrounding working peasant population - and still abode by strict Jewish religious laws. The fact that he earned his living in an exclusively Hungarian peasant surrounding showed that he must had been born in Hungary and only his parents or grand-parents could had come from some other country, maybe Russia or Poland.

Up to about the middle of the 19-th century there was a small Jewish community in Hungary, settled mainly in the cities and engaged in commerce, finance, small trade, etc. activities. From then on up to the First World War, in the "golden age" of the Austro-Hungarian Monarchy, there was an official, and an accompanying social, emancipation for the Jews: they could participate in the arts, and scientific activities, they could enter universities, etc.; practically there were no , or very little restrictions as regards their life, except one important item: they could not own agricultural land, which was firmly in the hands of the aristocracy and the various classes of noblemen. It has to be stressed that all the official emancipation and removal of restrictions did not change the anti-Semitism of the people and the

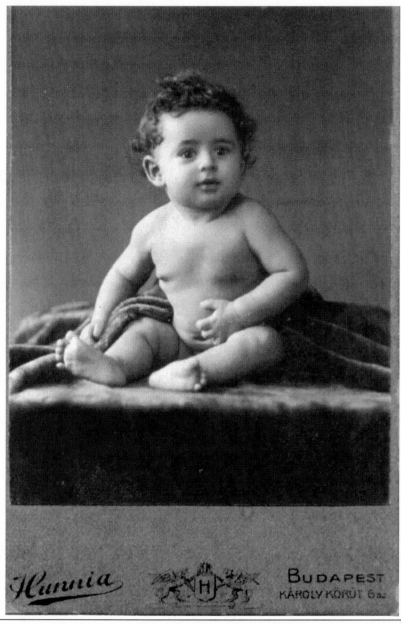

Picture 4 – Alex age 1

various church authorities: it remained in existence, only it became less aggressive and less pronounced. Optimists believed that with passing time it will entirely subside.

Anyway, during the "golden age" in Austro-Hungary, it was tolerable, especially in comparison with its level in Poland and Russia. Besides, there were no official restrictions on immigration. All these facts attracted an increasing number of Jews of Poland or Russia to make their escape from the official oppression and frequent pogroms of these countries to Austro-Hungary. Besides the very closeness of the place of refuge, there was one more quite important advantage in settling in Austro-Hungary, namely that the older, already settled Jews from decades or centuries back, did not behave inimically towards the Jewish immigrants; they did not feel more nationalistic Hungarians than the real Magyars, and they did not scorn the newcomers - as was the case, for instance, in Germany or England. One of these immigrants must have been the parents or grandparents of my grandfather.

Out of all my ancestors I have the most knowledge about my father. He was born on June 12, 1867, in Tiszanana. He told me about his life at those occasions when I was ill, in bed, and I asked him to tell me a story. He was, among other things, a very warm-hearted person, with a gift of style; so I learned from him a lot about his life-story.

So, for instance, at the age of 13, at his Bar-Mitzva, his father selected for him a Jewish grocer of good standing, somewhere in a country town and they made a contract, that my father will serve as an apprentice for five years and the boss will teach him the trade-know-how, besides allowing him to attend some school, mainly the Jewish cheder. It was not an easy way to learn a trade, but who had willpower and intelligence - succeeded. So did my father. After having finished the apprenticeship, he went to work to other grocery stores, in bigger cities, and after a while he joined the army. What I do not know: whether this was in consequence of compulsory conscription or voluntary enlisting. Anyway, he spent long years in the army, participated in the occupation of Bosnia, and reached the highest possible rank achievable for a person with no high-school matriculation: sergeant-major, a non-commissioned officer. Most probably this was due partly to his very good knowledge of the Hungarian and German language; he wrote with perfect spelling, calligraphy, and had a good style.

He married my mother in 1896, in Eger. The family name of my grandfather and my father was Lehrfeld; my father changed this name to a real Hungarian family name: Balla, with his first name: Marton. My father had a brother, a few years his junior: Lehrfeld Emil. Since I remember him, he and his family: wife and three daughters lived in Budapest; they were one of the quite few close family members with whom we had regular, although not too frequent contacts: visiting each other once or twice a year, on Sunday afternoons. My father and his brother were very affectionate to each other and Uncle Emil came very frequently to visit us, at least once every second week. He could do this because he was some supervisor at the Hungarian State Railway and in this capacity he had to visit each railway station from time to time, and thus he could come during weekdays. Besides personal and family matters, they always discussed religious problems. Every year, before the High-Holidays (Rosh Hashana and Yom Kippur), they traveled to visit the graves of their father and mother. These travels were big undertakings: they planned them carefully; starting by train, and then changing them at least once, then a certain station they had to hire a horse-drawn cart to take them to the cemetery of the small village of Tiszanana where their parents lived and were buried.

That to make a journey from the capital to a small village, not more than some 130-150 km away, to spend there about one hour, and to return back again, should take two days, including one night accommodation at a roadside country tavern: says a lot about life in Eastern-Europe in the first two-three decades of the twentieth century. But there should be no mistake: for the journey described, this was the only possibility. There was no other public transport facility. Rich people at the provinces had horse-drawn carriages, but the few automobiles in existence were at the disposal of a few very high-ranking officials only, and they could not be used on dirt roads, with knee-deep dust, mud, or snow-ice, as the seasons changed.

I remember to have known personally the father of my mother: he lived in Eger, one of the bigger provincial towns at the north-eastern part of Hungary, at the foot of the Matra Mountains. Eger is a beautiful town, with a quite long history, founded sometime in the 12-th century, at a then important strategic cross-point. During centuries (XV-XVII) of Turkish occupation Eger was one of the central points of their empire, proven by a big number of interesting and marvelous historical monuments: a fortress with strong walls, minarets, bath-houses, water carriers, etc. still in existence.

My grandfather had four daughters from his first marriage: my mother was the youngest of them. She was very young when her mother died, and after some time her father remarried. Unfortunately for the sisters, the step-mother was even more wicked than they are depicted in nursery tales; as I heard many times when my aunts and my mother recalled their sorrowful years of their girlhood. As it was understandable, my mother, the youngest of the four sisters, had the worst lot. Their family name was Czeisler, my mother's first name Charlotte. Her father had a big shoe-store on the main square.

The sisters were married strictly according to their age: first the oldest: Bertha. After marriage they moved to a village in the north, near to the Tatra Mountains, by the name of Rimaszombat, a region which after the First World War became part of Czechoslovakia. The next was Aunt Terry, who, with her husband who was a tailor, settled down in the same town Eger. The third sister, aunt Peppy, married a prosperous grocer and they moved to Budapest, the capital of Hungary, and opened a grocery store.

My mother married my father in 1896, in Eger, and they opened a grocery store there (Picture 7). My brother, Gyula (Julius in Latin), whom everybody called Gyuri, was born in May 27,

Picture 7 – Alex's parents in later years

1901. A few years afterwards, sometime in 1903-1905, they moved to Budapest, what they thought a big, but necessary step in order to be able to provide their son the best possibility for advancing on the social level, to get the best education, even university and get a diploma as a doctor, lawyer, etc.

They got encouragement for taking this step by their brother-in-law who had made such a move a few years earlier and had a grocery store in Budapest, in the IX-th, one of the industrial districts of the capital. Their store was on the main thoroughfare to the south. Along this and one or two parallel roads a big number of factories were located, refineries, workshops, slaughter-houses, etc. There was an electric city tramway line leading into the center of the city, and an electric district tramway line to the southern neighboring towns and villages. Dwelling houses were, almost without exception, along the cross-connecting streets.

These were generally big, oppressive two- or three-story houses, all around big rectangular plots, surrounding an inner courtyard, with one long front-side along the street, and the other three sides facing only the inner courtyard. Entrances to the tenements were only from the courtyard-side, through open corridors. The tenements were intended, without exception, for leasing, and most of them were one-room tenements, consisting one kitchen and one room nothing else. At one corner at each floor there were a number of toilet-cubicles, each one to be shared by two-three tenants. These were the dwelling places of the workers, employed in the factories of the vicinity. For a small percentage of the workers, having bigger families and higher incomes, there were two-room flats, prepared simply by connecting two adjacent one-room flats and converting one of the kitchens to an additional third room. The kitchens were equipped with wood- or coal-fired cooking fireplaces; lighting was made by kerosene lamps; the only central supply was water: one facet and sink in the kitchen. Cubicles with a door, one in the attic and one in the cellar belonged to each tenement.

A janitor cared for the cleanliness and order in each house; he collected monthly the rent from each tenant. Every house had a strong street-door that was locked from 10 pm till 5 am, and everybody who wanted to enter or leave during the night-time, had to ring for the janitor and pay a certain entrance-fee.

My parents moved in and opened a grocery store in one of such a big house, at a corner of a bigger southward leading road and a cross street. In this big building there was a spacious tavern (pub) with a lot of tables; a butcher; a hairdresser; and our grocery store. I do not know whether the premises of our store were earlier used for the same purpose; anyway the floor space of the store was quite big, at least 12-13 m by 7-8 m, with two entrances and two windows to the street, plus two big store rooms. Alongside the store was our flat, composed of two one-room units connected together, making up to one kitchen and three rooms; a connecting door between the flat and the store, so that the store could be opened and closed from the inside.

The store was at a distance of approximately 1 km from the store of my uncle. Still there was a substantial difference between the two stores: his store was on the main thoroughfare, thus one part of the clientele was casual, whereas the clientele of my parents were steady, composed almost solely from the tenants of the neighborhood.

Five such big tenement houses were along the street, but only at its opposite end were a few shops: a writing-material and school-supplies shop, one shoe-repair- and one tailor's-repair shop. Not too far away there was a pharmacy, and a little more distance away: a small post-office, and a cinema.

And in the post-office there was a public telephone apparatus. A wooden box, roughly twice the size of a shoe-box, was fixed on the wall, the middle of it at a height of a grown-up person. On the front side of this box there was a conical mouth-piece, a microphone that could be adjusted up and down to a small angle. On the left side of the box there was a hook, holding the receiver: a mushroom-like wooden piece. At the lower right side of the box there was a small crank-arm. Now: if you wanted to call somebody: you had to remove the speaker and rotate a few times the crank-arm - and wait. After a while a voice asked you what number you want to be connected to. You told the number and after a while you could hear a ringing sound and if you were lucky: it was the correct number. But more often than not, you got a wrong connection - but you had to pay for one call anyway. After an unsuccessful connection: you had to repeat the whole process again.

Such a call could be made only within the city's boundaries: interurban calls could be made only at the General Post Office. The pharmacy was for me a very solemn place. Men when entered took off their hat; everybody spoke softly and waited silently until spoken to. Prescription was obligatory for almost everything. Practically there were no ready-made or pre-packed medicaments, everything had to be mixed, prepared, and packed into small paper bags or glass jars, bottles, etc. In very urgent cases such preparations took a few hours; generally half-a-day or a full day was needed. In order to avoid the bitter or unpleasant taste of the medicaments in powder form, very thin wafer squares were used, approximately 3 cm by 3 cm, which had to be dipped in water, put on the palm of the left hand, the powder strewn in the middle, wrapped into the flimsy wafer, and swallowed with some water.

The cinema was a very simple rectangular building, more a shack; a corridor along the long axis, the simplest wooden benches on both sides, and a few chairs at the back. Piano music accompanied the picture, and the projection machine was operated by carbon-arc light that sparkled quite often. My parent's store carried the conventional spices, tea, coffee, sugar, flour, candy, bread, butter, milk, etc, cleaning materials, fuel wood and coal, etc. - but no vegetables. In one of the store rooms there was a big ice-chest, to be filled every day with blocks of ice.

One of the peculiarities of those times was that a small percentage of grocery stores were officially authorized to serve to its customers alcoholic beverages, poured out in small cups, to be consumed inside the store and solely in standing position, that is no tables and chairs were permitted in the store. My father had such a permit and some 10-12 sorts of hard liquors were carried, e.g. rum, several brands of fruit-brandy: apricot, plum, etc.

They had one-two skilled employees plus one delivery-man; besides both my father and mother worked full time in the store, which was open from about 6 am till about 9 pm, six days a week, plus until 12 am on Sundays. They worked very hard, with very little time left for entertainment - not to speak about vacation. One household help and one nurse-maid were employed.

My parents must have been doing passably well, although they could not get much pleasure, because they had to attend the store, there was no let-up, especially not for the two of them together. The maximum what they could afford was that my mother went once a year on a one-two week vacation, generally visiting one of her two sisters who lived in the provinces.

Their life was quite typical and characteristic of their fellow small shop owner Jews then and there. They worked hard to raise a family with the main ambition to give their children the possibility to the highest level of education, to become doctors, lawyers, artists, etc. Generally they had little interest and even less time for entertainment: most of them worked a lifetime without even once having a vacation for a few weeks. Most of them were religious, although not orthodox: had kosher household, kept the holidays, except the Shabbat, the Saturdays, when they had to work because this was the busiest day in the shop. They lived a very limited social life: mainly close family members visited each other, the frequency depending on the distance: an out-of-town visit was a big event made once or twice a year. They went to theaters at special occasions: they brought their children to a circus performance or to amusement parks once or twice a year.

My own earliest recollections are connected with the store, mainly on Sunday afternoons, when it was closed and I could play there; pulling open the many drawers containing funny smelling spices, etc. Next I remember well the big grandfather-clock in my parent's bedroom, striking every half-hour. Likewise I remember well when our district - and so our home - was connected to the expanding central gas supply system and when for the first time the brilliant white light of the gas-lamp was lighted on: it must have been sometime in 1913-1914.

But my most vivid memory goes back to the outbreak of the First World War (Picture 8). In July, 1914, my mother, for the first time in her life, went for a well-deserved vacation to a sea-side resort on the Adriatic Sea: Lovrana, and took along one of her cousins and my brother, who was then 13 years old. During their stay there war threats between Austro-Hungary and Serbia became stronger from day to day, and so they decided to return home. After long waiting and fighting at the railway station they succeeded to climb on a carriage, standing on the corridor, pressed together like sardines. As it turned out theirs was the last train that got through before the actual shooting started. What I remember well is their arrival, after more than two days travel: we were waiting at the railway station but I could not recognize my mother, only after she changed clothes after arriving home.

Then World War One broke out and life became more and more difficult, for almost everybody, but the problems to our family became really serious. One after another, almost all goods, but especially foodstuffs, were put on rations; thus running a grocery store became very complicated: ration-cards had to be collected and handed in to the proper authorities. Allocations of supplies had to be obtained by bureaucratic fighting, etc. And then, sometime in 1915, our father was called up, and it became obvious that our mother alone could not manage the store. It must had been a very difficult and painful decision, but the only solution was that my brother switched his regular school attendance to an external status, and so he could stay home and help our mother to run the store - and in addition to learn, do his homework and enter at the end of each school-year for an examination.

I remember quite a number of things he did in the store, and when, after 10 or 20 years I recalled those actions of him, I realized fully how original, resourceful, and brilliant were his

Picture 8 – Alex age 6

actions, especially as regards organization and planning. Needless to say that he did not know anything about planning as a scientific management tool, that was still almost non-existent at that time, and I could not have understand it anyway. But I very vividly remember what everybody: my uncle who had the same problems, my mother, our employees, and all our clients told each-other about the brilliant performance my brother accomplished in those difficult times: how he organized work to be done at home and at the offices with which we were connected to in the cyclical steps of carrying out the rationing process. In retrospect I am deeply convinced that a fair number of organizational and planning steps my brother performed were deposited in certain cells of my brain, that were tuned to them by inbred talent, and thus my brother, through his talent was the initiator of my interest for and accomplishments in using them in my later work.

In the fall of 1915 I entered elementary school that was housed in a big brownstone building, not far away from home. I remember well my teacher (Uncle Kuthy) who stayed with the class till the end of the four year school period. During those four war years we had long intermissions each winter, because of fuel shortages (Picture 9).

Needless to say that as a boy of 6 to 9 years of age, I did not know at that time what I was missing because of that war situation; I rather felt - and that I remember well - that our family had a very difficult life and we were helplessly subjected to unknown forces and people - and I hated this. This feeling started during those war years, and stayed with me all along.

Although my family had very limited social contacts and these only with the closest family members, due mainly to lack of free time, I as a child had a lot of free time at hand and it was quite natural that I was allowed to go out and play with the children of the neighborhood. There was plenty of empty area around, empty building lots, etc, where we could play. All the children, except me and one or two other boys were the children of the neighborhood's working class people. Without knowing about social classes and

Picture 9 – Alex age 8

differences, still I could feel that somehow I did not really belong to the group: I wore slightly different clothes, I followed the warnings of my parents, I never played the bully, etc. Once, when playing we came to blows, and when I complained to my father about it, he told me that if I take part in the group's play, I should care for myself, he will not interfere on my behalf: I should judge what is correct to do and should not let me drag myself into situations I do not like and could not handle myself.

Already during this childhood period I behaved a little-bit different from the other children of my age and company. But I want to stress now that in retrospect I see clearly that this difference was not because I was the only Jewish boy among all the Christian boys; a fact that all of us knew, but I cannot recall one single case when this religious difference was even mentioned, in spite of the fact that my own and the whole family's Jewish religion was not concealed, for instance on the High Holidays our shop was closed.

Still, besides the religious difference, there were other aspects that unconsciously made me feel distinct from the other boys. One of them was my very early interest or affection first to children periodicals and later to books. The biggest present I could imagine was a book, any book, even those that I still could not understand. Most probably I was influenced by my brother's affection to books. But besides such influence, I must have had my own inborn interest, love, and affection to literature and its physical manifestation: books.

Such, and similar other, differences or distinctions grow during my age of 6-12 years, that later I could only define as elitist. I can recall a very characteristic remembrance related to my affection to books. One of the basic goods in short supply during the war was tobacco, and ready-made cigarettes. One premium item on the black market was cut tobacco. Cylindrical cigarette-papers were also available on the black market, together with a filling device to fill tobacco into the cylindrical paper tubes.

Now, two or three relatives of our family happily farmed out the tedious chore to fill hundreds of cigarettes, and were ready to pay for the work. We made a deal, beneficial for both parties: for filling a few hundred cigarettes I received a payment: a book. My preferences were: Jules Verne, Fenimore Cooper, Carl May, etc, and Hungarian authors.

Since within a few months after the outbreak of the war almost all able-bodied men were called up, more and more women had to start working instead of the men, in factories, offices, etc. And in general, mainly in the cities, life suddenly became more dynamic, for instance I remember seeing more and more automobiles and trucks running, of course, almost all of them military. They were extremely simple in design, for instance, trucks had steel wheels with solid, hard rubber liners around them; the very simple differential gearing was somewhere at the middle of the truck and the two half-shafts had spur-wheels for chains to drive the rear wheels. The two front lamps were acetylene fueled: I remember well the flickering bluish-white lights and the smell of them.

In our close family there were five military-age young men: all of them were called up; three were discharged after two-three years, with deadly disabilities, who died shortly afterwards. Slowly the cities and the country were full of disabled soldiers, and slowly simple people started, first thinking, then questioning: what are we doing in this war and why.

Soldiers coming home, either as wounded or to short leave, spoke about the heavy shortages in supplies at the fronts, almost in everything: weapon, ammunition, clothing, food, etc. Nobody could understand the static war: many hundreds of kilometers long trenches on three fronts, that were moved front and back a few kilometers by hundreds of thousands of soldiers-lives sacrifices, and in the meantime another hundreds of thousands soldiers died in the trenches by bombardments, gas-attacks, and simply by standing and living in cold mud for years. Simple people at home asked among themselves such simple questions as: why all the war and the killing - and they could not find the answer. I remember hearing their bitter questions, feeling their hopelessness, and seeing their -mainly the women's - sad eyes.

And I remember one more item of silent but very disturbing talk about people who looted fortunes by supplying faulty, unsatisfactory materials to the army, or profiteering by other means on the war. Needless to say that as a child I could not understand what was going on around us, but what I felt was a general, disquieting, and frightening insecurity.

Then came October-November 1918: revolutions on all fronts of the Central Powers: Germany, Austro-Hungary. What I remember: marching huge groups of soldiers, with flags, shouting and firing in the air; day and night. The already reduced supply of foodstuffs and other commodities were completely disturbed. Some foodstuffs were brought from the provinces by the peasants - but not for money, only on the basis of bartering, for clothes, furniture, tools, jewels, etc. I remember clearly hearing from people that "we now eat our winter-coat!".

What went on the political life in Budapest: I do not remember, I could not have understood as a child. What I remember having heard that some politicians were assassinated because they were charged bringing the country into the war. We, the children of our neighborhood had some fun during the early days of the October revolution. An arsenal in our district was broken open and weapons and munitions taken. Still much material was left behind and so we also could get a few packages of gunpowder. At one evening we spread it on a zigzag line in an open plot, struck a match and threw it to one end, it was quite a spectacle!

The revolution had a direct bearing on our private life too. Business was almost non-existent: there were no supplies. Our house-maid left us and went back to her village. And then came a terrible epidemic, called the "Spanish Influenza". My father, mother, and I were struck down at the same time, only my brother remained healthy. All of us had very high fever; doctors were overloaded and could visit only occasionally; the only medicament was Pyramidon. I remember very vividly that three of us were in bed, with very high fever, and my brother, almost without sleep, tended all of us for almost a whole week, doing everything necessary - single-handedly. I felt then how much better "doctor" he was than our visiting doctor.

A few months after that one of my cousins, who served in the Navy, came home and stayed with us for a few weeks. He was a plumber by profession, and he installed for us a bath-room: a big step for us then and there, some relative delight in the general gloom.

The upheaval continued, life was extremely difficult supplies of everyday-life's necessities were very scarce, most of the factories were idle and people had no money. By the end of October the Austro-Hungarian Monarchy was dissolved, the king made to resign, and a Republic was declared. Governments changed a few times, until sometime in March-April, 1919 when a communist regime took power in Hungary. It seemed for a short time, at least in the capital, that life will start again: a few factories started to work, public transport was partly restored, etc, but at the countryside there was much fighting, and thus, sometime in September the same year the communist regime was overthrown by an extremely reactionary regime, led by an officer who was the last admiral of the Austro-Hungarian Navy: Horthy, who paraded and entered Budapest on a white horse. But the actual leading forces were those people whose power and existence was endangered by a communist regime: the aristocracy, the noblemen, high-ranking officers, civil servants, politicians, etc. - encouraged and supported, overtly and covertly, by the various religious authorities.

It is understandable that during this revolutionary period contacts among our family members had been increased and even enlarged: all of us had been anxious to exchange information frequently. We met almost every second evening with my uncle's family, that was enlarged by marriages of one daughter and one son: the son-in-law was an insurance broker, the son a bank clerk, and the daughter-in-law a nurse in a sanitarium, thus they were able to collect news and information from the entire city, in contrast with our very limited possibility in our close neighborhood. And although I was only a child of 10, I was always present at those nightly meetings. Another boy of my age living in a country not affected by war and revolution would not understand situations and happenings to which we had been exposed, but because of our circumstances, children of my age in Hungary were mature much earlier, thus eventhough I could not understand the full meanings and consequences of the turbulent events less than the grown-up members of my family - nevertheless I perceived somehow the actual, real, plain causes and effects of the fights, on a "good-guy" - "bad-guy" basis.

I do not remember when and how the new government was formed after the communist regime, because that had no direct bearing on our daily life, but we found quite strange - together with everybody else - that Hungary was declared a kingdom, without a king, but reigned by Miklos Horthy as a regent. It seems worthwhile to mention here a small event that happened some ten years later, at the end of the twenties, for characterizing Horthy's regency, dictatorial behavior and his acting out of being offended by the events around him.

Budapest had been famous for its very high level theatrical life and performances, plus for its special witty cabarets. Sometime at the end of the twenties, one of the most famous comic actors told his audience the following story: (My rough translation:)

Once we had an open sea,
And we had on it a man.
The sea was lost,
But stayed on the man.
He mounted a white horse,
And climbed up the throne:
And since then he does not want
To come down from the throne.

The actor was thrown in prison the next day and when he was released much later, he had to emigrate and stay abroad for a long time.

What I remember clearly are the many details of the terrible, wanton killings and tortures of Jews by the terror groups that under the banner of fighting communism, carried out unprecedented terror campaigns, worse than the Polish or Russian pogroms. These terrorist groups blamed the Jews for everything that befall on Hungary during and after the war. Nobody cared that their propaganda accused the Jews for being communists in one sentence and condemn them for profiteering fortunes on defective war supplies in the next. Terror brigades roamed the country, took the properties of wealthy Jews, who then disappeared together with many intellectuals, without a trace and - of course - without the slightest semblance of official investigation. These terrorist were searching for well-to-do Jews for the double purpose to rob them of their possessions and brutally kill them. There were a number of such terrorist groups that rushed mainly to summer resorts, villas, wealthy neighborhoods, with ready lists of Jews. They struck at nights, first took everything valuable, and tortured mainly women to disclose hidden treasures, using indescribably brutal methods; and then indulged in their revenge - they killed all the people: men, women, and children. One of the most infamous location was the forest of Orgovany, where one night 300 Jews were hanged. One of these terror groups had their Headquarter in a big hotel in Budapest, the Britannia, where tortures and executions were carried out, and from where Jews, caught in the city and after brutal tortures, were led to the river Danube and with a stone on their neck were thrown into their death.

A number of Jews succeeded to escape by going abroad or went into hiding at remote places by paying large sums to farmers. Based on many information, reached not only us but during a few weeks exchanged by many other people, it became clear beyond any doubt what the reasons and motives were for this sudden organized and unprecedented brutal, bestial anti-Semitic terror campaign, premeditated and continual, as compared with the Polish and Russian spontaneous and sporadic pogroms.

Within a few weeks the following picture became clear, not only in Jewish circles, but for a large portion of the society who were not, or at least not completely indoctrinated by the blind hatred of this novel type anti-Semitism.

The aristocracy and noblemen owned in the 19-th century more than 90 % of the land in Hungary. However, a considerable portion of them squandered away their wealth and the ownership of their land by overspending, big gambling in casinos in Europe, by lack of any sort of knowledge in agriculture, commerce, finance, industry, etc.; they even despised every sort of profession or skill. As they were losing their wealth and got into debts, they claimed - and got - government- and municipal-jobs, swelling excessively the number of public servants and increased bureaucracy.

Since Hungary was on the losing side of the war big portions of the country and land were transferred to the successor states, these declassified, propertiless and penniless public servants took the flight to the diminished Hungary, increasing thereby even more the number of redundant public servants.

During the last few decades they felt themselves more and more endangered by their loss of property, wealth, declining living standard, etc, and for all their self-inflicted troubles they blamed the Jews, one portion of them, with no connection whatsoever to the economic troubles of those noblemen, but as a consequence of the slightly liberal atmosphere of the previous decades, had become active and successful in commerce, finance, science, etc. The fact that the Jews could not own land and therefore the loss of land-ownership of the noblemen was caused by their own lack of knowledge and other reasons, exemplified above, but not by the Jews: have had not too much effect on their opinion. Due to their ingrained anti-Semitism, they blamed the Jews for their own failures.

And when during the short-lived communist regime after the

war in 1919, their fear from further decline and eventual complete loss of their still remained wealth was even strengthened on the one hand, and since unfortunately a certain number of Jews were among the communist leaders: they even more blamed the Jews, en block, for their loss of wealth and power.

These were the combined reasons for their hope and resolution that after overthrowing the communist regime, the time was ripe for an organized and concentrated attack against the Jews for regaining their previous wealth and power. Needless to say that the church authorities, who earlier benefited from wealth and power of those aristocracy and noblemen, were more than eager to allay with those reactionary activities and forces.

As it is evident from the above described development in the previous few decades, in 1919 there was a large reservoir in Hungary of people who lost, fully or in part, their holdings, money, and power, at all strata of their society. It was common knowledge that the higher-level aristocracy only organized, sponsored, and recruited the lower strata of impoverished previous "noblemen", enlarged by the scum of society: soldiers who were jailed during the war broke out at the revolution, small clerks in government municipality jobs who failed even there and were thrown out, and the like. These people were organized, provided with arms and vehicles, and guaranteed them undisturbed reign for their terror actions: and thus they bestially indulged in taking vengeance on the Jews for everything they were unable to attain in their life.

As we felt it at that time, together with those non-Jews who did not let themselves deceived by the virulent anti-Semitism, the ferocity, intensity, and extent of their organized, resolute, and deceitful terror campaign, after a few centuries of slow emancipation, was unprecedented, compared even with pogroms elsewhere.

During all these mortally grave persecutions we perceived one noteworthy consoling occurrence, corresponding to the experiences of all other Jewish shopkeepers in industrial worker's neighborhoods, everywhere in Budapest and in the bigger cities of

Hungary. It was a long established practice that in such neighborhoods the steady customers made their daily purchases on credit and they paid the accumulated debt once-a-week, when they received their weekly wage. Every steady customer had an account-sheet in a book, the sum-price of each purchase was entered in the book and the accumulated weekly debt had to be paid. This practice worked very well; I do not remember a single dispute or accusation of over-charging during all the long years of my father's activity. The only problem that happened sometimes was for my father. When somebody lost his job and could not pay his debt in time, my father not only prolonged the date of payment, but gave the family what they needed as usual. I remember my father's difficulty in his inner struggle before he decided to stop further credit until some arrangement could be found.

This correct atmosphere was not influenced and changed, and not one single anti-Semitic remark or accusation was made even during the most furious anti-Semitic terror campaign. It seems to me in retrospect that those proletariat of WWI generation were not anti-Semitic, neither on social, nor on nationalistic or religious basis. The anti-Semitism of that period was dominated mainly by religious indoctrination, but church and industrial proletariat have not had too much affection to each other; for instance I cannot remember one single church in our neighborhood.

Although its form and methods slowly changed during the coming years, with the basic intention remaining, Hungary holds the ignominious role of being the first country in the world that devised and established that barbaric, bestial, modern type anti-Semitism, far preceding its Nazi and Fascist followers.

We were shocked and frightened by these terrorist pogroms against the Jews. My parent's generation who was born in Hungary had not experienced pogroms, nor militant physical atrocities against them, although they knew well the long history of Jewish persecutions and were well aware of the pogroms in Poland and Russia just before and during WW1. But they still felt that somehow that terror would only be a temporary misfortune that will be over and our very existence will not be endangered. One of the reasons of our belief was the fact that almost exclusively rich Jews were hunted down, plus Jewish intellectuals who somehow participated in the short-lived communist regime. Another encouraging sign that set us slightly at rest was that in our neighborhood, where our Jewishness was not a secret: not once, not even the slightest anti-Semitic remark, not to speak about incident, occurred during all that period.

Out of the very many news and rumors that reached us and were discussed, and from which we tried to draw some explanation and conclusion, the most puzzling one was that the existence, the activities, and atrocities were not only not concealed, but were disseminated. There was even a periodical with the title: "What should happen with the Jews?".

The irony of the situation, that would us make laugh were our plight not so grim as it had been, was what everybody knew, based on quite a number of examples, that the safest place for a Jew or for somebody who had been charged with some minor complicity in the communist regime, was a police detention or even an imprisonment. Namely, public administration, such as municipality activities, public transport, police, etc, were generally not affected by the revolution and pogroms; they functioned on the traditional fashion, maintaining discipline and long established bureaucratic order.

Although our close family was not physically affected by the terror campaign still my brother, and together with him the entire family, suffered such severe blow, from which he could never again recover. He got his matriculation in the summer of 1919 and wanted dearly to become a physician. In the fall of 1919, right at the beginning of the reactionary Horthy regime, no single Jew was accepted in anyone of the universities. My brother tried to overcome this obstacle, first by visiting lectures, hoping that after some time he will be accepted as a student, but he was thrown out. It was an almost everyday occurrence that already higher semester Jewish students were subjected to a gauntlet run by the other students standing on both sides of the stairway in the university building and mercilessly beating the descending few Jewish students.

These Jewish students established their association, officially for fighting legally for their rights, and actually organizing defense groups to fight back the aggressive anti-Semites. My brother was a member of this association, and they succeeded to stop the brutal Jew-beatings. They developed and equipped themselves with a simple, but effective hand-weapon: a heavy-wire steel spring, with the diameter of a finger, some 40-50 cm long, similar to an expander-spring, and a cylindrical lead block of some 2 cm in diameter and 6-8 cm long cast on both ends of the spring, and the whole stick-like weapon covered with a thin leather slip. It was an improved version of a truncheon. Disguised in the arm of the jacket, the Jewish student group gathered on the top of the staircase and then swiftly descending they swung the springy lead clubs against their waiting "Jew-beaters". After a few broken arms and heads - they got the message and the Jew-beating first changed to brawls, and then slowly stopped. Police was never involved because universities were out-of-bound for the police.

Unfortunately, all the defensive fighting did not help my brother in his ardent aspiration to become a physician; he tried to enroll in the university in Vienna Austria, but he was rejected. A Jew from Hungary at that time was considered unacceptable and suspicious: as an alien, a Jew who was probably a communist, etc. He returned from Vienna, very down-hearted, and slowly he had to give up his aspiration first as he thought only temporarily - and had to look after some occupation for earning a living.

I have no recollection of the details how the Horthy regime had built up its government machinery, how and what sort of political parties had been established, etc, generally how the country's life had been attempted to get normalized. But I remember well and could never forget, together with everybody else of my generation, the creeping monetary inflation and its effects on our everyday life. Since everything was in short scarce supply: foodstuff, clothing, fuel, etc.; money started to lose its value and inflation increased at such pace that, for instance, one loaf of bread, that had a certain price one day - became twice as expensive the next day. Salaries and wages became valueless within a short period, and for trying to keep abreast with spiraling prices, the paper money was upgraded, by stamping periodically multiple values on it, e.g.: a 1 unit paper bill was stamped after a few days as a 10 unit value, then 100, 1000, and so forth. Practically nothing could be bought for paper money; the whole country changed - unofficially but actually - to barter trading: basically foodstuff from the peasants for clothing, furniture, jewelry, gold, tools, etc.

THE FORMATIVE YEARS - 1919 - 1927

In September 1919 I entered a high-school that was oriented for the exact sciences and modern languages, preparing mainly those students who intended to enter university to learn exact sciences. This school was for eight years and gave a matriculation (graduation) certificate. Emphasis was laid on mathematics, physics, geometry, chemistry, laboratory experimentation, and German and French languages.

The school was in the eight district of Budapest, at a great distance from home, so that I had to take two street railway lines, which - especially in the morning rush hours - took at least one hour. The school was an old established and a rather conservative institution, with middle-aged Professors, almost all of them having Ph.D. In the lower four years there were two parallel classes, each of them with 30-35 pupils. In each class there were 7-10 Jewish boys. Religious instruction was obligatory; Roman Catholic, Protestant, and Jewish religious instructions were held simultaneously for the combined parallel classes, one hour once a week.

The school was well known for its high-quality education, its curricula were extensive and we had to learn very much and well, however hard it might have been. School hours were from 8 am till 1 pm, and we had much home work. The general social atmosphere in the school I would characterize as restrained, conservative, trying to remain impartial in general social problems and in the ever-growing, spreading, and intensifying anti-Semitism.

I was not an outstanding student. Three-four boys competed always for the first three-four places; I was in the fifth-eighth place; mathematics, physics, chemistry, geometry were my favorite subjects, but in history, geography, etc. I had much less interest.

Although the horrifying high-peak of the anti-Semitic terror was already over, almost every day some new aspect and target was concocted and spread among the population. Leading in the campaign was the periodical "What should happen with the Jews?", and except a very few high-level progressive daily newspapers, all the others carried quite straightforward anti-Semitic propaganda articles. Everything was a good reason for them to condemn the Jews: because they were capitalists - and for just the very opposite also - because they were communists. The Hungarian version of anti-Semitism went so far that they blamed the allied countries' leaders for being Jews, because at the Trianon Treaty they allotted parts of the old Hungary with non-Hungarian nationalities to newly formed countries with the same nationality: the northern part of Hungary to Czechoslovakia, the south-eastern part to Rumania, the south-western part to Yugoslavia, and a small western strip to Austria.

This modernized type of anti-Semitism, devised and established by the Horthy regime, that later on swept over almost all Europe, became a new, high-resistant seed-grain that grew and spread and by its increasing multiple yield became the substructure of the ultimate Hitlerian anti-Semitism. Auschwitz did not start with Hitler, and Auschwitz could not have happened without this Hungarian concocted modernized type anti-Semitism since 1918. This anti-Semitism slowly permeated both Christians and Jews; the former accepted the legality and uprightness of all sorts of anti-Semitic activities, whereas the Jews slowly, step-by-step, adapted themselves to the creeping and growing anti-Semitism: they became acclimatized to it.

Unfortunately, my brother was one of the first victims of this anti-Semitism, when right at the beginning of its rise; in October 1919 he was not accepted for studying medicine. If there ever had been a born talent for medicine - my brother was a real one. He had not only an exceptional talent for medicine, but additionally he had an excellent talent for inventiveness, technical inspiration, and moreover he was a warm-hearted human being, who always looked for opportunities to help people. And these three traits are the ingredients of a good physician.

He did not give up hope easily; tried everything, and even

when he had to switch over to book-keeping, he still continued to read, learn, and even to work in the field of medicine, in private laboratories, as helper of physician-friends of him who were a few years older and thus they already finished their studies. He had four-five very good friends, all of them already practicing in hospitals, and at least once a week they spent an evening at our home with my brother.

He had excellent technical ability, he was inventive and a tinker. He installed for himself a small laboratory; his friends provided him with a few tools for laboratory work, the most precious one was a used microscope. He designed a device for making very thin microscopic slices of various materials, and he spent many a night studying and experimenting.

Needless to say that I was very much interested to look at - and thrust my nose into - his experimentation, which he quite often did not want to permit, as a precaution. I can vividly recall my appeals to our mother, asking her: "Please, tell him to let me in."

Around that time a joyful event happened: our neighborhood was connected to the city electricity grid. The electric lighting made our life, both literally and symbolically, brighter.

Photography at that time was either the business of professionals or amateurs who had to perform all necessary steps themselves: developing the glass-plates, fixing and drying them, making copies, etc. The photosensitive emulsion was deposited on glass plates only; film was a matter of the future only. And there were no shops or laboratories where already exposed photographic plates could be given for processing. And such processing on an amateur basis was quite a complicated task. A few kinds of chemical-solutions had to be prepared, using precise weights of chemicals, keep the solutions at proper temperatures, handle the plates during the development- and fixing-stages in special red light only; etc.

As an example of the remarkable technical talent of my brother: I recall an integrated set-up that he designed and built for easy processing. He took a conventional drawing-board and glued on it a big box, out of red glass plates; the front plate having two black textile sleeves, ending in thin leather gloves, inside the box. Through these two gloves it was possible to work inside the red glass box, seeing everything through one pair of goggles built in the inclined red glass plate above the glass-openings for the gloves. By this glove-box one could do the photographic processing with ordinary white light in the room. This was his photo-laboratory that we used for many years with good success.

I found this principle adopted in chemical laboratories for the so-called glove-boxes many years later. I am convinced that there was no connection whatsoever between these two applications, but it is all the more reason for appreciating his remarkably innovative talent. In that atmosphere of economic hardships, galloping inflation, and anti-Semitic propaganda - but with decreasing atrocities, especially in Budapest - I attended school. We were quite contended, especially my parents, that in the school the Professors, although had not changed their conservative attitude, but still almost perceptibly disapproved the brutal atrocities perpetrated by the terror gangs.

The atmosphere among the students was good, we had lessons every day, six times a week, and we had to work hard, there was home-work every day. The school was known as a strict and demanding institution, but the Professors, at least most of them, were dedicated people, for whom teaching was not simply a way of earning a living. Discipline was strict, especially as regards our behavior.

As is usual in schools, small groups of three-four children became very friendly with each other and they studied together, helped each other, and spent their free time together. I was a member of such a group; we visited each other at home and so our parents got to know the friends of their son. Our group consisted of four-five boys. After having finished our home-work, we made long walks in the city.

Now, in retrospect, I think it worthwhile to mention that although we had some common interest, we used every opportunity to go hiking to the surrounding mountains on Sundays and Holidays, but each of us had different personal interests: one liked and had ability to literature, the other geography; and I was the only one with interest and passion for everything connected with all technical topics (Picture 10). As is common with boys, they always liked to make fun of each-other's personal interest and knowledge, because seemingly this way it is easier to accept the other's specific superiority. At least, I clearly remember, how they made fun of me every time when I mentioned something technical that they did not notice and did not understand. Out of the many cases I recall now one characteristic item.

The newspapers wrote about a new bridge that was going to be built across the Danube, in Budapest. Since the width of the river at the site is something between 500-550 m, the bridge was designed with two pillars in the river bed. Pillars cannot simply be put on the riverbed; they had to be anchored some 5-10 m deep in the river bed, to stand on solid rock foundation. To accomplish this would be extremely difficult, if not impossible, in the sweeping flow of the river.

The papers described briefly the solution that was novel at that time, the so-called "caisson" design. The solution as I figured it out for myself was as follows. The idea was to build a big, heavy, water-tight steel structure, in the form of a slightly conical rectangular pyramid, with one, the bigger side open; in principle resembling a huge goblet. Now, if this goblet; the caisson, with its open side downwards, is lowered in the river, its inside will remain filled with air, although somewhat compressed by the pressure of the surrounding water. The caisson is lowered down to the bed of the river and compressed air is pumped from above for compensating the outside pressure. This way, inside the caisson, through proper doors, workers can enter and work on the river bed for digging out the earth, which, through proper elevators, could be lifted to the outside. Simultaneously, steel reinforced concrete structure could be built on top of the caisson, for constituting the future pillar of the bridge. The caisson thus goes down into the

Picture 10 – View of Budapes

river bed and on top of it the pillar goes up. This way a strong pillar can be built into the river bed while the water of the river flows by.

By intuition, I grasped the idea, in principle, and was enthusiastic about its beauty. I could hardly wait to explain it to my friends, who were first silent, but soon started to laugh and mock at me: obviously they did not understand why I was so enthusiastic about the caisson idea, and made fun of me for being self-conceited.

I mention this, out of a series of similar examples, in order to show two characteristic features: one is my inborn interest in everything "technical", and the other is my inborn intuition to grasp principles of technical problems and their solutions - without actually knowing their scientific or engineering basis. And exactly this condition was the cause of many debates with my friends, because in many cases I just could not explain and prove my standpoint, since I only felt them by intuition, but did not know them - not that it would have made a difference in persuading them: they would not understand anyway.

As I mentioned at the beginning, my brother was my senior by eight years and this fact had profound, far-reaching influence on my whole life. At the beginning, at my elementary school age of 6 to 10, his being my model was sentimental. I looked up to my "big brother" and admired his actions. But during my high-school years, from 10 to 18, he took upon himself to care for me, in every respect of upbringing, education, discipline, devotion, trustworthiness, etc. He was among other things, a very good pedagogue, and he was quite demanding, so that sometimes I almost rebelled against his method, but I felt that he was right. As an example: when I asked him to help me in one of my home-works, he always told me that I should do it as I can, and when finished, we would go over it together and he would explain what was incorrect, how can I do it correctly - but he never did a work instead of me.

As the years passed, he took me to theater performances,

matinee concerts, lectures, exhibitions, museums, etc, but always after making preparations, such as explaining the subject, the history involved, the artists, the moral of the subjects, etc. He gave me books and other reference materials to read before each such event, and always found some opportunity to discuss with me my reactions. Already during that period I felt and appreciated his very beneficial and otherwise not attainable educational program on my behalf, but I awoke to the full consciousness of its real significance and result only later.

What he gave me became a lasting immeasurable treasure-house that I never could properly acknowledge. Also as a result of his approach, another equally important trait has been become a permanent part of my life: to initiate and indoctrinate me in the classical and modern literature, Hungarian and foreign in Hungarian translation. He was well aware of my "love-affair" with books; what he wanted to do was to turn my attention and guide me to the real, high-value literature. He gave me books to read, but he knew how eager I was to read everything I could lay a hand on, so he left a great many selected books on his bookshelves; but those books I was not old enough to read: he locked in his cupboard.

In the meantime, in the twenties, a unique phenomenon took shape and spread over Europe and a few more countries elsewhere: radio-amateurism. Without analyzing: when, why, and how radio broadcasting developed after WW1, a few stations started broadcasting in several European countries. It quickly became a completely novel way of rapid news dissemination, supplemented by artistic performances: concerts, theaters, lectures, etc. Public interest and attraction was enthusiastic, still its spread was limited by the high cost of the receiver equipment, produced by only a comparatively few companies.

One basic feature of the receivers gave rise to an amateur movement; namely one of the two types of receivers, using a small piece of a crystal, generally one of a lead-alloy, was very simple. Such equipment could be used for receiving radio broadcasts within a few tens of kilometers of distance from the sender station. Such so-called "crystal" receivers were quite cheap, using unsophisticated components and this fact initiated people to build, assemble such receivers and take part in the fun of "hunting" for broadcasts. The components that had to be bought were a set of earphones, although even that could be improvised, and a small piece of the crystal; all the other components could be made on the amateurish way by everybody with technical interest and skill.

The other type of receiver used so-called electronic tubes and these needed two sorts of direct current electricity supply, and many sophisticated components, most of them could not be produced by amateurish way, but needed a small special workshop with instruments or had to be bought at expensive prices. Sometime in the early twenties my brother got and gave me some written material and the basic ingredients of a crystal receiver. Needless to say that I enthusiastically joined the radio-amateur movement and spent much time and experimentation with my crystal receiver. Once I fall asleep with the earphones on my head that almost strangled me.

I had two classmates who were radio-amateurs too; one was the son of a patent-attorney, who quite often got interesting news on the subject. The three of us exchanged experiences.

This was the situation sometime in 1922-23, when still there was no broadcasting station in Hungary. This situation urged us to speed up our efforts and start dealing with the more sophisticated receivers, using electronic tubes. I made very much effort, spent much time, and with the understanding and financial help of my brother, I made quite nice progress. So much so that in 1925, at the First Radio Amateur Exhibition, held in Budapest, I participated already with a 4-tube receiver, built completely by myself, giving very good performance and was awarded a certificate of distinction.

In the next two years I built a few big, 8-tube, sophisticated (ultra-heterodyne) receivers on orders, earning good money. This world-wide radio-amateur movement was a peculiar phenomenon, unparalleled in the history of technological development, and I am of the opinion that the pace of development of the electronic industry in the twenties and thirties was much accelerated and enhanced by it.

In the meantime, in the school, as I referred to earlier, I had been very good in a few subjects, such as mathematics, geometry, physics, chemistry, laboratory works, and average-above average in the other subjects, so that in summary, I was in the fifth-eighth place in my class.

When I was in the seventh grade an unusual thing happened. One of our subjects was "descriptive geometry". This is actually the "jargon language" of engineering, that universal, international sign-language, in the form of drawings, exclusively capable and used for describing machines, buildings, bridges, etc, specifying their features, dimensions, functioning, etc, and make possible their production. We had to learn the basics of this discipline. Our teacher was an old man, who was earlier an assistant at the Technical University. He had a beard and he mumbled something to the blackboard during lecturing and drew a great number of lines, points, and letters on the blackboard. Nobody understood a word; there was no book or note to learn from; and he always drew stereotype figures, with a few questions to be answered at examinations, that my schoolmates learned from questions of the previous years' results - and everybody was happy, but nobody grasped the principles of the subject.

I was quite unhappy; I did not like copying homework without at least understanding them. During that school year I got a few times the best marks and a few times I failed. In order to get a picture about my real knowledge of the subject, the Professor decided to examine me orally for one full hour.

And so it happened. I knew that I did not perceive the basic principles of the subject, but a few details that I understood fascinated me. So I decided to get to the bottom of the problem, I succeeded to get a fine, complete notebook from the Technical University. I went over on it and suddenly everything became completely clear and I grasped the basic principles.

Without going into the details, a few explanatory words seem to be in place - and suffice - to provide the basics of one of the most important and extraordinarily beautiful theorems of descriptive geometry: the theorem of "central collineation". Central collineation describes all regular plain geometrical configurations as members of a family, where each one of these regular plain geometrical configurations (point, straight line, triangle, circle, ellipse, hyperbole, parabola, etc.) corresponds to another (or more) similar configuration; each point of them has a corresponding point on the other one; the connecting lines of each these corresponding points meet each other in one point; etc. This entire theorem can be visualized by a cone, constituted by an infinite number of straight lines on the surface of the cone, cut by two (or more) plains. The cuts of the plains with the cone are the regular plain geometrical configurations.

I not only understood the principles, but could make a mental-visual picture that showed clearly all connections, relationships, and correlation; moreover I could mentally make cuts of the cone by inclined planes and clearly see how the various regular plane geometrical configurations constituted the correlated members of one family. This sudden insight was for me like a revelation; it was my first discovery of how proper understanding of the principles of a geometrical problem - that "par excellence" lends itself to visual presentation - can be visualized, held in memory and recalled at will.

I went with full confidence to the examination, where, after a few preliminary questions that I answered and drew the correct sketches on the blackboard, at the first serious question I started to say that the proper answer is a special case of the general, so-called "central collineation" theorem, and I wanted to explain the details. But our old Professor suddenly became quite excited and told me - with undisguised malice - "what do you know about that theorem, which is not compulsory even for University students?" I asked him to hear me out and gave a lecture on the subject with gusto; I enjoyed the feeling to be able to explain something that I learned and made my own and kept in my memory by my inquiry a few days earlier. It was my first lecture I gave; it took maybe a quarter-of-an-hour, and I saw that a number of my classmates understood the subject for the first time. The Professor mumbled something that I should have learned the answers to the other questions earlier as good as the answer I gave on the central collineation, etc. and gave me a "very good" mark.

I felt then for the first time the wonderful, delightful feeling of mastering a technical subject that looked for almost a year escaping my understanding, but I did not know - and could not have known - that my mastery of this subject, the descriptive geometry became one of the most important and decisive factor in shaping and supporting my entire engineering career.

Recalling now my high-school years, especially the last four years, I am amazed that besides all the quite heavy school work, plus the off-curriculum activities mentioned above, I still had time and energy to pursue sports, such as fencing, tennis, and skiing. During the last year of my high-school studies the question of my future profession was discussed a few times at home, based on the prevailing realistic assumption that I will not be able to enter University to study engineering, because of the "numerus clausus". I was so steadfast in my desire to become an engineer that the problem was reduced to trying to find another way to this goal instead of looking for some other occupation that could be attained. I was of the opinion that I should enroll a low-level technical school to become a technician, start working at that level and maybe, some time later, a possibility could be found to enroll the Technical University and eventually gain a diploma in engineering. My brother did not like this plan, and he spoke about making strenuous efforts for gaining the patronage and support of somebody of high rank for getting included in the 3% group allowed for Jews.

The school year ended sometime in June, 1927, and we had to pass the matriculation examination. I got a "very good" mark.

One small scene, quite characteristic to those days, seems to be worthwhile recalling. When a group of boys, happy about finishing school, went to leave the school building, our physical instructor, one of the few real anti-Semites among the Professors, stopped us and asked me what I wanted to become. My answer was a definite: "I will be an engineer!" He answered with a glee in his eyes and with an undisguised laugh: "You will not be accepted in the University!" To which I answered: "Don't worry, I'll be an engineer, and I'll then visit you to show you my diploma!"

I applied for acceptance and I had hope against hope that I will be admitted, since my brother got some promise, through an intermediary, that somebody "high-up" will support my application. In the meantime we could not do anything but to wait until the decision, sometime in August.

Partly as a present for my good mark in the school, partly a sort of consolation in advance for my dubious and not too joyful future - I was allowed to accept an invitation from my cousin and her family, who lived in Rimaszombat (Czechoslovakia), to spend a few weeks with them. I traveled alone abroad, for the first time in my life, and with her three children: two girls, about my age, and one boy, somewhat younger, we spent a joyful vacation together (Picture 11 & 12).

Picture 11 – with Friends

Picture 12 – Boy scouts

FORMAL   EDUCATION   -
1927 - 1932

Returning home from my vacation, where I had a very good time, playing tennis, hiking in the mountains, climbing the high peeks of the Tatra mountains, etc, I had to start dealing with our most important, the decisive problem: will I be admitted to the Technical University or not, and if not: what shall I do - or more properly - what could we afford to do.

Sometime by the end of August I got their decision: rejected. Although we forebode such decision, still the final word was an appalling fact.

The same day, after dinner, I told my family about the rejection, and returned to my previous plan to learn for becoming a technician. Then my brother, with his calm and unhesitating manner, said that "one victim is more than enough in a small family" and based on this principle, he pledged to support financially my studies at a suitable university abroad, and told us about his investigation he carried out in the previous two months about possible locations. Considering all pros and cons, the selection fell on the DTH (Deutsche Technische Hochschule: German Technical University) in Brunn (Czechoslovakia), (Brno in Czech), well known for its high standard, in a truly democratic country, the closest to our home, with comparatively low living- and schooling-costs. My parents and I myself were deeply moved; I thanked him more with my eyes filled with tears than with my saying him "thank you".

He got a letter from that University saying that I will be accepted if I report until a certain date with specified certificates regarding my previous studies. My brother already had the necessary certificates be translated into German, and all what we had to do was to prepare and pack my clothing and set on my way in a week or so. We set the date, my brother cared for the tickets and then it turned out that one of my class-mates wanted to join me going to Brunn and we intended to take a lodging jointly. My brother kept as a surprise his decision to come with us to help us in the initial difficulties of inscription, finding lodgment, etc.

We took the train on October 2, 1927 and on the 3-rd of October we were already enrolled as regular students, accepted and received personally by the dean of the faculty. The next day we rented a double-room, with breakfast and with all necessary services.

Thus, we were placed at the starting line and were waiting for the starting-pistol - and were left on our own devices. The very first lecture was mathematics. This was given in the biggest auditorium; and a few Hungarian colleagues were sitting in a group, nervously waiting the impact of the lecture on us. All of us had more than average knowledge in mathematics and since we had been learning German language for more than six years in high-school: we supposed to understand somewhat spoken in German. We followed the lecture with utmost attention, but our nervousness and confusion grow step by step - and at the end of the lecture we just sat there, completely shattered. After a few minutes everybody asked all the others the same question: "Did you understand?" And the unanimous answer was: "Not a word."

We parted silently, everyone deep in thought; each one of us felt that some conclusion should have to be made by us, alone, for the first time in our life, hard, weighty, and eventually decisive. I evaluated the problem for myself as basically the language issue that had to be solved. We learned during six years German literature instead of conversation. I knew by heart many tens of beautiful poems in German, but had difficulty when I wanted to buy a loaf of bread. And this was the case with almost all of us.

I decided on a double action program: (a) to improve my German conversational knowledge, and (b) to study the higher mathematics - and the other subjects too - in advance of the lectures. This point needs some explanation as there were no lecture-notes on the lectures our Professor gave us, because that was his first year at Brunn; he came from another university, from

Germany. On the other hand, there were quite a number of well-known textbooks that we could have on loan from the library of our University. The difficulty was only that all the books dealt much more extensively with the subjects than the lectures, at least four-five times as much. Consequently, learning from the books meant to sit and deal with the subject by spending at least three times the time that would be needed to learn the more selected version of the lectures. But such learning on the hard way would inevitably have the very beneficial advantage of gaining a very profound and wide knowledge, included the added advantage to understand the lectures in its spoken German. When discussing the problem and my proposal with my colleagues: most of them agreed.

Additionally: I made a firm decision for myself only. Since the arrangement at the University was such that everybody had to pass separate examination in each subject at the end of each semester, I resolved that if I fail my mathematics examination at the end of the first semester - I shall give up and return home, because I did not want, under any circumstances, to squander away the money and trust of my brother and family.

The remedial method I selected was a very efficient one, although it was the hard way to attain the goal. But I understood later - and could not over appreciate it - that this method proved the superiority and the true, scientific method of "advanced, university-type studying" a subject - by learning and comparing different interpretations of the same theories. Such deep and wide "studying" in contrast to the simple "learning" of any subject is the proper, the true way of university level acquiring scientific knowledge. What started out of necessity to overcome a difficult situation became later, during my entire career, as a very beneficial blessing.

Actually this method proved to be successful during the first semester: I passed my first examination in mathematics at the end of the first semester with a "very good" mark, thus I proceeded in my studies with good conscience.

As I learned the first few weeks of my university student's life in Brunn, our Institute was a real asylum for Jewish students, persecuted because of their religion in Hungary, Rumania, Bulgaria, plus a number of Hungarian speaking fellows from Slovakia, and Transylvania.

Brunn was a not a very big city, but was very dynamic, with bustling traffic. It was the textile center of Czechoslovakia, had an industry with high quality standards (cars, weapons, etc.), but first of all a big university center, with 5-6 universities, with a high level cultural life - two operas, a number of theaters, big concert life, exhibitions, etc. It was a rich city - but very democratic – same as the entire country.

Life was comparatively not expensive. We, students with meager financial means, had basically two possibilities for cheap sustenance: there were two students' canteens, one in the University, for every student, and another, supported by the local Jewish Students' Welfare Organization, for needy Jewish students. Lunch and dinner was quite inexpensive.

Since Brunn had been a university center for many-many decades even centuries - all sorts of ancillary installations and services had been established, such as dwelling rooms for rent, restaurants, inexpensive snack-bars, coffee-houses, etc, thus it was no problem for us to find room to rent, together with breakfast and services.

Brunn and its surrounding had been heavily populated with German-speaking people since the time of the Austro-Hungarian monarchy, and even earlier. Until the end of WWI, no threatening antagonism existed between the two groups, and during the Czechoslovak democracy they lived quite peacefully, each one using and preserving its own language heritage; for instance there were two opera houses: one Czech and one German; there were a number of separate theaters, etc. and there was our DTH and another Czech Institute of Technology.

For obvious reasons I tried to live very sparingly, economizing both time and money; concentrating all my energies on my studies. So, for instance, I gave up playing tennis or skiing, which were expensive and time-consuming sports. On the other hand, I, together with all the other students, was lucky to have many opportunities to obtain theater-, opera-, and concert-tickets on reduced prices through the various students' organizations. Brunn was a big music center, having its own high-standard orchestras, besides being on the itinerary of all famous musicians playing in Vienna, Prague, Brunn, and Budapest. In the seasons, not one week passed by without going to a concert or to the opera. This was made possible partly by a very intelligent arrangement of the Concert Hall, namely from exactly five minutes before the beginning of a concert, tickets still unsold could be bought at half price. And since generally more high-price tickets were available: we put on our best clothes and sat at good seats for half-price.

Among the big number of Hungarian speaking colleagues there was one fellow: Gottesman Ede (called "Roetl", because of his red hair), known and liked by everybody for both his extraordinary nice personality and his exceptionally artistic musical talent. He composed music, conducted choirs at concerts, and he was the conductor of the second biggest synagogue's choir in Brunn. He was a chemistry student, but his main interest and engagement was music. We became friends and after a few visits to each other, once he sat down at his piano, started playing and singing songs and made me to sing along (Picture 13). A few days after that he asked me to accompany him because he had to arrange something that will not take long, and after that we shall spend some time together. I agreed and as it turned out the person he visited was a famous music teacher, Professor Auschpitz. He went in, I waited in the hall, and after a few minutes he called me in, introduced to the Professor, who, without any explanation, placed me beside him and ordered me to sing the sounds he played on the piano. I was unwilling to do so and started to explain that this is a mistake, I did not come to take singing lessons, and ... but he cut me short, ordering me to sing what he played, and all this in such an authoritative tone that I had to obey. After a short time he

Picture 13 – University years

ordered me to note to come twice a week, at certain hours, for singing lessons. I tried again to resist and told him that, besides I was not interested to learn singing, the main point of resistance was that I was a poor student from Hungary and I couldn't afford to assume financial obligation beyond the inevitable costs of my studies and a modest sustenance. He answered saying that he would accept tuition fees if I were the son of a wealthy industrialist in Brunn, otherwise I would do him a favor by taking his lessons because his hobby was to teach a few selected young people who had potential in singing develop their talent - and with this he sent me away. My friend Roetl was only smiling that he succeeded to outsmart me, and added that I will be accepted to the synagogue's choir as a bass-baritone singer and I will get some modest salary too.

And so it happened; I got lessons from Professor Auschpitz and became soloist in the synagogue's choir. I enjoyed immensely the singing lessons and those occasions when 10-12 friends and colleagues celebrated something, and two or three of us, with Roetl as conductor and tenor, sang classical songs, by Schubert, Bach, etc. This musical love-affair of mine accompanied me during all the four study years and signified a joyful counterpoise to my engineering studies. Besides, it provided me with a steady income, covering at least one fifth of my outlays.

In short: I was quite happy; I applied my good experience with the method used for my mathematics studies, by going over and studying in the library several works on each subject, and additionally I enjoyed my singing lessons. This way time just flew by and we came to the end of the second semester, when we had to pass a number of examinations. Among them was my favorite subject: Descriptive Geometry. I went to the examination with full confidence. Eight or ten questions had to be answered, in writing and with drawings, and the finishing time was marked on the answer-sheets. I finished all questions very quickly, checked them, handed in, and went away. In two days the results were posted on the faculty's notice-board, but to my astonishment: my name was not mentioned. To my inquiry I was told by the assistants that I was suspected by the Professor of having inside information on the examination's questions, otherwise I could not have solved all the questions within the short time as I did, and they implicitly were suspected too. They asked me to clear myself and all of them from this suspicion by voluntarily undergo a special, individual examination. Needless to say that I was ready, and within a few days I was given a drawing board in the assistants' room and got in writing (in a closed envelop) a very complicated problem to solve. The starting time was marked and I was let to work under the watchful eyes of the two assistants. I well remember the question: given was a sphere (a ball) that had to be cut by a tilted plane. The task was to draw the three projections of the configuration of the cut, plus to draw the shade-line, by so-called "technical light" of the cut on the horizontal base plane, plus the self-shade line on the sphere. Within an hour or so I drew a few representative points of all three configurations, and the drawing sheet was already more gray than white, because of the many construction lines. I went to the assistants and explained that to draw more points of the three configurations were the repetitions of the already constructed points, but for doing this: so many secondary construction-lines were needed that the sheet would have a solid gray color. But if they insist - I am ready to do it. First they wanted to scrutinize my work, alone, without my participation, that took at least 10 minutes. Then they went to see the Professor, took my drawing and told me to wait. After another 5 minutes or so they came out, together with the Professor who told me that he hoped I understood his hesitancy to accept my first examination work that seemed to him too good to be true, but seeing my present special work: he wanted to congratulate me on my superb work and knowledge of the subject - and gave me an extraordinary "mark of distinction". I was happy, mainly because I remembered my encounter with my high-school Professor on the same subject and I felt that I had some specific aptitude for the subject that was now proven for the second time.

My case was a matter of talks among my colleagues and when they asked me for details and we discussed the subject matter beyond the specific occurrence, the descriptive geometry in general, it turned out that almost all of them had more or less difficulty in understanding and applying it. They told me that descriptive geometry was one of the few subjects that were considered extremely difficult to comprehend and consequently many students failed at their examination. Generally there was common practice that students who knew they did not have sufficient knowledge in some specific subject, organized study-courses, lead by a higher-semester student who was an established expert in the specific subject, for preparing themselves for the exams. Within a few days, some 10-15 first-year colleagues came to me, asking to set up a study-course in descriptive geometry. All those students who failed by the end of the first year or did not even attempt to stand for the exam, then could sit again during the third semester. Since the second semester was going to end within a few days, I agreed to organize a course in the fall.

My first study year was going to wind up within two weeks after that noteworthy event and I set about to give some thought to draw up a sort of a balance sheet of my performance versus the goal that I had set for myself. I made a thorough soul-searching on the question: what did I do and how; did I achieve what I was obliged and wanted to achieve; what could and should I had done better; and so on. I came to the conclusion that basically I fulfilled my duty, first of all towards my family; although I could have done a few things even better. Besides, I felt that my progress during this first year, proven by all examination-marks of "very good" throughout, except the one "distinction", confirmed my aspiration to become an engineer. Summarily: I could go home with good conscience and report to my family - especially my brother - on my work.

Besides scrutinizing my own work, achievements, and a few things that I have also attained, I could not help to ponder about my way of day-to-day private life: how I managed to live alone, not within my family circle for the first time in my life, at the age of 18. To find the proper answer to this question was quite easy, because I knew closely at least fifty colleagues with whom we started together our first year's student's life - in "exile", all of us having exactly the same outside circumstances, whereas maybe half of them had good financial background and the other half, including myself, had to live a rather modest life. Judging their performance, not from the scholastic point of view but basically their persistence, firmness, steadfastness of purpose, their stamina to studying for becoming an engineer: gave me a ready scale for comparison. I had no reason whatsoever to feel ashamed of my performance during the first year of my student life aboard, alone.

The very liberal system at our University enabled students not to attend lectures; consequently, fellows with less than average willpower fell back in their studies. There were no roll-calls at lectures; the principle adopted was that to attend lectures was not obligatory; anyway, everybody had to pass examinations and the University was not interested to check where students got their knowledge from, the crucial question was sufficient command of the subjects by the students, that had to be proven by the more than fifty individual subject exams plus the two examinations by independent state examining body. Nobody was obliged to attend lectures, because, as a matter of fact, nobody was obliged to enroll the University that had not the goal to bring up and train students in discipline.

So far I spoke about our duty and work, success and failure, etc. but for the sake of completeness I have to mention that all of us, including myself, had cheerful, merry times too. We were freshmen after all, young, healthy chaps like other freshmen all over the world, although our life was somewhat overshadowed by our "exile" status. Tricks were played on us and we played tricks on each other, in a time-honored traditional student's fashion. We went hiking in the nearest mountains, making picnics, drinking the famous Pilsner beer, and singing "gaudeamus". To tell the truth: we were quite a happy lot most of the time - in spite of everything.

I had two-three good friends among the many colleagues and when winding up the first year, not I was the only one who made some sort of soul-searching on the performance in the past first academic year. This subject came up during our conversations and I felt some slight, delicate perception of my interpretation of "work" we did, which was in a way different from theirs. "Work" has quite a wide spectrum of meaning; at one end it means toil, drudgery, travail; at the other extreme it means mental activity directed toward accomplishment of a specific scientific or artistic achievement or understanding. I felt that I had not "worked" during my studies, I had all the time been eager and impatient to find answer to problems; and so I did not feel my search for solutions as work, the same way a boy do not "work" when he tries to assemble a puzzle picture. I could not define it clearly, I had only some hazy conceptions, but in one thing I was sure: studying was for me something resembling a state of mind, not confined between start and end-time in a day; it was a continuous mental activity, fluctuating in intensity - having even gaps - that I could increase or degrease, but not switch off from my mind: it went on subconsciously, and ideas, images etc. just popped up, any time, suddenly, with no connection to my thoughts at the moment. Thus, I did not feel and consider my studying activity as "work", since it was something exciting that I enjoyed and it gave me a delightful feeling.

I did not mention these of my raw notions to my colleagues; I could not explain them properly, and I did not want to appear showing off. Anyway, I had been taken by my colleagues for a silent, of a rather reticent person, who preferred more listening and less speaking in general conversations, and got more talkative only when technical questions were discussed.

By the end of June the second semester ended and I traveled home, and let my dear little mother to pamper me for a few days with her sweet tender care. I learned in the meantime that the biggest heavy machinery factory, the "Ganz Machine Works" organized special summer "engineering students' apprenticeship courses". I rushed to apply - and miraculously I was accepted. The course was intended for three months (July, August, and September), in each of three consecutive years, to provide a survey of production processes of heavy machinery building, to be made by the students themselves, by their actual participation in a big assortment of production works; such as : making casting forms, operating lathes and other machine-tools, welding, etc. etc. There were no lectures; one or two students were assigned to one shop or group, for one, two, or three weeks. We had no privileges whatsoever, we were in the same category as the workers, had to punch the clock in and out, were assigned by the foreman to machine-operators to assist them in their work and thereby learn something about their trade, in reality, by making our hands dirty. We got our weekly pay slips with 0.00 Korona wage; but the benefit of our own direct experience in actual day-to-day practical workshop-work promised to be inestimable. I was very glad in doing such work, where I learnt very much. A few times I got plain proof that I succeeded, when a machine-tool operator, to whom I was assigned, let me work alone on his machine for a few hours, or half-a-day, while he went away. Interestingly enough, very few students took part in this course, we were not more than 15-20 people; the reason could have been that it was not publicized; maybe the plant was obliged to organize such a course, but actually they were not too much interested in it.

For the beginning of October I returned to Brunn. Subjects in the third semester were organized, what could be called, in two parallel lines: one consisting theoretical studies on a high level and the other practical works in laboratories, and designs of basic machinery. Each of us had a drawing board and a desk, in big design halls and was given various problems to be solved. Working side by side we discussed each other's work, and after a while, seeing and analyzing a number of designs: I started to realize that my basic approach in designing even the smallest machine components was different from theirs. It did not even come up in my colleagues' mind when designing that the drawn picture of a component, of any component, of even the simplest mechanical device or machine is not automatically the actual, real, existing piece. As a contrast: for me the drawn picture of a component signified a sort of command to produce the actual piece, specified in the drawing. The difference between these approaches is basic: their approach, devoid of production considerations, can have damaging effects on the component or the entire device or machine; whereas my approach was to design each and every component in such a way that it could readily be produced.

This of my approach was obviously the result of my experiences gained by working during the summer months in the Ganz Factory. Looking at a drawing of a component induced me a quick mental process of thinking: what raw material is needed for the item in question, what machine-tool - or more than one in succession - is to be used, what sort of tools, jigs, etc, are needed, what other technologies have to be applied, etc. etc. And vice versa: my goal was to design machine components in such a way that they could be produced efficiently. Obviously: this was the consequence of the knowledge, still in its initial phase, that I acquired in the summer course, but which was still enough to direct my attention to the problem: the need to "design for production" concept. Needless to say that my perception was only the first, faint step, but I felt that it was in the correct direction, and that I decided to pursue further. Closely attached to this idea was the next logical step, the question: why mechanical engineering was taught, everywhere in the world at that time, as a monolithic discipline? It seemed to me more than obvious, even at that early period of my knowledge about engineering that the design phase was clearly different from all other phases of mechanical engineering. This of my early notion was proven correct much later when machine design became a distinct subject.

It has to be emphasized that the above outlined "designing for production-concept and practice was supported and advanced by my firm command in my unusual ability to visualize spatial configurations in my mind and thereby doing most part of a design work by imagining.

Of course, our student life had now and then its light, cheerful events, especially when we went out to fool and take in each other. The scene of the favorite jokes, used every year on the new freshmen, was the drawing hall, where each of us had a drawing board and we worked sometimes on one of the drawings for quite long time. Now, colleagues came often to discuss details, stood by the desk and after having finished - they left. And then that one at whose drawing board the discussion took place, was frightened to death when he noticed a big black blotch of India ink covering critical part of his drawing, seemingly caused by an accidentally overturned India ink bottle. The trick was a piece of paper with irregular outline, painted black by india ink, and placed unnoticed on the drawing the moment when they left the victim.

Besides studying, I continued with my singing lessons, and singing in the choir. The male choir consisted of young boys with soprano and alto, adults with tenor and baritone voices; two of us sang bass-baritone. We had one or two rehearsals a week and sang on Friday evenings and holidays. I received a modest salary, which was a great help in my budget. Studying singing, but especially singing in the choir was an extraordinary delight for me. As I mentioned, my friend Roetl, our conductor, had a phenomenal gift in music. Singing under his baton gave opportunities to me experienced only by musicians, especially by singers, performing under famous conductor. These musicians and singers referred to their most memorable experiences when they achieved peak performances they never could even hope to attain otherwise, only conjured up by a very few conductor. Similar experiences had I many times by singing beautifully under his spell, what otherwise I could never have achieved.

Those colleagues, to whom I promised the previous year to organize descriptive geometry courses, spread the word and so some twenty people came who wanted to participate. In the meantime I inquired about courses given by "perpetual" students, who collected examination questions from the preceding years, and they "trained" their students to answer those questions without actually teaching the subject. I was reluctant to give such courses, and at a meeting with a few of the interested colleagues, I explained my standpoint and offered them a course to teach the basics of the subject in such a way that they would understand the principles and would enable them to work out the proper answers to almost all predictable questions, at examinations or otherwise. In brief: I promised to bring them home and make them the master of the "frightful" subject. They accepted my proposal and I started to give a series of lectures, once or twice a week, to some 20 people, in a room we rented from the YMCA. I had to work a lot in preparing the lectures, but it was a success, already after the third-fourth lesson. They just grasped the basics and connections, and - as they told me - they could not understand how it was possible that they had not seen and understand them earlier. They were happy - and so was I; first of all because their success verified my understanding of the true structure and the proper explanation of the principles of descriptive geometry - as I grasped it in my seventh senior high school year, and developed it further for myself. By the way, all of them passed their exam, and I became a confirmed expert in the subject (Picture 14). Besides, although I asked modest fee, still I earned a sum of money that was a great help in my budget.

The year 1928 was the tenth anniversary of founding the Czechoslovak Republic, celebrated all over the country, but one of the highlights was a big national exhibition in Brunn, on a big exhibition ground, built specially for this purpose. A number of beautiful modern buildings were designed and constructed on the exhibition ground, and some staff members and students of our University also participated in the designs. Based on my reputation as an "expert" in descriptive geometry, I got the assignment from the faculty to make a so-called "photogrammetry" drawing, which means to redesign the ground-plan and front-view of a building shown on its photo. It was a very challenging and interesting task

Picture 14 – University class

that I carried out to their full satisfaction - and to my own enjoyment. Additionally to my studies, singing, and lecturing: I still had time to go to concerts, the movies, the Opera, and once or twice a week to a coffee-house where we had reserved table, to read newspapers and just have a chat.

Sometime in November, 1928, an unusual affair happened at the University. As we learned the previous year, together with all other peculiarities of a German University, all the students, almost without exception, were members of one of the many student fraternities. At one end of the long line of fraternities were a number of the traditional German-Aryan dueling fraternities, then a few quite neutral ones, and at the other end there were two-three liberal ones - even in their names - plus two Jewish-Zionist student societies. One day some anti-Jewish poster was hanged on one of the extremist Aryan-Nazi society's board in the hall of the University that was ripped off by a Jewish student and quite a brawl broke out. On order of the Rector, the hall was cleared, the building closed until orderly behavior guaranteed by the fraternities. Outside the building, the extremist anti-Semitic German students announced that next morning they intend to fight out the dispute with the liberal-Jewish group. We prepared ourselves for the fight, although with caution, because the Czech law was very severe as regards violence, etc, the use of a stick or cudgel was considered a weapon, and we as foreigners, did not want to be expelled as a consequence of such minor crime. Thus, we took attaché-cases full of heavy books, to be used as weapon, etc. A large crowd of students gathered in the front garden of the University's Old Building. The confrontation started with speeches on both sides. But within minutes pushing and hand-fights started. The forces on both sides were roughly equivalent. Then a quite surprising thing happened: we got a note from the student organization of the Czech Technical Institute (also in Brunn), pledging that if we ask for it they will immediately come to our help in full strength. This promise was quickly spread out among our fellows and this gave us the necessary shot in the arm and so we started to push the Germans out of the garden, to the streets. And then the hidden waiting police intervened the two fighting groups. We quickly organized ourselves to an orderly protest march to the Police head-quarter and to the Mayor's office, demanding they stop anti-Semitic actions of the German-Aryan fraternities. The following years I spent in Brunn: no other anti-Semitic action was made at the University.

This event prompted me to join one of the two Zionist student organizations, the "Veritas". The majority of its members were German speaking Czech Jews. About a year later I switched to the other Zionist fraternity, the "Barissia". The fellows of the Veritas were all boys of well-to-do Czech Jewish families and because of my more modest financial situation I could not - and did not want - to keep abreast with them; whereas the Barissia consisted mainly Rumanian (from Transylvania), Hungarian, and Slovakian fellows. The two fraternities had the same platform and were on very friendly terms with each other. Interestingly enough, no inter-Zionist political line was mentioned, only the overall Zionist disposition.

These two Zionist fraternities were not involved in any political activity, national or municipal. They were active only at a very low profile, at certain occasions and at the request of the general Zionist Organization of Czechoslovakia. As a matter of fact: foreign students did not participate in any Czechoslovak political party's life and activity; to do otherwise would have been incompatible. Still, we slowly became aware of a small group of colleagues, mainly from Hungary, who were active at Jewish students' deliberations, for instance, at meetings of the management of the Hostel or the Menza. They criticized a great deal, made a lot of proposals, etc, but somehow the great majority of the students could not see their point, their rationale; they felt rather confused by this group's ambiguous behavior. For a time no clear-cut action pattern emerged and the group's members were not disclosed. Only some time later did we learn that they were communists, who had to work clandestinely, they had their undisclosed goals, but enlisting new student-members was not one of their tasks.

During the third and fourth semester I passed all examinations with "very good" marks, and by the end of the fourth semester I set for my first "state examination", which I passed with "very good" mark also and thereby became a "candidate-engineer" (Picture 15 & 16). I went home for the summer vacation, and after a few days I re-entered the Ganz Works for the second period of the three-year course. During this second period I experienced the more complicated technological processes together with assembly works of general machinery, such as pumps, freight-cars, road-making machines, etc. I appreciated very much this second period too; I more felt than knew: to what great degree this first-hand experience contributed to both my university studies and my future professional work.

The third study year could be characterized by a continuously increasing scientific level in the treatment of the steadily more and more sophisticated subjects, and in addition to it: increasing occasions of organized excursions (by the University) to various big machine works in the country, such as: Witkovitz Steel- and Machine Works, Zbrojovka Automobile Plant, Skoda Plants, etc.

Traveling to and back between Czechoslovakia and Hungary during the first two years, we collected, step by step, much experience on the topic: democracy versus more or less dictatorial reactionary early-stage fascism. We, the "exiled" students, were lawfully citizens of Hungary, who, by law, were not restricted to obtain a passport. Still, in reality, no one of us could foresee what obstacles were laid in the way to issue or extend the validity of a passport. I had a first-hand experience: the first time when I applied for a passport at the age of 18, right after my graduation from high-school, I was called in before a police officer and was told that I not only cannot get a passport, but I am going to be arrested on the spot, charged with concealing of stolen goods for a prolonged period. I was just shocked and dumbfounded, but somehow still could stammer that there must be some mistake, I

Picture 15 – University class picture

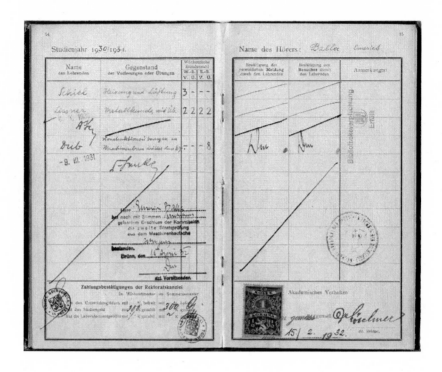

Picture 16 – University grade book

just now finished my high-school and passed my graduation two days ago. Fortunately, I had with me the certificate - and so I was sent out of the room to wait and after about a quarter of an hour - what amounted for me an infinity - I was called in again and without any further explanation my request for a passport was approved, and so I could proceed to the next step in the long process. As a comparison with such - and similar - treatment from "my own country", obtaining a long-term visa from Czechoslovakia, with which Hungary was officially on hostile, if not straight war situation, was a question of a straightforward operation, taking 15 minutes, when the purpose of the visit or stay could by some simple way shown as bona fide.

That was democracy in action. During our stay in Brunn, we happily and easily adapted ourselves to the true democracy of Czechoslovakia. Democracy manifests itself in countless ways, but it cannot be my intention to write here an enumeration of that infinite number of ways democracy works. Still, one small example from our, the "exiled" Jewish students life, seems to suffice to characterize a small number of people's unostentatious humane and intelligent deeds, that was also evidence of their true democratic frame of mind and sincere determination: how democracy shall act. As I mentioned, there existed a Jewish Students' Welfare Organization that cared for - among other things - a Hostel, a Menza, etc, and gave monthly contributions to needy students. And there was an interesting phenomenon: nobody knew the Organization, the names of its leaders, its address, nothing. The Hostel, the Menza had their elected managing body, and from year to year, an appointed agent cared for proposing needy students for receiving monthly allowances and distributed the allocated sums. In my third year, I was informed in a letter by the Organization that I was appointed as agent. I had to inquire, very discretely, about the real need of financial allowances of a number of students in a list and I had to propose additional names, and rank the names in sequence of neediness in descending order. After a short while I received an approved list with the sums of money, and was informed that the sum total will be sent to my name to the address of the University, every consecutive month; I had the task to distribute the sums to the students in the list and return the signatures to a specified address. We never found out who the people were who donated the money, we could never thank for their contributions, not for the monthly sums, neither for the more substantial sums the Hostel and the Menza were allocated to. The monthly allowance, presented in such extraordinary way that was devoid of the feeling of accepting a gift or alms, still provided the students with that additional money that enabled them to spend it on things such as books, theater, concert, etc, that made all the difference between a somewhat cheerful and intellectual life and a simple subsistence. And to let these needy students just find some money in their pocket in a very humane manner - is also one way how real democracy works.

And now, an extremely important thing has to be mentioned here and be kept in mind throughout these reminiscences, as an attempt to prepare a basis for a correct comprehension of my, secondly my fellow Jews, and generally my whole generation's immediate and long-range attitude to political movements and all other events happening outside our own country (or country of residence). Big dislocations, serious social, economic, and political disturbances were happening in the post-WWI period, in the twenties and early thirties, in Central- and Eastern-Europe; to mention only a few of them: scarcity of foodstuff, raw materials, fuels, industrial products, etc.; monetary inflation to unprecedented levels, unemployment, etc.; all these - and others - at various levels from country to country. Reactions were different, with diverse remedies. People lived and reacted to the happenings within the confines of their country or district, and their reactions were rather slow in coming. Pace of life was generally almost as slow as in the pre-WWI period, except a few revolutionary outbreaks.

Today, in retrospect, I would express my opinion that one of the reasons of the "slow-motion" unfolding was the state of art of the information technique. Newspapers, radio-broadcasts, and weekly news-magazines in the movies were the only methods of information, all of them characterized by more or less local, if not provincial, disposition. And besides, these informations were quite slow in coming, brief, and colored by political interests of the sponsors. In summary: the world was still a very big place and - as its complementary phenomenon - time was slow moving. An event of minor importance that would happen somewhere in Central-Europe today - would be broadcast live on TV and would be watched all over the world at the same time - or within a few hours -, analyzed and debated immediately by the entire spectrum of political and other interest groups: that is by everybody, but literally everybody would be informed about the event. The same event then, in the twenties and early thirties, would, in the best case, get a small article in a few local paper and shown in two-three weeks time in one of the movie newsreels in a few movie theaters. This enormous difference has to be borne in mind when events mentioned in this narrative are striven to be properly comprehended. But information distribution and reception is only a means to an end, and not an end itself. Information is one of the most important basis - and trigger for action. Action, or the lack of it, correctly and at the proper time depends on timely and reliable information. This is the ultimate goal, in general. But restricting my recollections to my - and to our family's history: I am convinced that the main reason for our and almost all of our Jewish fellow-sufferers, catastrophic fate was caused more by the single-factor of lack of proper timely information, than any other secondary factors.

This is not the proper place and I am not the competent person to analyze the above mentioned notion, but I still venture to raise the question: what would have happened if the Jews of Austria, Czechoslovakia, Poland, Russia, Hungary, Rumania, Bulgaria, Greece, France, Holland, Belgium, etc, would have got timely and reliably correct information about the intentions of the Nazis in the coming years after 1936-38 Maybe, this is not only an "unanswerable question" but an "unquestionable question"! One thing seems to be true: today's information methods would make the consequences and processes of incomparably less significant events completely different.

In the light of all these, the reader can comprehend properly our perception of the world around us there and then, when I describe it as follows. We knew, or at lest thought that we had some idea about the situation in general in the European countries, and somewhat more, but inadequately analyzed, about events in Germany, Austria, and Italy. We could understand that as a consequence of the post-WWI situation, there were difficulties, and various old and new political parties tried different solutions, that sometimes led to collisions. Some of us could agree or disagree with this or that standpoint or even action taken somewhere - but we did not have the feeling that those events had any impact on our situation; we did not suspect any connection or consequence of these foggy events to us. And under "we", the entire population of Czechoslovakia should be understood. Compared with all those countries mentioned, Czechoslovakia was a steady, reassured country, with a solid democratic government, and a clear-headed, composed population - and the informations, the news that reached us, did not make us anxious, either generally in regard of the country as a whole, or specifically for the fate of the Jews. To some slow deterioration of our social and economic standing in Europe, we Jews have already reconciled ourselves that we were, so to speak, conditioned to a down-swing in our wavy fate, but we had not the slightest fear of any dangerous or imminent misfortune. I did not know myself, and I do not know till this day about anybody else, who would know at that time, that there was a "writing on the wall", what we Jews failed to see at that time: 1928-33, and as much as it seems to be self-deception or exoneration, but I feel that the state of art of information distribution was one of the reasons of our, the Jews, belated reading on that "writing on the wall". I wonder whether the "writing" referred to the Jews only, or it had a more general augury, first of all for the WWI's victorious powers that all of them failed to read at that time, and consequently did not react to it until it was too late.

In the tranquil, reassuring atmosphere of Czechoslovakia we continued our studies. I proceeded nicely, completed my design- and laboratory-works and passed all my third year's examinations. A rather funny habit established itself, mainly among the students from Hungary. He, who passed successfully a major exam, invited his friends to a brief celebration in one of the few Italian ice-cream bars, by buying a round of ice-creams, preferably "cassatas". Sometimes, at a joint celebration, two-three rounds were consumed, which was maybe a foolish thing to do, but still it was more sensible that drinking as many mugs of beer.

By school-year's end I went home for the summer vacation and within a few days started the third, the last, period of my "apprenticeship" in the Ganz Works. This time assembly- and testing-departments were in the program, such as locomotives, big Diesel engines, big water turbines, etc. Needless to say that I learned a lot and took much pleasure from participating in such high-level work.

Returning to the University for the fourth, the last year of my study - and for all other engagements - signified the completion phase of my engineering education. The subjects in that year were composed of sophisticated theoretical studies, complemented with high-level design tasks, for instance: water turbines, hoisting cranes, etc. I liked very much these sorts of design works and had been in a highly animated mood during the time while I worked out the correct solution for the problems. Without following with deliberate attention my own working style, I became aware of my eager and increased interest and activity during the sometimes lengthy finishing details. As I worked in succession on two-three designs, I became aware of another phenomenon, namely that I worked out the details of a design-solution in my head, by imagining. I could see clearly in my mind the components of the device or machine that I had been designing, and could combine and assemble them to a working unit, then keep all the details in my memory and recall them at will. This reminded me of the similar sensation with the "central collineation" theory of the descriptive geometry, which was my first extraordinary success at the end of the first year here at the University in the subject of descriptive geometry, and established my reputation as an expert in that subject.

An additional aspect of this working pattern was an also peculiar phenomenon, namely that the ideas concerning a specific design task at any time turned up consistently, at an overwhelming preponderance versus the well-known general pattern, where flashes of diverse pictures, ideas, conceptions, thoughts, etc. pop up with a definite program, at any moment, during whatever activity.

First, I tried to inquire and find out my friends' and colleague's perception or observation on their own working method, mainly the question how far could they progress in solving a design problem in their imagination, and what portion of a solution needs sketches, drawings for checking and finalizing a solution. The results of such observations could not be quantified, but a general conclusion could still be drawn, that roughly 50-50 % was carried out by imagining and drawing.

I had been following with attention this of my own emerging spontaneous working pattern, and to my happy astonishment came to the conclusion that by me distribution between imagining and drawing was something 80-90% vs. 10-20%. I felt uneasy about this result, I was very skeptical on relying and using such non-exact method in design, which could possibly cause defects and flows on the one hand, but at the same time I felt what advantages such a mental imagining method could offer. I decided tentatively to pursue my method, but - to be on the safe side - to check and re-check every solution before accepting it as being correct. I developed for myself a quite uncommon test attitude for preventing myself to make errors, mistakes, or completely wrong designs, relying on my solution by imagining only. I devised the principle of this test as follows. After having finished a design, I switched to the role of a very scrupulous opponent to my solution, trying to prove, by all conceivable evidence, that my solution was not correct. And I approved my original solution - or a corrected version of it - only if I could not prove it being incorrect. It was not an easy mental exercise, I had to play the role of the "devil's advocate", but the results of this method proved themselves very beneficial.

This was the beginning of a long period of quest, of search for my own method of designing. I treated that entire unusual imagining-dominated design method with a healthy measure of caution. On the one hand I felt that I had a certain specific unusual ability, already proven by two highlight-events, but still I wanted to check very-very carefully its reliable validity, and if so: its benefits vs. its risks. My reasoning was based on the uncontested doctrine that out of the two basic tools of engineering design: method of work and knowledge of engineering principles - the first, the method is predominant versus lexical knowledge of engineering principles and data, because textbooks and handbooks are always available with the latest information, but method of work is liable to become habitual, immutable, that would prevent progress. And since I aspired above anything else to become a dynamic, progressively oriented and devoted engineer: I decided to give this of my practically discovered ability a chance - but using the "devil's advocate's" method for checking and double-checking it for correctness and reliability.

I liked browsing in our University's library, looking especially for novel machine components, applications, etc. I had been just fascinated by the professional periodicals in the field. Many things that today are either forgotten, outdated, or well established: were at that time novelties. Slide-rule was at that time also a novelty; an early item in the mathematics lecture. A huge slide-rule was hanged above the black-board for illustration purposes. The first time the Professor used it for illustrating the simplest operation of multiplication, he took the example: 2 times 2; put the zero arrow of the sliding stripe to the number of 2 on the body and looked for the result opposite to the number of 2 on the sliding stripe and read aloud: three point nine, nine, nine, let us say: four. We just burst out laughing.

Novelty was for instance the various types of ball- or roller-bearings, to be used instead of the then conventional sliding bearings. I applied such roller-bearings in one of my design projects, but instead of getting praise for such an advanced design, I had quite a difficult time when my Professor did not want to approve it, and only the guaranteed loading data in the catalog of the producer helped me from redesigning the project.

Our Professors at the University were well known and recognized based on their textbooks that were used extensively by many European universities. The most famous and distinguished was Professor Kaplan, the inventor of that most advanced water turbine that had been almost exclusively used - and is being in use even today - in big power stations all over the world. I was fortunate enough having been his student. Another famous Professor was Dub, expert in pumps and cranes. His textbooks were extensively used at other universities in Europe. He was a rather rigorous, strict, and stringent engineer; everybody trembled when had to enter his office for a verbal examination. My exam was one of the cases that were related many times by colleagues who faced examination. He received each student separately. When I entered his office, he looked over my design project and asked me to draw on the black-board a few types of valves, what I completed within a few minutes. He did not look at me during I made the drawings and explained in a few words the application characteristics of the valves; he only raised his head when I finished speaking; looked at the sketches and said: "thank you". Then he asked some theoretical question - and again he lowered his head. I started my exposition that included an equation referring to a special theorem concerning fluids: viscosity. This theorem was not discussed and elaborated on in the lectures in all its fine details and its quite complicated theoretical implications. But during my studies, the question challenged my curiosity, and I became absorbed in its details. So, during my exposition, I mentioned a few details about viscosity and its influence on the topic I had to answer as part of my examination. But before I could actually go into details, the Professor, without raising his head, told me: "thank you" - and I stood there, stopped speaking, and waited for further questions, because I thought that so far the questions were so to speak only for "warming up" purposes. After a few seconds of silence, he told again "thank you, you can leave now". I left the room and to the questions of my waiting colleagues I could only answer that I had not the slightest idea whether I passed with high mark or flopped. Next day I got my paper with a "very good" mark, very rarely granted by him.

By the end of the fourth year, one day I stood for an examination on the last of my major obligatory subjects. My colleagues wished me luck; and when, after having finished my exam, I returned to the laboratory and told that I passed easily, they congratulated me. Incidentally, one of a German colleague, hearing that I finished with my obligatory exams, asked me, in students' slang: "In which one are you?" - and I replied: "In the eighth"; to his next question: "Year?", my reply was: "No, semester." He looked at me with visible disgust, turned around and left the room. German students generally finished their studies in eight years, instead of in eight semesters. That colleague of mine certainly thought within himself: "These dirty careerist Jews!"

I went home for the summer vacation, but this time I had to start to make a job-market research for the time next spring when I get my diploma. Unfortunately, the general economic situation was very difficult, thousands of people with university degrees were jobless, and thus the prospects were very unpromising. I did not despair, on the contrary: I was confident that once I succeeded in becoming an engineer despite big difficulties, I shall, sooner or later, overcome this obstacle too.

When I said good-bye to the people at the synagogue, they offered me my role of soloist for the coming High Holidays, with a special high honorarium, that I accepted, all the more, because I still had to stand for a few exams in non-compulsory subjects, plus I had to make the last, the second, finishing state-examination. Thus, I returned to Brunn earlier than usual for finishing these jobs. Everything went very smoothly; I made two very fine projects as the practical part of my state-exam, and at the beginning of April 1932. I stood for the oral part of it. I succeeded easily, and on April, 15, 1932, I graduated in Mechanical Engineering from the DTH (Deutsche Technische Hochschule: German Technical University), Brunn (Czechoslovakia), on the 15-th of April, 1932. - one week after my 23-rd birthday (Picture 17).

As the adage goes: a dream came true.

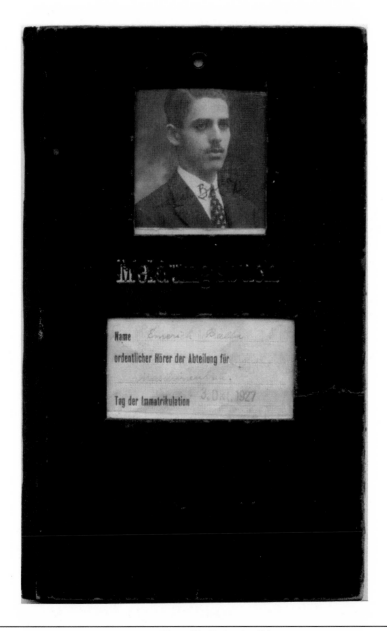

Picture 17 – Engineering diploma

SECTION 2 - THE RUMBLINGS OF WORLD WAR II

JOB HUNTING UNDER PREJUDICE - 1932 - 1937

Out of a wide spectrum of a dream's interpretation, my "dream" was an aspiration, a striving for becoming an engineer, which started earlier than I can remember. On the question of why and how this of my aspiration came about, I have been pondering a few times for the last fifty-odd years and I could not find a better explanation than that I was born to become an engineer, as some people are born to become painters, composers, etc. During all those years there was not once, not even a shadow of doubt in my mind that I shall be an engineer.

But even an innate talent can and even should be guided, controlled by outside influences. And that is what happened in my case, when one single person, my late brother, had shown me, intentionally, by his own superb, talented, exemplary deeds how talent differentiates between outstanding and mediocre people and stimulates aspiration to ever increasing improvement. As regards the "how" my dream came true: actually it was almost nipped in the bud when due to the anti-Semitic law of Hungary at that time: the "numerus clausus (restricted number)", I was not allowed to enroll the Technical University in Budapest. Then my brother, by his firm and resolute determination, took me to a Technical University abroad for enrollment, and by his continuous, unselfish financial support enabled me to achieve my aspiration to become an engineer. By the last analysis: without my late brother's decision and support my dream could never had come true.

Within a few days after graduation I settled my outstanding obligations: returning books, drawing-board, etc. to the University; said good-bye to friends - and to Brunn; and set out to travel home.

The half-day travel time gave me a respite for contemplating on my short-range plan at that first milestone event of becoming an engineer. I was fully aware that this was only the pre-requisite of being able to work as an engineer, but in itself it was not an automatic assurance for it, not even under normal economic conditions. And I was not under an illusion that in the prevailing economic and political situation in Hungary, my chance to get an employment would be favorable.

Still I did not give way to despair - on the contrary: recalling my hopeless situation four years earlier regarding my prospect for a university education - I took courage from the fact that I still succeeded to become an engineer. I resolved to continue and even to strengthen my fight for enabling me to work as an engineer, and keeping this resolution as my base line, I started to search for an opportunity, be it ever so small.

Remembering the last encounter with my former physical instructor at high-school who did not believe I could become an engineer, I wanted to proudly show him my new diploma, but he was no longer with the school.

Within a month or so it became clear that to get an engineering job, for anybody, at the then existing economic depression, was incomparably worse than I could foresee. To be accepted as an engineer by state-owned, big, or middle-size factories was conditional on being a member of the Chamber of Engineers and Architects, for which only engineers with Hungarian diploma were eligible. Thus: engineers with foreign diploma - meaning all the Jews having studied abroad - were not eligible as members of the Chamber, and there was no sense to apply for a job at those bigger enterprises, even if a job would be available. Practically there was no legal obstacle against employment of engineers who were non-members of the Chamber by factories that were not suppliers of state-, military-, etc. - authorities, that is by small- and middle-size factories, operating on the free, private market. Consequently, this sector, with its limited volume of opportunities, was the hunting ground for a job.

We left no stone unturned to find a trace of the slightest possibility - but in vain. After a while, only as an interim arrangement, I tried to earn some money by a few sorts of selling e.g. household appliances: vacuum-cleaners, etc.; or books; health insurance policy; and a few odds and ends - with the overall result that I myself bought a few books.

Then another approach occurred to me: I wanted to obtain a driver's license, and try to get a job as a driver. Within a few weeks I passed the necessary examinations and in June, 1932. I got my first driver's license. I was received by a few people: businessmen, architects, lawyers, and although I concealed that I was an engineer, they somehow got information from somewhere - and I was turned down. Their reason reached me through a number of people, that most of them were uneasy and disturbed to have an engineer as their driver: a feeling I could understand - only it left me jobless further on. Still, there was one lawyer, with whom I had a quite lengthy meeting, when he told me in detail, what he wanted me to do for him. He was a very talkative guy and he warmed up when he told me his conception. As he proceeded, my blood became on the boil, but this time I wanted to play to the end and tell him my opinion openly and unpolished, so I only smiled and let him speak. What he said was roughly as follows. He was a lawyer, lived and had an office in Budapest and had a villa somewhere, 70-80 km away along the river Danube, still being under construction. My duty would be to work in the office as a filing clerk; to lodge appeals, petitions, etc. to the courts of justice; to make copies of documents; to drive his car whenever needed; and - last but not least - to drive him on weekends to his villa and help him in his amateur stonemason's enthusiasm. For all these he offered some pitiful wage. I swallowed a few times to calm myself, and then I asked him whether he would have dared to request from a professional driver all these works done and offer such a dastardly wage - and added in unmistakable words, what he should do with himself and with his money.

For earning some money, I accepted the offer of a distant relative of our family, to do some administrative work during the summer season, in their business. They had the famous delicatessen shop at the Svabhegy (Swabian Hill), the exclusive villa-quarter of the aristocracy, diplomats, and wealthy people.

Their delicatessen business had a rather unique character: some 10-12 salesmen collected orders from the kitchen-chefs of the villas, for everything: foodstuff, including e.g. lobster (which was delivered only for the firm every day, live, in seawater containers, from the Adriatic See, by the daily express trains), foreign liquors, including French champagnes, etc. etc. These orders were then delivered during the next day, by 10-12 lorries and carts. And very often calls came during night hours, asking for delivery, within an hour or so, cold buffets, wines, liquors, fruits, etc. for 20-30 people. The work went on round the clock; payments were made once a week and preparations of the bills was quite a job, by the only help of manual adding machines. I was responsible for the book-keeping and billing.

During my about three months spell there, the owner of the business, a widow, a charming grand-lady, who was on close-friendly terms with all the aristocrat-ladies on the Hill, mentioned my singing affair of my university student years to somebody - without my knowledge. And so one day, a lady came in the shop and wanted to speak with me. She told me that she arranged an interview for me with the choir director of the Opera house, at a certain date - and wished me luck. I was perplexed, I felt that I must not decline her cordial help, eventhough I had no intention whatsoever to enter into a singing, instead of an engineering, career. I realized that both ladies were laudably full of goodwill, and if they had asked me before their benevolent move - I would have explained my standpoint of devotion to engineering against my amateurish affection to singing. But once they acted so kind-heartedly, all I could do was to express my sincere thanks - and go to the appointment.

The choir conductor - after hearing that I had been studying for four years at Professor Auschpitz, and singing in a choir and as a soloist - asked me to sing a few songs by Schubert, Mozart, etc, with his piano accompaniment. He was an elderly gentleman, very kind, spent quite a long time with me, and explained very frankly that I had a higher-than-average good voice and musical ear, and he would be ready to accept me in the choir as a full-time employee. But he made it clear that out of the about 100 choir members, not more than 10-12 develop into soloists and out of the 20-30 soloists not more than 2-3 reach internationally known level, after many years of hard work - and good luck. And he made no secret about it that a singer's life is very difficult, and it is exactly the opposite of the common belief about the wonderful life of famous opera singers.

He did not have to tell me, I knew it and I had no hesitation or regret in my clear-cut and final decision to pursue engineering - and engineering only. I more felt than knew that in a situation like mine: there could be only one choice: either-or, and there was no place for a secondary occupation.

I told this to the director and thanked him for his kindness and wise warning. He appreciated my decision and wished me luck in my engineering career.

My morale was very down after about nine months of joblessness (except the three months summer administrative work), when one day my brother told me a good news that through his friends he was informed that the owner of a small workshop promised to see me, because he had been considering to expand the activities of his shop.

Early the next morning, sometime in February 1933, a cold winter day, I went to his workshop. The offices were situated below street level; in a cramped outer office room three-four clerks were diligently working, bent low over their small desks; a few bare electric bulbs gave a pitiable lighting, but as a funny contrast: a round iron stove was red hot, fueled by wooden blocks, out of a carton-box beside the stove.

I told them that I was looking for Mr. Popper; I had an appointment. One of the clerks told me to sit down and wait, since Mr. Popper was busy - and made a nod with his head to an adjacent door. I sat down, and after a short while a quite loud and heated debate was heard from behind the door of the adjacent room. After a few minutes two men came out, one of them left the office and the other, a rather short fellow with a big cigar in his mouth, red in the face, looked around - and with a sudden move: opened the entrance door, took the box with the wooden blocks - and throw it out, shouting that the heat was unbearable. It seemed to me that he was near to exploding form anger - and the few clerks seemingly would have liked to become invisible, and tried to duck as low as possible to vanish from sight. The short man with the cigar, obviously the boss: Mr. Popper looked around and asked me what I wanted. I told him my name and reminded him to his message sent to me by one of his business connections that he wanted to see me.

He told me to wait and went into his office. During my wait in the outside office room, I tried to contemplate on the scene I witnessed, and I could only conclude that what I saw was a scene in a real workplace - and not that of a lunatic asylum, and would I have not absolutely determined to start working as an engineer, by whatever price - I felt like to get up and leave the place without further ado. But I waited, much impressed by what I experienced and what at the same time aroused my inquisitiveness to find out the real reasons for the actions of the big boss with the big cigar.

After a while, Mr. Popper called me in, offered a seat, and asked a lot of questions, such as: about my family, education, diploma, experience, etc. He was composed, quasi-jovial, with not even a trace of his previous towering rage. He examined me on a few technical subjects, e.g. how much the specific weight of wood, and other questions relating to wood as raw material. Then he alluded to his plan to increase the capacity of the present production of wooden-heels for ladies' shoes and to the other, more ambitious future plan, to expand the capacity of repairing and refurbishing all sorts of shoe-machines for the shoe-industry. He mentioned very proudly that a new factory-building was being built for those purposes and as the first step of starting work there shall be to transfer the wooden-heel making machinery from the present place to the new building. He took me then to have a look at the present workshop, of very cramped rooms, full of workers -

and very noisy and full of dust.

Then we went over to the new two-story building, almost completed; with a big hall on the ground floor and a few adjacent smaller rooms; the first floor almost similar, the second floor more divided between bigger and smaller rooms. Basic services were already installed: water and electricity. As he explained: the wooden-heels department was going to be located on the first floor; the second floor was foreseen for store-rooms and offices; the ground floor was the location of the future machine shop, for repairing, refurbishing used machines, and eventually producing new shoe-machines.

When we returned to his office, he told me that he was willing to accept me, for a term of probation, with the first task to organize and manage the transfer of the installations to the new factory, in such a way so as not to lose time and production. With a smile, he said that the machines should not stop running even during their transfer; he told this as a joke - but he meant it earnestly. I understood it clearly, although I was not a psychologist; but I took it as my first challenge, even if seemed to me a "mission impossible". The task offered to me was at the farthest extreme of a young engineer's conception of the classical field and mode of engineering activity: to work in a nice office, designing machines, organizing production, and so on - as contrasted with the presently offered task, hopefully only for the beginning of my work. I took on the challenge - I remembered in a flash my encounters with the "descriptive geometry" and "mathematics": precarious challenges in which I succeeded; so I felt having a quite firm background. I told Mr. Popper that I shall do my best to serve his interests. To his question: when I was ready to start - I answered: right now.

During the time from accepting the offer one morning and starting the actual work the next: I tried to check and recheck whether I decided correctly. The first and weightiest point for my consent was that after almost a year's waiting - I got a job, my first one. That the assignment was far from a classical or conventional engineering assignment: would be a negative point on a traditional, conservative scale, but the challenge of the present case versus a traditional slow upgrading on a donkey-ladder was an overwhelmingly positive factor for me. Thus, as a consequence of these, and a few more secondary considerations, I confirmed my consenting answer, and started working the next morning with high hope, enthusiasm, and confidence.

I bought a work-coat of gray color, as a symbolic display of my desire to collaborate with the workers, instead of playing the role of a commanding engineer. Anyway, my primary responsibility will be to set up a machine shop, with new skilled workers - and less, or almost nothing, with managing the present staff of the wooden-heels' facility. But the transfer of the present equipment and starting the production in the new building was my first responsibility, and for succeeding in this of my first task: I needed the full cooperation of all present people; and for achieving this: I had to proceed carefully, because an existing group of workers are always suspicious of a young new "engineer-boss" as an adversary. I wanted to allay their antagonism, by proving with my actual participation in their work that what they will get from me will be for their benefit, for instance: safety installations, equipment to make their work easier and less tedious, etc. At the first glance on their old place of work, I noticed a series of items which in the new factory I could easily improve, such as lighting, vacuum-removal of the huge quantity of wooden-shavings and dust, safety glasses for grinding work, etc.

Thus, I started next morning, at 7 am. A big trailer was due to arrive at 8 am to move the first machine. The factory had some 50 workers, with an only foreman as their direct boss: Mr. Lukacs. It was clear to me that he was not too enthusiastic to get somebody, a young engineer, as his future superior. In order to dissolve his antagonism and fear for his status: I told him about my actual duty and program to design and build shoe-machines in a separate department of the factory; the present production line of wooden-heels will remain his domain, and presently I wanted to help him in arranging the machines for a more efficient and convenient production procedure.

As the first step: we went over with Mr. Lukacs to the new location and there I asked him how he intended to place the first and the successive machines, and expressed my agreement with all his preparatory instructions. I asked him for his opinion: how to move in the long machines, which end to steer first, in order to save difficult rotational movements inside the room afterwards, etc. My main purpose was to let him have the command for the entire transfer and learn as much as possible about the production process in detail. A few details I already saw that could and would be advisable to improve, but I felt that I had to move very carefully.

My instinct told me that I face a precarious situation. On the one hand I was unfamiliar with the production process of their main product, the wooden-heels, although it was not something complicated - but still it had a lot of small but important details, that had to be considered when transferring and arranging at the new location the big number of machines and accessories. Thus, I had to act with much cautiousness so that not to give away my lack of expertise. But on the other hand, I had to build up, slowly but consistently, my hierarchical status, which I could achieve by proving before them my professional expertise. More by instinct than by consciousness, my tactics evolved along the lines that I asked them, at proper occasions, questions like: what are the reasons and the advantages to do certain things as they had been doing, as compared to other methods the competing factories were doing it. This instinctive questioning method proved to be doubly advantageous: they made out from my questions that I was familiar with production steps applied by other factories, and by their explaining the reasons of their methods, I could easily learn everything I needed for completing my understanding of the entire production process.

The transfer of the machines progressed well; on the second day a few of the machines were already running. On the third or fourth day an accident, that could have had fatal consequence, was prevented by my sticking to that basic, strictly defined safety rule: do not touch electric wires without first checking them whether or not they were "live", that is connected to an electric circuitry. What happened was as follows. The wiring and switches for the electric motors of the machines had been completed by a contractor a few weeks earlier. By pure chance I passed by a machine, newly placed on its foundation, when two people wanted to connect the prepared wires to the electric motor. By an innate instinct I stopped and asked them whether they checked the wires for voltage. They showed me that the switch on the wall was in the "off" position. I told them that it was not sure enough, and the wire-endings had to be checked. Since no measuring instrument was at hand, I took a hand-lamp and carefully touched the prepared wires to those of the lamp. And the lamp lighted up - with the relevant switch in the "off" position! The few workers were just shocked, they looked at each other, and I did not need to explain to them how easily they could had been electrocuted by touching the "live" wires; they experienced in their past similar accidents. This completely chance event, that I passed by at a particular time point and had an instinctive curiosity to see what they were doing: turned out in such a way that established my competence and reputation very firmly. Calling the electricians who did the work, it turned out that, by mistake, that particular point was connected to two distinct electric circuits, and the switch on the wall controlled only one of them.

This occurrence was my first encounter with safety rules in my capacity as responsible for workers under my command, and it stayed with me all along: "safety first!". Besides this safety aspect, the many small events during the starting days on my job, including my investigations by questioning the details of the production technology of wooden-heels, properties of raw material: the type of wood, its storage, its steam-treatment, etc, made me pondering about a few aspects of the events that occurred during the previous days, mainly as a consequence of my preponderant "intuitiveness".

Intuition, a sort of capacity for guessing something correctly in a flash, or a sense of something not evidently exposed, or a faculty of knowing without the use of rational processes, a sharp insight: seemed to me a faculty that may be useful in engineering work - but I was hesitant to accept it as a reliable scientific factor for considering in engineering work; I had my doubts - but at the same time I wanted to clarify the matter in depth.

I considered intuition as a very important, specific, innate human feature that certain people possess, while others have not; in other words: it cannot be acquired, but may be used when available. I thought that its use can be beneficial or harmful, depending on the manner how it is used. Spontaneous and unchecked, haphazard acceptance and use can be harmful, even damagingly dangerous, whereas intuition checked by strict logic, scientific scrutiny and double-checking could provide valuable factors for professional, especially engineering, problem solving.

The above described events were not the first encounters with my inborn intuition, but at the start of my engineering activity: I felt I had to scrutinize it. Countless intuitive impulses occurred all along my engineering career, and most of them, after careful scrutiny, proved to be beneficial for my work.

Closely connected and sometimes maybe a trigger to intuition is another trait, also inborn and instinctive: subconsciously practiced observation and taking notice of all sorts of things, with no discernible reasons for selection, in a flash, unintentionally, when moving around or just sitting at a place and the world passes by. Characteristic is that you do not watch, you are not on the lookout you just notice things around you. One symptom of such observation is that you become aware of even small changes of things that had happened since you saw the same spot previously, or that they are out of the ordinary. Such instinctive observation must have been the reason of my intervention when the workers wanted to connect a motor to the electric circuitry.

Within about three weeks the factory was running at the new location. We had nearby a big plot as a storage place for the wooden rods; big quantities of various cross-sections.

The offices were located on the second floor: one smaller room for the boss and one big room for all the clerks, including myself, getting the same type and size of desk as all the others - and no drawing board. I did not complain, because I thought that when the need will arise for doing real engineering work: design, drawing, etc. - I shall get the necessary tools.

The next step in the development program was to transfer the big number of used shoe-machines that had been stored at a few shoe factories that had become bankrupt and closed down and their machines, with spare-parts and accessories, had been bought up by Mr. Popper. Transferring the machines, placing them in a big store room in the new factory building, and especially placing on shelves the huge number of their spare-parts and accessories in drawers of cupboards - was a big operation, during which I learned a lot about two important factors. One was my learning the machines themselves, their tasks and functioning, helped partly by Mr. Popper's explanation and partly from the operating manual books, containing the lists of tools, changeable components, and accessories.

The other thing I learned was Mr. Popper himself. He was a self-made businessman, very clever, shrewd, and tough; a real dictator, who terrorized his workers and clerks. There and then, employees were totally unprotected; there were no regulated working hours and days, neither regulated nor contracted wages and salaries. A health insurance organization was the only working body for the benefit of the employees.

Mr. Popper made some agreement with his workers as regards the working hours, but he alone fixed the wages of each group, from time to time. When one or more workers begged for some increase - he became extremely agitated, red in face, started shouting, banged tables, and accused the workers of being communists - a dangerous charge at that time. And as I learned from other work places, the situation was similar in nature: the workers were completely dependent on their bosses' unilateral decision, mainly as regards wages.

Mr. Popper's frequent sudden outbursts, yelling, and thundering first confused and troubled me. In my inexperienced naiveté, there just was no place for such unreasonable behavior: you either agree or disagree with opinions of others on something - and you tell your standpoint and decide as you want - but bullying and terrorizing your adversaries was, in my opinion, not a civilized way to negotiate. I was very-very naive and by every week I learned more and more that I did not like and did not want to accept and adopt for myself, but I had to be aware of its existence.

Mr. Popper was great in sham-acting. Every time, when he wanted to establish or strengthen his sole, absolute, and final supreme commanding position, or felt that such of his position was threatened or questioned: he hollered, red in face, rushed up and down, slammed doors, banged tables, etc, until people were so terrified that they gave up any request they had and they were happy to be able to escape before being thrown out bodily. Then he went in his office, lighted a big cigar and changed right away to his regular, quite normal behavioral state of an almost jovial businessman. I saw him, not once, to chat and speak about business at a completely normal, cheerful manner, one or two minutes after he made a big show.

I could not see and perceive it clearly at that time: what his reasoning was that the only person in the company, to whom he did not even try to apply this of his artificial and purposeful practice of terrifying people, was me - but this was the situation right from the first day. Maybe he sensed my disapproval and aversion to his sham-acting, or maybe because our relationship started by my silent but extremely diligent and tireless work which not only surprised him, but went far above his expectation. He never said a word of appreciation to me - and with intent; what he wanted was to examine me and my work for ascertaining whether or not he can rely on me to carry out his ambitious plan to establish a shoe-machine factory. He was smart enough to see through me, right from the first day of my work, that I was there, a young engineer, who was more than eager to work, but was timid to request anything, not to speak an adequate salary.

One other reason for our special relationship, distinct from that he had with all other employees, could had been that I took all his requests with a laconic O.K, never made any comment, even when details of his requests were wrong, unattainable. I carried out the work as I deemed it correct, and - especially at the beginning of my work there when I presented the result, I saw in his eyes that he noticed the changes that I made contrary to his demand, but he was clever enough to perceive that his request could not had been implemented, or that my solution was better than he expected to attain - and he never objected to my method.

My silent but plain refusal to assent to his bullying behavior had been exposed to view by a number of, in themselves insignificant, but for the other, older office employees' startling occurrences.

Since there were no regulated working hours, the office workers started at 8 am; there was no official lunch break: everybody ate sandwiches, etc, at their writing desk, and continued working. Mr. Popper went home for lunch and a nap, and returned at about 4 pm; was seated in the big common office room, among the clerks, smoking a big cigar, either working silently or discussing business matters with his people. Until he got up and called his driver to drive him home - nobody dared to go home. Thus, sometimes it was 7 or 8 pm when the people could leave.

The workers finished at 4 or 5 pm; then I went up to my desk in the common office room, to finish my drawing, etc. work. When I felt that I finished my work for the day, I cleared my desk, went to the locker room, changed clothing, passed through the big room, said "good night" and left. True enough that sometimes I worked till 10 pm or even later. The first time when I left when all of them were still working, my colleagues could not believe their eyes, and were waiting for a big show from Mr. Popper. He just looked at me

- but did not utter a word.

Another small example of the same sort of interaction was when, for some reason, Mr. Popper played one of his terrorizing shows, nobody dared, for instance to eat his sandwich, or do anything but extremely diligent work, silently, and lay low. If it happened at lunch-time, I washed hands, laid out a napkin, took my sandwich, tomatoes, etc. - and ate my lunch. He noticed my act, but accepted it without the slightest comment.

I was then a young guy, who after almost one year's chasing for a job, was first of all more than happy to have a place of work, where I highly valued my first chance to be able to do engineering work and enjoyed every single one of the challenges put up before me - and succeeded to overcome them: thus I definitely did not want to endanger this of my first job by resisting to Mr. Popper's requests or instructions. Moreover, I was in need of the money I earned, which was another reason for not defying Mr. Popper's supremacy. But I could not see any reason why I should behave and demean myself for Mr. Popper's just or unjust, real or artificial anger against somebody or something, not related to me. I felt that any sign of fright or fear would mean confessing some sort or part of a misdeed or offense that I did not commit. Thus, I did not join the frightened people who, maybe, had some reason and felt that they were guilty or wrong in something that brought about the outburst of Mr. Popper.

Mr. Popper was intelligent enough to perceive the rightfulness of my behavior and was convinced that it was not a provocation or insult to him. So our special relationship evolved.

On his credit: Mr. Popper had an extraordinary power of memory; for instance, he knew and remembered exactly all details of every single one of the many used machines, and what is more: about their spare parts, components, and accessories that had been taken together with the machines when he had bought them.

The transfer of the big quantity of the used shoe-machines had been finished within a few weeks, and they were nicely stored, together with their spare parts, etc. When they were sold, one or two at a time, Mr. Popper told me to prepare the particular machines for delivery, including spare parts. Referring now to his extraordinary memory, he took it as something absolutely natural and obvious that I should know about the existence of each single spare part and component, the same way as he knew it. This was an almost impossible task, but since I hated even the thought to admit that I did not know about this or that spare part, etc, I had been making extraordinary effort to get to know and identify and keep in memory every single one of those components, and present them when needed, as a mere trifle, nonchalantly. Mr. Popper made no comments, but he was very much impressed. In the meantime, we employed two technicians, who had worked as maintenance workers in shoe factories, and we set up and equipped a workshop for repairing and refurbishing the used shoe machines. With the help of these technicians I had to muster all my ability to carry out the task to remove from store, clean, refurbish, and test the proper machines; to find the spare parts and accessories, and put the machines in good working condition.

This went on for a few months, when one day Mr. Popper told me about his ambitious plan to set up a real machine factory with the task to produce shoe machines, except the really sophisticated automatic machines. For this task I prepared a list of the necessary equipment, and we started to buy machine-tools, such as lathes, milling machines, planers, various sizes of drill presses, etc.; hand tools, measuring equipment, etc, etc. It sounds quite simple to say: "I prepared a list of the necessary equipment, machine-tools, etc.", but actually I (or any other young engineer fresh from the university) would not had been able to compile such a list, were it not for my actual workshop experience from the three-times three months "engineer's apprenticeship" in the Ganz Works, during my university years. During these months, I worked on all machine-tools, used every measuring device, etc, I made my hands dirty on actual production of machine components. For me a machine-tool was not a concept, but a real device, about which I knew what it could be used for and how.

Simultaneously, we started to look for and employ skilled workers. This happened about three-four months after I had started to work at the factory. For the first month I got a very small sum as salary, but from the second month on my salary rose month by month, without my asking.

When we started to set up the machine shop, I felt that my time was ripe: I got the green light and could start doing real engineering work. My task seemed to me an ideal one: to start from zero, to set up a machine shop for producing a quite well defined assortment of shoe machines; to equip the shop with the necessary machine tools and all other equipment; to organize the work; to employ skilled workers and establish a good working team. Unfortunately, there were difficulties: first of all Mr. Popper agreed to everything I proposed, but I had to make a lot of compromises mainly because he wanted to reduce investment cost to an almost absurd minimum. I had no other way than to proceed step-by-step, adding one machine after another to form the constituents of my future total plan.

Installing the first assortment of machine tools, work benches, etc. was proceeding quite rapidly, and we started to use them for repair works of the used machines. One day Mr. Popper called me in his office, where he had been negotiating a business deal with the owner of a shoe factory, and asked me whether I remembered one particular shoe machine that we had refurbished some time earlier. To my affirmative answer, he asked me: what would I say if we start our own production with that particular type, to which I answered: "O.K." Then he said: what would I say that he already sold two units of that machine to Mr. X, who was sitting there, and promised to deliver them in six months time. I remember well that moment, when, without thinking and without the slightest hesitation, I simply said: O.K. Then we shook hands and I left the room and went down to the workshop.

And there, I started thinking about what happened, what I took upon myself, and what could be the most optimistic result or how I would fail ignominiously; why did I agree to accept a "mission impossible" when I knew full well that our workshop was still far too scarcely equipped, with too few skilled workers for such a job; I had not even a drawing board and instruments, etc.; every single requisite for such an undertaking was insufficient if not lacking, and consequently, any engineer in his right mind would have declared such a request as unreasonable and turned down the responsibility.

And I accepted it. I could not properly analyze the reasons for it, I rather felt that this was my first, and decisive, real challenge; all the previous tasks were "small fishes" only. And then I concluded that the challenge, that I took on in the office of Mr. Popper, I shall carry out and resolved to myself that I shall succeed, at all costs, regardless to any other consideration and reason. This was my first real test, to myself, that I was an engineer, who could cope with uncommon tasks, and I was strengthened in my resolve by remembering and relying on my ability of designing by imagining, in my head, planning carefully but changing and improvising as the need arose.

Since we had no more such machine on stock, I went to a shoe factory the next day and made as many sketches and measurements as was possible without dismantling the machine. Then I prepared a list of those machines and tools that had to be bought within days - and Mr. Popper could not resist. There remained one item, definitely the smallest one of all investments: a drawing board and instruments for designing. In this point I was defiant: I did not repeat my request, I wanted to show off, by designing on simple stationary, by free-hand sketches. Within the framework of the general challenge, my free-hand designing on letter-paper sheets: was a headstrong duel between me and Mr. Popper, whom I suspected that he stage-managed this whole situation in order to ascertain whether or not he could build his development program on me. It was a fight, a silent one, and I went about happily to fight and win it.

I designed the components, each one on a separate sheet; but I could not make any assembly- or sub-assembly drawing on those regular office size sheets; these drawings were made mentally, in my head, and stored there in my memory bank. I completed first the set of drawings for the cast-iron pieces, for which the casting forms had to be ordered; then the cast pieces themselves. We ordered necessary raw materials and started machining the components. Some operations I had to farm out due to lack of proper tools. As work progressed and we had to put together sub-assemblies, sometimes I felt strong twitches in my stomach before assembling - but did not show any emotion and played calmly by taking it as the most natural thing on earth when there were no hitches and everything went smoothly. Deep inside, of course, I was very happy and I credited the accurate design on account of my talent of the "descriptive geometry" complex. When I saw that everything progressed finely with the machine, designed originally on the model of the conventional machine in general use, I became bold and added a few improvements to it.

Mr. Popper came to the workshop quite often, asked questions, but was intelligent enough not to intervene in the technical details. He was waiting for the final result. Then, one day, a few days prior to the deadline, I invited him to the workshop and presented to him the two machines in operation. He just smiled, went around the machines, asked for a few shoes and tried out the operation. He was satisfied and thanked us for this first product of his shoe-machine factory.

I felt that in that unconventional challenge and duel: both of us won. I had all the reason to be content with my success against all obstacles, and felt my self-confidence enhanced. "Descriptive geometry" and my ability to design in my head, keep details in my memory, and manipulate the components at will: won the day. (By the way, when I mentioned to a few of my colleagues my challenging work, they simply told me that I was crazy.) Mr. Popper considered himself a winner too; I was convinced that he did not believe originally that those machines will be performing well and be ready at the set delivery date - but I proved that I succeeded in both.

After having finished my first real, veritable production machine, a result of my engineering work, comprising the following main constituents: design, machining, and assembly, plus ancillary steps and succeeded in it - I spent some time pondering about my feelings on being a mechanical engineer. Out of a number of branches of mechanical engineering: design-, production-, programming-, maintenance-, etc, I landed by chance in a work place where I had to perform not in one, but in all these branches. Were it not for my "descriptive geometry" expertise and the three-times three months "engineer's apprenticeship" practical experience - I definitely could not had been able to carry out my duty and succeed in it. By the end of my almost one year work, comprising every conceivable branch of mechanical engineering, I wanted to find out: whether or not I had any preference to one or another branch. And I came to that definite conclusion that I had none; I enjoyed all of them, especially and preferably in their totality. What I felt was that I aspired to do "problem solving" as the primary goal, and mechanical engineering only as a means to that end.

At that time I already got a quite decent salary, and within two-three months I was registered as factory manager in the "Hungarian Machine Factories Association", and I was given the legal right of procurement, together with our accountant, in the absence of Mr. Popper, who traveled to Germany at least once a year, on business. He was the sole representative of those shoe-machine factories in Germany whose products were predominantly used in the shoe industry, such as: Atlas Werke, Fortuna, etc.

Simultaneously with designing and producing the first type of our own shoe-machine assortment, another challenge was put before me. The factory building was designed by a well-known architect, who happened to be a friend of Mr. Popper. They started some two years prior to my entering the picture. The architect had a friend - whom I did not know - who was some sort of technical businessman and who seemingly acted as a technical consultant for Mr. Popper and the architect. The wooden-heels were produced out of pre-cut wooden blocks, and in the process an average of 30-35% wooden-waste material was left over, that had to be collected, stored, and generally caused a headache: how to get rid of it. That friend of the architect had an idea of not only to solve the problem of getting rid of the waste material, and in such a way as to result in a certain financial profit - instead of expenditure. He proposed to utilize the wooden waste material for producing wood-gas, in a gas generator and to drive with it a gas engine. He procured a used, 6 cylinder, Diesel engine, with an original 150 HP power, that had to be modified for wood-gas as fuel; they ordered a gas-generator and a three-phase electric generator with 75 kW output, and the building had been designed for housing these equipment in a sub-terrain machine room.

These machines were delivered by separate suppliers, but the technical consultant, who persuaded Mr. Popper and the architect into ordering these machines, was already not available, and consequently, nobody was responsible for the proper functioning of the whole set-up. Thus, the task dropped into my lap. I sensed that the concept was good; and anyway the machines were there and I felt as if they were mockingly looking at me, saying: "now, you wise guy, what are you going to do with us?" So, I had to deal with the problem.

A Diesel engine fueled with wood-gas: whoever heard about such a thing. But the problem was there, challenging me stronger than all the other, previous ones. I had already been deeply involved in similar, albeit smaller tasks - so I decided to take on this new and heavy one too. I was running from one library to the next one to find references, but there were very few. We employed an old guy, who had been a Diesel locomotive driver, and started experimenting.

The total problem was divided into two parts: gas production and engine running. The engine had a starter arrangement by compressed air, stored in two huge cylinders. We had no testing arrangement for the wood-gas quality other than the actual engine running.

Many a days were spent to start the gas generator and after a while, when by the smell we thought the gas quality was proper, we started, by the compressed air, the engine. Our initial happiness when the engine, after some coughing, started running, first slowly, then at near normal speed - turned sour when within 2-10 minutes the engine started stalling and then stopped altogether. After a few similar performances, I diagnosed that both quality and quantity of continuous gas supply was insufficient. After a few more trials, I added an injection air blower to the gas generator, increasing thereby both quality and quantity of the gas stream, that could be regulated - and this supplement solved our problem.

We made an arrangement with the Electric Supply Company, so that we could run our factory either with our own generating unit or switch over to the central electric supply system. Besides, we built and installed a deep water pump for the sole purpose of cooling the engine and supplying the gas generator. From that on, the factory was run by our tiny generating unit, fueled by the wooden waste.

This success added another feather to my cap. But, I had no doubt about the predominant role of my intuition and inventiveness versus my actual knowledge and praxis on the subject, which had been very minimal at the beginning. The success made me feel good, but at the same time, I was full of doubt and uncertainty about how far may I proceed on this way; how can I ascertain whether or not my intuition was warranted. And such sort of hesitancy was not a question of a few minutes or hours to decide either way: this stayed with me continuously, day and night, and became the complementary to my mental process of designing by imagining. The steps of the entire process established themselves on a spiraling line as something like: stating the problem; choices of solutions; eliminating not promising choices - by intuition; designing promising choices - based on precedents, or partly by intuition and partly by inventiveness; playing the "devil's advocate"-role by trying to prove that the selected solutions are not good enough, and proceeding with ranking the remaining winning solutions; and finally completing their design. I felt that the flash of ingenuity is a marvelous thing - but it is far from being sufficient for the final design.

We hardly finished those two units of the first type of our own shoe machines, when Mr. Popper came with the news that we shall start with another type. And so it went, on and on; by the end of the fourth year of my work there: I made a statistic: I designed and we produced as an average one new type every month. It goes without saying that among them were simple machines, the design of which did not take more than a few days; but there were a few types necessitating months of design and six-eight months of through-put production periods.

The basic characteristics of the design process remained the same as I used it for the first type: I worked out every detail in my head, by the imagining process I had found out in my early student years in connection with the "central collineation" theorem of the general "descriptive geometry". During the years, as I worked on more and more designs, the method developed and matured further, mainly in the direction that I could work simultaneously on more than one design problem. This design method, which I had discovered by chance and had played with it consciously for visualizing space configurations, mainly in their relationships with each other, had become during the years and as a consequence of more and more applications, a quasi-unconscious process. It permeated my mind; the process, once triggered by a need, had been transformed into a continuous one, going on and on, day and night, using more and more mental capacity. I became aware of the growing collimation when, for instance, sitting in company of friends, chatting, and after a while they told me: "Imre, where are you?" My mind was busy with design problems and thus switched off my brain from incoming sound and visual signals. By such occasions I started to realize that that was the price I was compelled to pay.

In the factory we proceeded with designing and producing more and more additional types. Maybe understandably I was a little bit overjoyed with my successes, but I warned Mr. Popper that the pace he dictated cannot be kept unless I get proper design equipment and at least one or two young engineers and technicians. But Mr. Popper was much more overjoyed than myself; in his sanguine dreams he had not hoped to achieve as much new machines produced in his factory as we actually did, thus he was contented. I, on the other hand, was more headstrong and defiant than before, and was stupid enough by wanting to show him that I can manage without a drawing board and accessories, and designing everything by free-hand sketches. So, our silent duel went on, without change.

My designing by imagining had proved its worth right from the beginning, when dealing with the sole first type of our machine production program, but became really beneficial and even indispensable later on when I already had to design simultaneously more than one type at any given time. Besides designing, I had to deal with production also, in all its aspects: material procurement, programming and scheduling, etc, which I did the similar way. When I arrived every morning at the factory, I had already worked out in my head a complete program for the day: what to do, in what sequence, etc. Later, when designs of two or more types of machines occupied my mind simultaneously, the daily programming had to extend to the combination of programs of all types in work at the time, where the emphasis was on the priorities: what to do first, what next, etc. As a matter of fact, this method was, in practice, an early sort of programming steps of works, a method that much later became what is now called PERT method.

By the fall of 1935, Mr. Popper offered me to go along with him to his next business trip to Germany, to visit a few shoe-machine factories we represented in Hungary, especially because he wanted to produce a few types on a cooperation basis (Picture 18). There were a few types of quite sophisticated machines, having a number of components that neither we, nor any other factory in Hungary, could produce at acceptable prices in the yearly quantities needed.

Picture 18 – Chief engineer at Popprt

Needless to say that I accepted the invitation. I prepared carefully the questions to be discussed. We visited all factories we represented, and negotiated successfully all items: we would get all crucial components for the machines to be produced under license in our plant.

We were received by the owners and directors with courtesy and hospitality, although they knew very well that Mr. Popper and I were Jews. During our business negotiations we never entered into politics; but at nights, when they invited us to dinner in elegant restaurants, they came up with those questions. They, almost without exception, told us that the excesses of the Hitler regime were only a passing phenomenon; by reducing unemployment and increasing living standard the need for anti-Semitic propaganda and restrictions will automatically recede - and anyway, the majority of the people were against those excesses. Whether or not they were sincere in what they told us - we had no way of knowing.

The factories we visited were of middle-size, with 500-1000 workers. They produced only shoe-machines, each of which, by their nature, were not bigger and heavier than maximum 1000 kg, and both of us knew very well the entire assortment of their products. During our visit they showed us the whole plant. In one of the factories, by passing through a quite big machine hall, I noticed that some heavy change-gear boxes were produced on a long assembly line. To my question they said, by trying to dodge the question, that they got an order for a big quantity of change-gears for heavy trucks. It was more than obvious for me that those were units for tanks and not for trucks: their size revealed that fact without any doubt. This happened in the fall of 1935, when Germany was still forbidden to arm itself.

We had no contacts with Jews or Jewish institutions; all our informations we got from the daily newspapers. What they wrote with respect of the Jewish problem at those days referred mainly to the question that Germany offered to let their Jews to leave Germany, but, except those who had family contacts abroad, very few, almost no Jews were allowed to immigrate into foreign countries; and they wrote with much malicious gloating their propaganda evaluation of this behavior of all foreign countries. When the two of us reflected about these news, unfortunately we had to admit that all foreign countries, almost without exception, responded negatively; what we could not understand, and, in our naivety we hoped that some political arrangement must had been underway which would bring some solution to those hundreds of thousands of German Jews, by letting them emigrate to somewhere.

Our trip to Germany, from the business point of view, was successful - but as regards the Jewish problem, we returned home with depressing feelings; we felt very uneasy, we consciously wanted to be optimistic, or at least not too pessimistic, but the facts so far did not support optimism. The spread of Nazism and Fascism was a threat, but we, all of us in Hungary, did not feel it imminent, and whoever had some minimal means and circumstances of livelihood at home in Hungary: was under the spell of - what was called in Jewish circles - the "side-board" complex; meaning briefly a reluctance to leave behind the existing "side-board" because of the fear of a potential threat. This complex was one of the manifestations of the creeping process of conditioning the Jews to the slowly, step-by-step worsening economic and social situation, at different rates in various East-European countries, except in Germany, where it erupted with a heavy blow.

After having returned from our trip, the pace in designing and building machines increased. I visited the bigger shoe factories quite often and tried to draw lessons from the experiences of their production processes, especially those directly connected with the working of the machines and the cumulated comments of their operators. Consequently, every new type I had to design became the subject of a few modifications, improvements - they were not copies of existing machines. Each new type became a new challenge for me to be taken on. And with all due modesty, I cannot recall that any one of my designs left anything to be desired for further improvement. The pace increased steadily, but only at certain time points did I perceive and been troubled that I was going to become a person with a monochromatic, collimated mental interest and activity.

A very illustrative example started to be emerging when I listened to concerts. I went regularly to concerts, and to the Opera. And I started to notice, to my disquiet, that instead of following and fully enjoying the music, my mind became busy dealing with technical problems of my agenda then. And I started worrying about it.

I started to become aware of another phenomenon that annoyed me - but which I could not change - or maybe I did not want to change, because changing it, at least I felt so, would have meant to become aggressive, demanding, bossy, etc.: traits I had had loathed from my childhood. I recognized it - I thought: correctly - as a weakness, a drawback in life, but still I preferred, obstinately, my elitist, unassertive, pliant, and passive behavior. In retrospect, I think, I made a mistake when not fighting strongly against my stubbornness; but somehow I never could find a compromise between those character features that had been lacking in me and the supreme objectivity, one of the unwritten laws of engineering, that had been one of my leading principles in my entire career.

Maybe the most characteristic example was the following. Our small electric power plant was operating regularly. The engine needed lubricating oil of a suitable quality, so I asked three suppliers to submit samples for testing. I sent the samples to the Technological Testing Institute, and we made a supply contract with the supplier of the best quality oil. At Christmas time in 1935, the agent of the supplier firm came to me, with good wishes, and presented me with a very elegant set of crocodile attaché case, purse, and belt. I told him that for preventing any doubt of a bribery charge, I can accept it only if he presents it to me in the presence of Mr. Popper. So we went to see him, where he wished us very Christmas, and he showed to Mr. Popper the present he intended to give me. Mr. Popper opened the box, found it very nice, and even told the agent that I really deserved it. The agent left us, the box on Mr. Popper's desk. He kept it, and never gave it to me and I was just disgusted even at the thought to ask for it.

In the meantime, designs and production of additional new types continued at an accelerated pace. A young technician was employed, to help me in the growing liaison duties between me and the workers and suppliers; dispensing hand tools, caring for deliveries of raw materials, etc.

One day a decision was made to embark upon the biggest, most difficult task in our machine designing and building program up to that time, to produce a so-called "punching press" machine. At that time the only material for shoe-soles was leather that had to be cut to suit shape and size of the shoes. Thickness generally used was between 3 to 5 mm. In factories, the soles were cut, called "punched", on big, heavy punching press: one sole by one stroke of the head: the "ram" of the machine. The leather sheet was placed on a wooden block, of some 15 cm thickness, placed on the big base plate of the machine. The actual cut was made by strong steel punching forms of the desired shape of the sole, some 15 cm in height, its bottom ground to a sharp cutting edge. The punching form was placed on the leather sheet and the heavy ram was lowered to the form's upper surface by the help of a pedal, and the huge rotating fly-wheel of the machine exerted a heavy blow to the ram, and through it, to the punching form that cut out the sole.

This work, conforming to almost all other work steps, was paid by the piece. Consequently, workers were eager to increase the quantities they produced, and due to the danger involved in the cutting process, one could hardly find a punch-press operator who had not lost one-two fingers, that were snatched on top of the punching form when they rotated and placed it on the leather sheet, and pressed on the pedal for punching. A conventional safety device was adopted: a collar, fixed around the punching form near to the top; but it did not help too much.

Mr. Popper wanted to copy - at least the principles - the type most in use in the industry. This machine was going to be the biggest and most complicated machine in our production program up to that time, the biggest challenge to me at the same time.

I did not deliberate too long and made up my mind to make every effort to design this machine as safe as possible, for preventing cutting off fingers of their operators, along with shoe soles. I resolved to try to find a solution for achieving a safe operation, because I felt it irreconcilable with my private and professional conscience to design a "mini-guillotine" of fingers. This was my self-imposed goal, as a super-challenge, complementing the "routine" challenge, placed by my boss and took upon myself. But I had to devise my solution in complete secrecy: Mr. Popper would not want to hear about it, even less to agree to it.

As it turned out - I was too naive when I started to design a "safe" machine. On second thought, it became obvious that the few bigger factories that produced those machines would have made them safer a long time ago if they could find a solution. I was disheartened at first, but in my headstrong pride and self-respect I continued my struggle. A few times I was sure to have found the correct solution, I had only to test it - but it turned out to be flaws; some crucial detail always eluded me. During these trials I had to learn what anguish and agony put a design engineer on his mettle. But I persevered. By comparing my basic goal with other similar tasks, I concluded that the crucial step to be adopted was the first in the sequence of consecutive steps: warning on danger!

Similarly for instance to the red light and sound signal on oncoming railroad at street crossings, and this idea proved to be the correct aim. Without going into the quite complicated details of my solution, suffice it to say that I built in the machine a warning feature that functioned in such a way that a clutch, which was my novel mechanical safety device, would not activate the ram unless the ram touched the upper edge of the cutting form and was exposed to a strong (some 50 kg) resistance. The machine operator, when pressing the pedal to actuate the ram for the punching blow, would have to squeeze his finger first if he did not remove it from the upper edge of the cutting form, before pressing the pedal further, in order to overcome the strong resistance and thereby activate the ram for carrying out the cutting operation. It seemed to me highly unlikely that anybody would or could squeeze his finger by his own pressing on the pedal and thereby injure it without letting off and releasing the pedal: ceasing the squeeze and not activating the ram.

I got overjoyed when many trials proved without a single exception that my solution was correct. As proof I used pencils, instead of my finger, and unless and until the pencil was first squeezed by the foot pedal so thoroughly that it was cut into two parts: the newly devised clutch in the fly-wheel did not engage and the ram did not exert the blow to the cutting form.

When I presented this remarkable functioning to Mr. Popper - he did not know what to say. He was obviously less interested in the technical solution, but he immediately saw the prospects of commercial exploitation of such an improvement. After a while, we agreed that a patent application had to be filed, on my name.

I was happy; not only because of my success, but mainly because I succeeded to reach my self-imposed goal: a safely functioning machine for punching shoe soles - without cutting fingers.

With passing time, the pace of developing additional types of machines, smaller and larger, did not decrease, in spite of the fact that the factory was producing all previously developed types too, and managing these production activities was my duty also. I had been quite busy all the time, and I felt a slowly increasing pleasant and gratifying satisfaction with my work and achievements. But, at the same time, I had become aware of a concomitant feeling, that I could not exactly define, but which annoyed me: a feeling of becoming single-minded, so deeply preoccupied with my technical problems and their solutions that took up too much mental activity, and with lessening ability to control and keep it within bounds.

This feeling had been counterbalanced now and then by the appraisal of my actual task and performance in my job, imposed upon me by a good chance, compared with a conventional job that I could have gotten by chance too. In an established factory I would had the task to slightly modify or redesign a few older machines during the same years - and nothing else; or supervise a small workshop with the sole duty to care for carrying out a production program, where the biggest challenge that could had happened would have been to find some help if and when one of the machine tools had broken down. Compared with such a job, the probability of which could had been at least a few hundred times bigger than getting a job like mine: I felt with justified reason that I had been very fortunate indeed that, by good chance, I got a job where I had been incited or induced, and compelled by my own enthusiasm and devotion, to work hard in most of the many branches of the wide spectrum of mechanical engineering. The need and resolution to set up a small machine factory, by a very pretentious self-made businessman boss, whose goals were not confined by professional knowledge and considerations - on the one hand - and my devotion and eagerness to do engineering work, through thick and thin; my practical experiences from the three summer's engineer's apprenticeship; and, last but not least, my talent, intuition, and inventiveness - on the other hand - : had been a perfect match, that could had hardly been dreamt of happening - except by good chance.

Since those times when the appraisal of my situation had been slowly evolving, the "chance" factor, as the most decisive factor in addition to the other, the real, actual requisites in determining and shaping anybody's fate, had been ingrained in my mind, and I recalled it at occasions since then.

From the professional point of view: I had every reason to be contented; the high aims I had been confronted and that I even increased - had been achieved, and I proceeded with further good prospects. One aspect of my activity that I could not appraise during the years was the enormous practical experience I had gained on my job, especially as a consequence of my "duel" with Mr. Popper.

We lived in those years under the spell of some many-sided political and social transitions, changes, mainly in Europe and quite near to us, that nobody could properly understand, because of their partly new, unprecedented nature, intensity, speed of their actions and reactions, and, last but not least, by the hesitancy and haphazard reactions or reluctance to them by most political leaders and governments, mainly of the West-European powers. This general feeling of uneasiness and a sort of fear of uncertainty and unknown threats overshadowed everybody's life, especially that of the Jews. And in this respect we have to consider that the general awareness of everything political was still at a very low level: this was the legacy of all previous decades' habit that politics is a matter for the politicians and not for the people. Besides we lived in a conditioned, filtered atmosphere where only news from the world reached us that were deemed suitable for dissemination by individual governments' or organizations' propaganda machines - as informations or dis-informations - and then screened by the Hungarian government.

Huge libraries are full of books, written by learned historians. political scientists, etc, abundantly analyzing and explaining the twist and turns of twentieth century history, so I could not add any new aspect to their findings. Still, I cannot get rid of the memory of one of the very many reactions and general opinions of common men in the street, when Germany, in March 1936, denounced the Locarno Treaty and by a small military force crossed the Rhine bridges and unilaterally reoccupied the Rhineland. Regardless of peoples' individual feeling about the Versaille Pact and the Locarno Treaty, the mere fact that an insignificantly small German military force reoccupied the Rhineland: people in Hungary said aloud that if the existing French army had sneezed in unison - they would sweep away the invading small German forces, which was at that time the total illegal army of Germany.

Sometimes, and especially at those years of the twenties and thirties, common, even simpleton peoples' reactions and opinions were right and sensible, as opposed to the idiotic demagoguery, irresponsibility, and hesitancy of political leaders of that time, who should had been discarded much earlier. It is an awesome and mind-boggling thought: what would had happened, were that first Hitler-bluff speedily and easily suppressed WWII, with all its horrors, would not had broken out, the history of the whole world would have been completely different, and maybe - just maybe - we would be today at a higher spot on the spiraling ascent in the history of mankind. Or is such reasoning not too simplistic: are we sure that the political leaders of the world powers at present are any better, wiser than those of 60-50 years ago?

What we could figure out for ourselves in those years of 1936-38: the Spanish civil war, with all its horrors, supported on both sides by Germany, Italy, and the USSR; and political, almost civil-war, clashes in Austria, and the assassination of Dollfuss, the chancellor. Throughout 1937, the Austrian Nazis, encouraged by Hitler, had stepped up their campaign of terror, and were to stage an open revolt. Schushnigg, the new chancellor, was called to Berchtesgaden (Germany) and there Hitler demanded in an ultimatum, to turn the Austrian government over to the Nazis. Schushnigg decided to hold a plebiscite, but Hitler invaded Austria on March 12. 1938, before the plebiscite. England, France, and Italy hadn't raised a finger to defend Austria's independence, in spite of their written obligation. We heard rumors about the atrocities perpetrated against the Jews there, but we didn't know about the full extent.

Irrespective of the threatening European political and social upheavals in general, and the additional danger to the Jews in particular, which very much depressed our mood in Hungary: I personally felt a relative contentment, brought about almost exclusively by my professional activity and achievements. Besides, my partly self-imposed, very heavy work-load, especially my single-minded preoccupation with engineering problems, I still managed to attend concerts, theater performances, movies; read books; and kept company with friends.

As one of the nice legacies of the Austro-Hungarian Monarchy, there were a great number of coffee-houses in Budapest, famous for their special homely but elegant atmosphere, where people could have excellent coffee and cakes, and could sit at a table for unlimited time, and could read all the Hungarian newspapers and magazines, plus most European papers. Some 15-20 colleagues who studied in Brunn during the previous ten or so years, established a regular weekly meeting in one of the best coffee-houses of Budapest: the "Japan", that was the meeting place of artists, writers, painters, the Opera singers, etc, and known intellectuals. A big table was reserved for us every Thursday evening.

I went to these meetings quite regularly. Most of my colleagues had jobs, but a few of them had their own business. It was interesting to hear about each-other's experiences, both professional and general. I was maybe the youngest of them, or one of the youngest, and as such I was given good advice and was questioned about my job. When I spoke about my enthusiasm in seeking technical problems and taking on challenges - their reactions were generally discouraging; they said: "Do not produce more than you asked for doing, otherwise you will be overburdened - with no reward!" I did not argue, neither did I accept their advice. After the first year on my job and when I mentioned happiness about new challenges and achievements: they thought and called me a little crazy. They heard some stories about my reputation during my university years in the subject of descriptive geometry, and at their request I explained the principles and technique of the matter, emphasizing my own "imagining" method of designing. From their lukewarm reaction I understood that since they knew me and acknowledged my professional capabilities: that was the reason why they did not want to express in words their skepticism. I was not discouraged by it, but understood it clearly that my professional concerns and doubts could not be subjects of discussion with anyone of my colleagues:

a premonition I had had anyway ingrained a long time ago.

One of my concerns and worries referred to my fear that I started to lose my control on my "imagination", that started to function predominantly on engineering problems and thus sometimes switched off for short periods my precautionary capability for all other impulses. Another thing that worried me even more was the increasing realization of a few character traits of mine that, I felt, would cause me distress bitterness, etc, besides putting me in a quite handicapped position, diminishing my professional competence and achievements, by my default to stand up against wrongs, dilettantism, etc, and against flagrant, fault, and malicious fabrications. I had the disquieting feeling that measured by objective, rationalistic yardstick: my professional talent and developing competence had been increasing, but I felt being damned with one insufficiency: I was like a creeping plant, with nice flowers but the stem soft and pliable, and in its grow, swaying and wavering for seeking a firm support to be able to climb up and burst to full flowers - or fade away with no support. It was difficult to reconcile myself to this sad, discouraging fate - but life went on, as usual: much work, some listening to music, reading books, chatting in the "Japan" at Thursday evenings, etc.

But all these were only small and in the last resort: subordinate signs, in comparison with the predominant feeling that my rationalistic and seemingly auspicious existence was actually a partly hollow, incomplete life. I realized this fact, but did not know what to do about it; I had been an out-of-season romantic-naive soul.

And at one of those Thursdays, sometime in April, 1937, by chance I went to our meeting in the "Japan". And this chance attendance brought about a change in my incomplete life, perfecting eventually my so-far rationalistic existence to a full, comprehensive, all-embracing, real life.

FALLING   IN   LOVE   -
1937 - 1938

On that nice spring-evening the two Laub brothers were also present at the Japan: Fred, the older one, and Paul, the younger brother, whom I knew quite well from the university years, although he was two or three years my senior. They brought their young sister with them. We sat at opposite sides of the table. She had beautiful, somewhat sad eyes, black hair, a delicate but strong figure; she was clad with fine elegance. She rather listened to the conversation around the table, but when she spoke, her remarks were intelligent, striking, and impressive. I had never met a girl like her; I sat there spell-bound, motionless, and I did not know what impressed me more: her beauty or her decency, her radiant intelligence or very decent, delicate modesty; her firm liberal opinions expressed in very amicable manner. I sat there and tried to look outwardly normal, but deep inside I was absorbed in thought: "My God, during long years I had conceived the image of an ideal girl with whom together we could make and live a happy, harmonious, superb married life, to love each other profoundly, to live and work for each other, to take delight in each other's work and achievements, to strengthen, defend, and fight for each other if needed. And now: she sits opposite to me - and I am afraid to speak to her, scared that since she does not know me - she would find me undeserved for her accepting even my slightest personal approach."

The week after our first encounter in the Japan was a very long one for me, my emotions fluctuated from the deepest pessimism to some miraculous high hope (Picture 19). I could not make any plan: I waited for the next Thursday: would she come or not. I wanted to be optimistic and was looking forward to our next meeting with hope and expectation. She came! This time she was completely relaxed and joined at ease in the conversation around the table, and I became more and more impressed by her exquisite

Picture 19 – Falling in love with Evi

personality, her wide knowledge, perception, and quick comprehension combined with modesty and decency. And to hear and see all these character traits, and even much-much more, from a girl so gentle, so delicate, so beautiful: made me captivated and enchanted. I felt to have found the ideal girl, as in a fairy tale, and at the same time I trembled from fear even at the thought that an approach would be refused by her.

The next week was much worse that the previous one. I worked in the factory like obsessed, but my feelings were swinging from one extreme to the other, but rather dominated by my inborn pessimism.

Next week she found a chair at a distance from me, so we could not talk; I only enjoyed her presence from afar. When we broke up to go home, her brother mentioned to somebody that they signed up to a group vacation tour to Italy, to Venice and Cortina d'Ampezzo. It touched me as a stroke of lightning: I joined in the same program a few weeks earlier. "Oh, lucky chance - or good fortune - that brought us together, for getting to know each other: thank you, thank you!". I told them about my previous, separate application to the same tour. But it turned out that we joined different organized tours, although to the same places, but with a few days difference. Then she told me that it would still be worthwhile to try to coordinate our plans - and she invited me to a cafe in their home, one evening in the coming week. I saw in this coincidence a joyous sign of a good fortune, but I never before had been so nervous than on the evening of my visit.

They lived in a two-story house, in a good neighborhood. The outside front of the house was something unconventional: on the first floor they were two balconies, slightly protruding, in a half-circle, and closed by stained-glass windows. On the second floor, in the middle of the house, there was a high room, an atelier, with big windows. As I learned later, the house had been built by a painter.

Her room was on the first floor, in a big apartment of her mother, and the younger of her two brothers: Paul. I was introduced to her mother, who was a widow, and after a while we sat at a table, at the stained-glass windowed balcony of her room, and compared the two programs of our vacation trip. It turned out that there was only one day shift between the two schedules, the hotels were different, but the sites were the same: first one week in Venice and then two weeks in Cortina d'Ampezzo, in the Dolomites. The travels, by train, to and back, were not the same. Neither they nor I had any acquaintance in our separate groups, so everything looked like an insignificant coincidence. Only I could hardly conceal my exuberant happiness; and was looking forward, in high spirit, to start the trip, in about three weeks time. I must had been in such a state of mind during this interval that I do not remember how many times and what details did we discuss, but certainly we had some phone contacts. We agreed that since I was to arrive one day after their arrival, I was to go the following morning, after breakfast, to their hotel to join them.

And so it was. I found them sitting at a table on the terrace of their hotel, in the bright sunshine, close to the seashore; there was a light breeze; everything radiated joy and happiness for me (Picture 20 & 21).

After a brief chat, speaking about our travel experiences on the trains, they told me about some of their impressions on the Lido, the long seaside resort of Venice, which they gained the previous day. Then we decided to go for a swim in the Adriatic Sea, and after lunch we intended to cross over to Venice for sightseeing.

At one point on the shore a wooden platform was moored at about 150 meters from the coast. We wanted to swim there, stay a while, swim back, rest, and go back to the hotel to change clothes and have lunch together. One had to jump a few meters height into the water: there were no stairs. They jumped in first and swam ahead. I was a little bit reluctant to jump in, because it was to be my first encounter with sea-water and I was cautioned against the salty taste. I knew swimming, and at home I went frequently to swim in pools and in the fine sweat-water of the Balaton, a

Picture 20 – Touring Italy and meeting Evi there

Picture 21 – Evi in Italy

beautiful lake not too far from Budapest.

The sea was somewhat choppy, but I took my chance and jumped in. It was a heavy shock for me, the salty-bitter taste made me lose my control, I gasped for breath and swallowed some water. I turned back and with some help climbed up to the coast. In a few minutes I regained normal breathing and rested in the shade until they came back in a short time to find out what had happened since I did not arrive at the platform.

It seemed that everything was in order, and so we went back to our hotels for a shower and then to meet for lunch. I was to go to their hotel at 5 pm for crossing over to Venice, as agreed in the morning. But when I reached my hotel after lunch, I hardly could walk to my room; I shivered and felt cold, my teeth chattering: everything indicated high fever. I went to bed and since I had a thermometer: I took my temperature - it was above 39 degree Celsius. I became grief-stricken. Since I got acquainted with her, my increasing enthusiasm and adoration and the happiness for my good fortune had been overshadowed by a slight foreboding, a fear that something would go wrong, a sort of pessimism that branded my whole life, a fear, a worry that I belonged to that group of people who always have to overpay for everything. Now I felt that my fate was already here to collect my debt, in advance. But somehow I did not want to give up without a fight.

I called the reception and asked to send a doctor for an emergency case. A doctor came within an hour and I explained to him, in German, what happened and told him my layman's opinion that my raging fever was the consequence of salt from the seawater entering the bloodstream through the lungs. He examined me and told that the fever will be over in a day or two; I should take 2-3 Pyramidon tablets daily for a few days, and everything will be just fine.

Then I called Paul in their hotel and told him my story. They both came to visit me in the evening, when I already felt somewhat better; the fever went down. We agreed to keep contact next day by phone, and hoped for the best.

The third day I felt quite in order, so after their early-morning swim, we had breakfast together and went over to Venice for sightseeing.   It took all my willpower to control myself and behave normally, befitting to a friend of her brother, who, by chance, were members of an organized vacation trip.

All three of us visited Venice for the first time. For supplementing my general knowledge about the Renaissance, its Venetian artists, some history of Venice, it's most important buildings and churches: I read a few books on these subjects before the trip. Still, the impression was overwhelming: it was impossible to absorb all the splendors of the city, the marvelous pictures, statues, and buildings; so instead of trying to rush over too much points, we selected a smaller number of them, to be able to spend more time to enjoy their beauties. Admiring their exquisite beauty and trying to perceive their messages, the highlights came from small, unpretentious comments of her. I understood then that all what the guidebooks wrote were correct, and artistic descriptions of the beautiful things the Renaissance created and we tried to understand and enjoy: were valid and objective - but all were dead words - and Eva spontaneously added to us a new living dimension. She was intuitively conscious of the Renaissance artists' feelings and messages, she was an artist by herself.

This was the main lesson I learned then in Venice, and it made me very-very happy and even more captivated at the same time.   All the time in Venice the three of us were always together, so even if I wanted to - I had no opportunity to speak even a few words alone with her. Besides, our conversation was generally quite impersonal. Still, what I learned about her was that she was a professional textile designer with a diploma of the Technological Institute of Vienna (Austria), and had been working as the assistant of the technical director of the biggest textile works in Hungary, in Budapest. Her special field was woven design. I learned further that she liked classical music. By the end of the week we traveled by train to Cortina, high in the Dolomite Alps. The two hotels where we stayed separately, were very near to each other, thus the general arrangement was that after breakfast I went to their hotel and together we set out every day to half- or day-long hikes, sometimes on foot, or by bus. We did not visit any night entertainment programs, neither did we spend the evenings, including dinners, together.

Seemingly, Paul took his chaperon role seriously, and I had the feeling that he wanted to emphasize that ours was not a jointly planned vacation; it was a chance occasion. It has to be stressed that at that time and at that part of Europe, in our middle-class, especially Jewish, social strata: we had to conform to quite strict social conventions, especially with regards young ladies and bachelors. Needless to say that I was very careful not to overstep the threshold, although it caused me much strain to keep my self-command at all times. It was clear to me that she too had to adapt herself to those conventions, what she performed perfectly; although sometimes, to my very great happiness, I noticed that she was not unfriendly to me.

Quite often we joined other young people to trips and at these occasions we had to be especially careful to avoid an impression that we two were somehow in any closer connection. Anyway whether only the three of us, or in company of other people, the subjects of our conversations were general, not personal. And during these conversations my admiration and esteem increased immensely; her superb intelligence, quick, intuitive comprehension and induction, her wide knowledge combined with her gentle, graceful, pleasant, and modest manner: intensified my love to an unimaginable extreme. I hardly could believe that such a miracle was really happening to me: to adore her with all my heart and soul - with one very heavy self-imposed interdiction: I had to conceal it even from her, in addition to everybody else.

Those three weeks were a wonderful time - and at the same time an increasingly difficult period for me. I felt that we were destined for each other, but my first and main concern was: how to protect her from any inconvenience and trouble as a consequence of following my sincere desire and proposing without first very carefully planning and finding some reliable, secure financial basis for establishing a family. And so I had to start what became a continuous and excruciating search for weighing and finding out whether or not I could provide her with a minimal amount of financial safety to start a married life. I had had a safe job, I was needed in the factory; I had a quite good engineering salary and an arrangement that when I marry: my salary will be substantially increased. On the other hand I had an obligation to provide, together with my brother, financial backing to our parents whom we persuaded to retire a few years earlier. Considering her salary as an addition to mine, but without taking into account any contribution from her family - I felt that we would stand an even chance.

During those three weeks I lived a dual life: outwardly a care-free vacationer and inwardly continuously fighting heavy battle with the problem of conscience. The evening before we were going to travel back to Venice on our way home: my emotions overcame my anxieties, the tide overrun the dam, and following my sentiments I wrote a poem to her - which was not the first one I played with previously, and although it was rather amateurish - but it mirrored my immense love. Here is a rough translation:

Whispering your name - Eva into the stillness of my room:
and like fairies group on magic-baton's beat
reason-shackled words of longing leap to life.
And I won't find peace any more in sleep or awake:
I'll dream only of you.
But in the morning I would have to ask you:
How did you sleep, you fair young lady?
I can't stand it any longer.
I feel: tomorrow I'll speak out or I die.
I'm done if you laugh away
and done if I can't speak out.
But I want to live, to fight and win

always for you!
Gaining everything, fair and beautiful
and give with both hands everything to you.
Queen of my heart - I love you for life.

July, 1. 1937.

That I have today the original of this poem, hastily written on a torn-out page of a note-book, is nothing less than a miracle. Years after she closed her eyes forever, I went over on her drawers and then I found a small folder containing this poem and a few letters and notes I wrote to her. She never mentioned about them but she kept and guarded them through the thirty-six years of our married life, and saved them two-three times when we lost literally everything we had. It was her most cherished treasure - they should be now the miracle-treasures of her heirs.

We met briefly after dinner to discuss the travel plan for the next day. I succeeded to pass on to her the folded piece of paper with my poem. Then we parted: I wished good night to them, went back to my hotel, and then . . . I hoped and feared the answer. In half-dream and awake, my feelings varied between anxiety and hope.

Then we met at the platform. Her eyes were shining and when I kissed her hand, she pressed mine. We could not speak to each other, but we did not need it. If thoughts could have been recorded - ours would have been identical. It was late afternoon. The train, a slow one, wound on its rail down from the height of some 2000 meters to the sea level. The scenery was beautiful. Slowly it was getting dark. In the clear mountain air the stars came out glittering.

Paul started dozing in our compartment. We stepped out to the corridor, stood by a window, close to each other, and slowly, shyly, without a word, embraced each other and kissed for the first time - and then just stood there and gazed and admired the sparkling stars in each others' eyes. I do not know how long we stood there, adoring each other, but its wonder is still with me and will stay to my last breath.

Arriving in Venice-Mestre, they took their train homeward and I had to stay one night in a hotel and go home the next day. We said good-bye and I promised to call them some time after my arrival. I looked for a long-long time after their disappearing train, and realized for the first time in my life a stifling emptiness because I will not see her for two-three days. Next day I took my train and during the travel I felt somewhat unwell. Arriving home to my parents, I already had a strong shivering-fit, went to bed and took two of the pills the doctor gave me in Venice. I had high fever in the morning, so I called a doctor and related the whole story about my encounter with the sea. After some examination, he suspected some sort of paratyphoid and definitely refused the possibility of problems with the lungs. Ordered some medicaments, but the next morning I spat blood, lost consciousness for a short time, and an ambulance took me to a hospital. I asked my brother to call Paul and inform him about my sad plight. It did not take a long time and they diagnosed an advanced pneumonia as a consequence of an infection by dirt contained in the inhaled sea-water.

Exactly as I suspected right when it happened. They told my brother that my case was quite serious. At that time penicillin and the other antibiotics were still unknown, and I do not remember what conventional medication was applied. What I remember still was that I was encircled in my bed in a sitting position, day and night, and cold compress was wound around my body every two hours. First they put me in a room in the internal diseases department, but the next day I was lucky that a young lung-specialist physician saw in my unconventional case a challenge and he let me be transferred to his department. He was a very intelligent man, besides being a good doctor, and he explained to me my case, its treatment, and the hope to recover; thus he involved me in the whole process. He came to see me 4-5 times a day. One thing troubled him: I had high fever peaks every second day. I asked for a sheet of squared paper and started to register my temperature curve. He liked this visual presentation so much that he introduced it in his whole department.

I was in a quite serious condition and I knew about it not only because of my very high temperature but mainly because I was sleeping or half-sleeping for long stretches, not aware of what was going on around me, or just had a foggy feeling of indifference or nonchalance toward my situation and fate.

But after being some time in such "impersonal", unconscious situation, I suddenly realized, as if by struck of lightning, who I was and what happened to me and to us in the last month or two - and then I wanted to fight my illness, at all costs, in order to get well and continue - or rather start - my life for my beloved Little Girl Eva. She was informed about my situation and she sent her good-wishes by Paul, who came to visit me and brought pictures we took during our trip. She couldn't visit me alone: it was not becoming as per the social conventions then and there. So, after a few days, I realized that one of our coffee-house-society colleagues came quite often: he was an "emissary" of Eva and through him we could somewhat communicate. For thanking the pictures, I sent her a letter:

Dear Little Girl Eva,

first of all: many thanks for the pictures you sent me. Please let me know the cost, maybe money transfer would be complicated from over there. As you know: I am now lying in a special department for lung diseases, since I suffer from a serious pneumonia. I am encircled to a sitting position in my bed, day and night, and get cold water compresses every two hours. My temperature curve imitates the zigzag of the Dolomites. The x-ray examination found extensive infiltration on both sides. Nevertheless, they say that I will be fine. I want to see it and something else too, and soon.

  Kiss your hands
  July, 20. 1937   *Imre.*

My illness was not only serious, but quite prolonged. As far as I can remember I got some sulfa-product medicaments - among other things, but one sort of injection I remember well: something containing camphor. This material has a very penetrating smell and it is very quick-acting: almost before stabbing the needle, I already felt the smell and taste in my mouth and nose. Maybe this helped: who knows. Unfortunately, it was a long stretch of touch-and-go, first mainly physically and partly mentally, with periods of pessimism and depression. But after a few days only physically, because of my ever growing will to overcome my illness and see again and adore my beautiful Little Girl Eva. There was not a shadow of doubt in my mind that she not only "kept fingers crossed" for my recovery, but I was deeply convinced that she arrived at a resolute will to stand by me and would like to help me in my fight.

Once she rebelled against the conventions and came alone to visit me and brought some flowers. I was sleeping, so I did not see her. She left a note with the flowers:

Speedy recovery!
Eva

When I awoke and saw her note and the flowers, I was very-very happy about the tangible sign of her tender kindness, and mainly about her bravery, and was very sorry at the same time because I had not been awakened to see her and speak to her. So I wrote her a letter that was forwarded by her "emissary":

Sweet Little Eva,
Friday afternoon old Charon, shrewd shipmaster, took me again into his boat to row over to the world of the dead silence of eternal darkness. But I braved him: my blows fell on him, thick and fast, to force him to bring me back; my

heart proved to him with a hundred beats every minute that I still have much to do here. We struggled heavily, the boat swung - and it seemed that I had no hope. Then suddenly from the hither bank, a fairy princess called me back, by forcefully signaling with a bouquet of flowers. This persuaded old Charon that I still have to do my duty over here - and brought me back.

Thank you, dearest, that you cared about me and thereby you strengthened me in my battle for my life. Thank you very much for the beautiful flowers that have given me immense pleasure and happiness.

Imre

Unfortunately, Sunday afternoon there was a relapse. Now, Monday morning, they told me that I am somewhat better, but when will I be really all right?

Dearest Little Beautiful Eva: I feel that I have very, very much to talk about with you; or three words would be enough?

Dear Little Girl, I send you many-many hand-kisses
July, 26. 1937.   *Imre*

As I suspected and learned later, she was reprimanded by her mother for visiting me alone. She was allowed though to see me escorted by her brother. Short visits, with no handshakes, and sitting at a distance from my bed, as hospital precautions; with conventional conversations, as I was sure she perceived in my eyes the messages of my heart.

My condition improved, slowly but consistently. After more than two months - I was released. She knew about it, but still I sent her a short note:

On the occasion of my release and my first walk in the streets of Budapest - I am sending you my profound reverence and hand-kisses
      Sept. 21. 1937.   *Imre*

I visited her at home and we spoke a few times on the phone. Then I suggested and she consented that I should spend one month reconvalescence-vacation in a hotel on the Swabian Hill, where her family had a villa and where they still stayed, at least until November. And that was what I did. She went to work every morning and arrived back at about 6 pm. I was waiting for her at the station of the cog-wheel railway that served the Hill, and walked her home, where I was accepted warmly as a daily guest, for giving me what they jokingly called: humanitarian help to me recovery. The members of her family who lived in the villa were: her widowed mother, the "Mama", her older sister Oly with her husband Erno, and their son George; her older brother Fred; and younger brother Paul. I stayed in a hotel-sanitarium, where I had dinner early, about 5 pm, in order to be able to meet her at the station, and I ate a second dinner together with them. This arrangement was not only wonderful, but was considered acceptable by the Mama, and was helped by Oly-Erno, who voluntarily - and without saying so - became our "accomplices".
      On one of the first days of this arrangement, I sent her a short note:

Thank you, Little Girl, for my recovery; thank you for my life which I shall guard from now on as your property lent to me.
      Sept. 24. 1937.   *Imre*

No wonder that within a few days I almost forgot that I had been seriously ill. I was happy, in spite of all limitations of the social conventions. We were always in company, so we could not even speak freely with each other. But we succeeded to stand up to that challenge, we were pleased to read each other's thoughts and feeling out of small signs, a few words, and tiny allusions.

Every day, after dinner, even in rain, we took long walks, Oly, Erno, we two, and quite often somebody else too. The Hill was beautiful all year round, but the most wonderful season was the fall. We strolled side-by-side but not arm-in-arm, but we were happy. Talked about many things, and I realized more and more: how much common interest we had and admired her more and more for her superior gentleness, goodness, integrity, modesty, decency, her superb intelligence, her way of thinking, views and beliefs, and everything expressed so modestly, in a way as if spelling out the partner's opinions.

Oly and Erno was a very easy-going couple, they were full of life, artists in making life worth living, without pretentiousness. They had four-five couples as very close friends who met, with no formality, once-twice a week, in their city apartment or on the Hill. They played bridge in the evenings, and in the week-ends they listened classical music for long hours.

They had a textile printing factory; Oly had excellent artistic taste. One of their friends was a gynecologist, one was a lawyer, one the Hungarian representative of the Bull bureau punch-card company (the forerunner of the computer punch cards), one an exchange broker, and one a director of a large company. All of them were 8-15 years our seniors and the fact that - after legitimate and understandable scrutiny - they whole-heartedly accepted me into their company of the Laub family's friends: signified a big success for me - and for both of us. When we made our plan to spend one month on the Hill, we did not take into account this company of friend's role, we were unawares of their interest and scrutiny - until I was accepted as a full, ordinary member of their company. During October Eva had a common cold and stayed at home for a few days. I sent her a bouquet of chrysanthemums with an attached prescription of "Dr. Balla", specifying direction of use:

Rp

Chrysanthemum Corymbosum X.
MDS.
Against common cold;
sniff every quarter of an hour.
        Dr. Balla
Oct. 14. 1937.

By the end of October I returned home and went back to my work in the Popper factory. They returned home too, and so a new scheme had to be devised to meet her frequently. My success with all members of the family and with their friends in the "apprenticeship" period on the Hill made the successive city-life scheme quite easy.

They had a very nice and at the same time a very practical arrangement at home. The whole family lived in their two story house: Mama had a big apartment on the first floor, for herself, for Eva, and Paul. (Pictures 22 & 23) The other, the somewhat smaller, but still big, apartment on the same floor was the home of Oly, Erno, and George. Four smaller apartments were located on the second floor; in one of them lived Fred and his wife Katherine.

The Laub family owned a factory of electric motors, managed by the two brothers. The factory was located on the same big plot: the dwelling-house along the street front and the factory building in a big U-shape, surrounding a common courtyard. The factory building had three floors; two of them housed the Laub factory and the third floor was occupied by the Relief textile printing factory of Erno and Oly. Mama liked to run a big household; she had one-two, live-in housemaids, and she just loved to receive regularly all members of the family's friends at her table.

Regarding my "courtship", actual if not declared, it was not simple and had many limitations, because of the strict social conventions, and especially because neither of us wanted to initiate

Picture 22 – Pali outside car, Evi & her Mother in back seat

Picture 23 – Evi's Mom

any program of ours which was likely to be denied by Mama. So, for instance, it was out of the question to go to a movie or a concert for just the two of us, we had to have company. Oly and Erno, and their friends helped us spontaneously and naturally, for instance, by inviting me frequently to dinner together with one-two-three couples of "our" friends, and of course called over Eva from her adjacent home. My happiness knew no bounds during this period, but still I had a very oppressive problem. Returning to the factory after my illness, I notified my boss about my intention to marry and asked him to implement now our understanding and raise my salary to a level appropriate to a senior engineer, managing a factory employing some 120-130 workers. He did not refuse my request, but he referred to the general economic depression and special problems as a consequence of his Jewishness in getting government orders, etc. - thus he started a delaying tactic. Although he was very much dependent on my continuing work, but he wanted to achieve this at a minimal cost for him.

Since I had an obligation that I wanted to meet at all cost on the one hand, and I was resolute to assure that my income should be adequate, even if a modest, but safe subsistence on the other: I felt that I must not propose until and unless I resolve this problem. And the worst aspect of my problem was that I could not discuss it with her, because of her family's superior financial situation.

And then, one day Erno took me for a walk. He was earlier a bank director, had quite extensive life experience; a rational, sober-minded man, with much commonsense. He came straight to the point and told me that in the last few months he, the whole family, and their good friends got ample occasion to know me and they unanimously were more than satisfied with my personality and character. He told me further, he felt that it would not surprise me too much to learn that during the previous few years two-three very fair, respectable young men tried to approach her with honest and respectful intention. But after not too long periods of time Eva turned them down, politely but firmly, without letting the family members to express to her their opinion, not to speak to discuss them. In such matters she had been uncompromisingly self-reliant and firm. Thus, her acceptance of my persistent attendance was a proof that she would approve my proposal. In addition to her approval, the family's and their friends' agreement would surely be accepted by her. They were sure of Eva's sentiments and mine too, since they did not need too much ingenuity to find the explanation for my eagerness to join their company; they just could not help to notice the room becoming brighter by our radiating love whenever we enter.

Thus, they could only presume that I must had some problem that prevents me from proposing, and if so, they would gladly help me if I were willing to disclose whatever oppressive cares I had.

I told him that there was nothing on earth that I wished more and more ardently than to marry my dear Little Eva, and that I fervently hoped for her consent. I described in detail my financial situation and problem, and explained that I want to make more and stronger efforts to enforce to get a salary due to me that would be a sufficient basis for a modest family life, and that then I will ask for her consent to marry me, that so far I did not dare to do because of my unsolved problem.

He appreciated my standpoint in my assumed responsibility, but he called my attention to the fact that due to the preoccupation with my own financial problem, I neglected Eva's role in our common future arrangement. He told me that I should had already known better her strong self-respect and firmness in dealing with her future, such as her devotion to her professional work and her will to take her share in any common effort such as sharing in earning the upkeep of a family's life.

Then he tried to calculate our would-be budget by the use of fact-figures; taking first my net income, after deducting my part of our parents' support, the nice salary of Eva, which I did not know, I never inquired about it. It turned out that these two sums together would have meet an average family's requirements. But he added that since Eva was a one-third heiress of her late father's estate, she receives her share in two ways: all bigger expenses, such as travels, luxury items, an apartment when she marries, etc, were paid by the company and the outstanding share accumulates on her credit. He made here some hint that would I join the company as the third family member of the management, then Eva's share would even increase. Then he concluded that the total net income from our salaries would be more than enough for our current expenses, and as far as one could foresee: our situation would be very good. He cautioned against squandering away our youth, and encouraged me by saying that two such professionals as we were: will succeed in all circumstances.

I accepted his reasoning - but with one proviso: I did not want to join the company, I want to marry Eva - and not the business. And so we agreed.

I went to my brother's home and told them about my talk with Erno and my decision to marry Eva. They were very happy, they noticed my ongoing struggle but they preferred not to intervene unless my request to do so.

Next evening I asked Eva to come with me, under the pretext of buying something in the neighborhood, and as we were alone, I asked the simple question: "Do you want to marry me?" She looked deep in my eyes and said: "For us two together with body and soul: everything will go well!"

We stood there in the big, long hall of Oly-Erno's apartment, embracing and kissing tenderly, and holding each other in silence, only our heart throbbed in unison. Before we entered the room, I asked her how Mama will react when I shall formally ask her consent to our marriage. Mama will agree, because she too likes you - she answered.

Then we went in, and I asked Erno to be my intermediary in arranging a private meeting with Mama. She received me - and I told her that since I very much loved Eva: I wished to marry her and asked for her consent. She asked in Eva, told her about my request and wanted to hear her response. She agreed, and so Mama kissed me and Eva, congratulated us, and we were allowed to kiss each other in front of her. Then she called together all members of the family who were at home, announced our engagement - and I was received very warmly into the family. Mama told the maid to bring in the champagne (which was already prepared for the occasion, as I later found out) and the whole family started discussing the subject which was going to be the main topic of discussion and action in the coming few months: how to arrange everything for us.

We called my brother and his wife - who already knew Eva - and told them the news. They were very happy and wished us much happiness. It was very late when I got home, my parents already were sleeping. After some hesitation I woke them up and told them about our engagement. They knew, of course, about my "courtship", although they did not know my problem. I considered it important to set their mind at rest about my contribution to their provision. They were very happy and asked a lot of questions about Eva and her family. Before I left Eva's home, Mama asked me to arrange an invitation by my parents whom she wanted to visit, to get acquainted with them.

And then we spent every free minute together, until late night when I had to leave for home. I had dinners with the family, in Mama's big dining room where, beside the in-house family members, a few of their big family, living in Budapest and at the countryside, took part. I want to make special mention about the oldest brother of Eva's late father, the famous specialist-surgeon of nose-, throat-, and larynx-diseases, whom everybody called "Laci Bacsi" (Uncle Laszlo), who was not only the favorite uncle of the entire family, but Eva was his favorite niece. The main, recurrent subject discussed was planning our near and distant future: how and where to settle down, what we would need, etc,. The very first point on the agenda was, of course, the engagement ceremony. Eva and I were resolutely for the most modest arrangement, and so we decided for a family lunch, with the closest members of our families, at Mama's city apartment and an informal weekend outing at the Hill villa for the friends.

She gave me an engagement present: a gold Swiss Doxa

wrist watch and I presented her with a nice diamond ring. (Both of which I succeeded to guard to this day.)

In the next few months, until our wedding day, we were quite busy. We continued working, of course, and evenings and weekends were carefully programmed for meeting with relatives and friends, from both sides. We went to the Opera, to concerts, theaters, movies, etc. although less than we would have liked to go. We could now go alone, without escort, still with some limitations. We felt as a burden those social conventions, especially since they were not spelled out or specified, but you had to know the rules if you did not want to get reproved and then apologize - acts that we were too proud to accept, but we rather submitted ourselves to these conventions for the short period.

We were deeply moved by the family's and friends' first and spontaneous reaction to start right away planning and designing our future home. And this made our final deliberations regarding our future plan doubly difficult, namely our decision to emigrate from Hungary, to outside of Europe. We came to this decision after difficult soul-searching. As regards ourselves, we were sure that we shall succeed, with our professions and devotions, and felt that the sooner we could leave the better were the chances; thus we must not settle down conventionally as for life, because that would jeopardize our future emigration. As regards our families, we felt as our primary and cardinal duty to tell them our decision, the reasons, our frightful struggle in weighing our hope to escape from an overhanging unknown danger against leaving them behind - and maybe we will not see each other again. We were not the first and the only who had such intention, quite a number of people left already: those who had relatives or other connections abroad. Thus, however painfully our plan struck our families: they understood it and tried to bear their pain bravely.

Unfortunately, we had no relatives in those countries where immigration was possible in a legal, official way. Both of us were aware of our lack of that sort of dexterity, slyness, or wiliness that has to be applied to succeed in illegal immigration; so we had to try the legal way. We found out at the Australia House in London that immigrants with agricultural and live-stock raising education and profession were eligible. So we enrolled in the bee-farming and rearing faculty of a university in Budapest, and on that basis we applied for immigration permit, to Melbourne, Australia. Besides, we were looking around for other possibilities.

In the meantime, a minimal program was shaped for our home. Our apartment on the second floor of the family's house was to be reshaped to a comfortable, modern, one-bedroom apartment. Modern, but modest Scandinavian furniture was ordered from the family's carpentry-master of long-standing. Oly designed for us some beautiful textile plating for the doors of the cupboards, and every single piece of furniture, tableware, china, bed-sheets, etc, was carefully selected.

We made visits to the many family members and friends, to fulfill social obligations. Our young friends we invited to Eva's home. She had a close friendly company of four class-mates who studied and finished together the Jewish Gymnasium for Girls, which, together with the Jewish Gymnasium for Boys, were the best high-schools in Budapest. Those five girls were the best in their class, but Eva was the first among them, acknowledged and loved by them without reservation.

We got everywhere very-very friendly and warm acceptance. But the real highlights were every meeting with our dear Laci Bacsi, Eva's oldest uncle. He was a rather short, small built, always the best-dressed gentleman, with impeccable but unobtrusive elegance; friendly, smiling, good-humored, lively: the eyes always sparkling with a touch of impishness. Besides being the top laryngologist, he was an artist, a painter. But he did not sell his pictures; he gave them as presents to their friends.

And what is more: he was a gifted inventor. He designed most of his surgical and diagnostic instruments. The ingenuity of his ideas I can even more appreciate today, after the immense improvements made on them during the decades since.

The waiting rooms of his city clinic were full of beautiful

paintings and art objects. He was the resident director of the nose-, throat-, etc.-department of the Opera House in Budapest. The singers, from the prima-donnas down to the choir members, came to beg his help before performances. He was everybody's Laci Bacsi and everybody greeted him by saying: "I kiss your hand!" He gave to each one individual treatment and when they happily left his room, the corridor resounded from their trills.

Another of Eva's relatives of artistic trait was her cousin Laub Juci, who became the best portrait photographer in Hungary. She was married to an orchestra-conductor Somogyi Laszlo, who became an internationally known maestro. Laub Juci, of course, made a few series of portraits of ours. Again, as a small miracle, I succeeded to guard through all the cataclysms two small pictures. Now, before the "changing of the guard" will take place, the "New Guard" shall be acquainted with us, as we looked like at that time. I will always have her image imprinted in my heart.

Our wedding date was set for March 14 and 20 1938. respectively, for the civil- and religious-ceremony, and we were going to set out to our honeymoon on the evening of March, 20. to Italy: Rome, Capri, Florence, and Venice, for one month. There were some considerations whether or not it was advisable or proper to make trip under the then perilous political situation in Europe, but optimism and sort of defiance prevailed and reservations were made for our trip.

During those few months of engagement, as we got to know each other in more and more detail: my love, adoration, and esteem grew more and more intense. She was the embodiment of human kindness and righteousness. She loved nature, people, flora, fauna; she had faith in the superiority and final victory of goodwill and love to evil and baseness. She spoke softly, never a loud or harsh word, even her firmness had been expressed politely and gently so that it could not but be accepted without reservation. For describing all her noble character and her warm, humane, tender personal traits - the entries of a "Dictionary of Noble Personal Traits" would have to be quoted, were such a dictionary in existence. Instead, a few examples would suffice, I think, to illustrate her specific marvelous personal traits.

Once we went for a stroll to the Margaret Island, a beautiful big park in the middle of the Danube in Budapest, where - among others there was a small zoological garden for a few species of deer. A young deer, a fawn, was peacefully pasturing some 10-15 meters distance from the fence. We paused for a few moments, watched the deer-kid, and it looked at us and made funny tilting with its ears. We walked on, but a few meters away there was a small gate in the fence; Eva opened it, stepped in silently, looked the deer-kid in the eyes, and slightly bending down, approached it. The dear came forward slowly to meet her and let itself be caressed, then sniffed and licked at her hand. When she left it and slowly came out through the gate: the deer-kid looked at her for a long time as if saying good-bye to a good friend. I was charmed and bewitched. She noticed it and explained it as the most natural thing in the world, saying that animals somehow feel when a man approaches it with friendly intentions. For her it was nothing special, just the most natural occurrence.

She had many potted flowers at home that she cared for regularly. Once she looked closely at one of her flowers and said, in a whisper, more to herself: "This flower got annoyed for some reason, I now have to find out why and pacify it". Flowers, besides animals, were her friends too; they understood each other well.

She spoke sometimes about her work and her profession generally: design of woven textiles, which needs a much higher technical knowledge - besides artistic talent - compared, for instance, with design of printed pattern on textiles. At one occasion, a few of us of the family saw a fashion show and were much impressed by two or three silk materials with modern patterns, harmonious colors, and unconventional compositions. Then Oly told me that these were Eva's designs; she did not mention it to me. This occasion gave me a subject lesson, basically on two things: one, that besides being an excellent professional textile designer, she was a talented artist; and two, that she was much too much modest.

Time was quite short for making all necessary arrangements for our wedding ceremony and our honeymoon trip. We wanted everything organized the most modest way possible. After the religious ceremony in the Dohany street synagogue, a buffet reception was held in a big confectionery, and a lunch at Mama's apartment for the closest family members.

The political atmosphere in the neighboring Austria was tense and chaotic in the last month, but nobody suspected such a drastic occupation by Hitler's army, welcomed by jubilant crowds, that actually was made on Sunday, the 13-th of March. Hungary was not involved in the case, but suddenly we Hungarian Jews awoke to the realization that some dark, grim danger was approaching us: Hitler was some 200 km from Budapest.

But we set out on our tour, together, having absolute faith in each other, and knew that we shall strengthen, stand by, and fight for each other for overcoming whatever difficult and dangerous fate awaits us.

SECTION 3 - WORLD WAR II

THE GATHERING STORM CLOUDS - 1938 - 1940

Sunday, the 20-th of March, 1938 we set forth to our honeymoon to Italy. Actually, no one of us wanted to make such an old-fashioned trip and to yield to conventionally obligatory social tradition - but the entire family was for it, by saying: who knows whether there will be for us another possibility to travel.

We stayed one week each in Rome, Capri, Florence, and Venice. History, culture, and arts in our educational system in Hungary had been very much influenced and shaped by the history of the Roman Empire and especially by the Italian Renaissance, and thus the historical and artistic monuments were quite well known to us; still, the actual, personal encounters were astonishing and we enjoyed them very much. As it turned out, my love, marvel, and wonder for my "Little Girl"-wife was very much enhanced by our conversations on all the beauties we saw together, and almost without noticing it, I became the happy winner and beneficiary of Eva's superb knowledge, evaluation, and her explanation on the interplay and influence among the various branches of Renaissance culture.

We wanted to forget and not to worry about politics and the world around us and the frighteningly arising winds of war - and in this we succeeded by and large. We enjoyed the first personal encounters with the marvels of the historic Italy and besides were enjoyed by the discoveries of each other. We had been convinced that we were one body and soul, and became slowly and profoundly more and more aware from day to day that our way of thinking was almost identical, so were our reactions and moral and intellectual evaluations, about the world around us, etc. We noticed that we started to tell something to the other at a certain moment - and what both of us wanted to say to the other: was the same. Our interests were almost identical, but in addition to mine, she had more of her own, such as tender passion to nature, animals, flowers, and, last but not least, she had been fond of people and believed in their goodness. Partly because of this world conception, she had been strong, bold, firm - and she incessantly tried to diminish my inborn skepticism, pessimism, feebleness, and anxiety and fear from the triumph of evil over virtue and goodness. I adored her and ardently wished her view of life shall become true.

On our return travel, sometime in April, 1938, at the first Hungarian railway station we bought a newspaper that wrote about the first "Jewish Law" in Hungary. I do not remember the details; it was about restrictions, mainly on the economic field. Speaking at home with the family and friends about the changing situation, they evaluated the new law and restrictions mainly as a comfortable means for the political leadership to compel enterprises to employ certain percentages of Christians as directors and in other leading positions. Within the slow sequence of our "conditioning" to worsening official anti-Semitic policies, all of the Jews in Hungary were of the opinion that "one can live with it".

We rented a small furnished apartment until our one-room apartment in our house is completed, that happened sometime in October. Both of us went back to work. I had to make an effort to make up for the period I was away, together with making a lot of designs of newly added types in our production plan.

In our family circle my two brothers-in-law inquired more and more about the details of my work at the Popper factory, and repeatedly discussed with me problems of their own factory, and asked my opinion on them.

The factory (the Laub Electrical Works) was established in 1898, by my late father-in-law, (who died a few years earlier, thus I did not know him) after he had studied and had worked in Germany. At the beginning they started producing small electric motors, switches, controllers, and a few other accessories. This factory, small at the beginning, was the second largest electric motor factory in Hungary at that time. The range of products slowly increased by adding bigger types and expanding the assortment of the machines, such as direct current motors and generators - besides three- and one-phase motors -, special types in addition to catalog items, etc. In 1938 their catalog-type motors covered the range from 0.3 up to 150 kW, for three- and one-phase alternating- and direct-current. Besides these conventional motors and dynamos, the factory produced a wide range of special grinding machines, from very small (dentist's) up to 10 kW heavy duty (foundry) types (Picture 24 & 25). But the factory's reputation was enhanced by its special products, individually designed and produced for uncommon requirements, such as galvanizing dynamos, middle frequency generators, rotating transformers, etc. In 1938 the Laub factory was the fourth in size in Hungary in that branch - but the first whenever special equipment became necessary in anyone of the factories, but especially in research work, at the universities, and in the military industry. The factory had a good engineering- and technical-staff: five electrical, three mechanical engineers, four-five technicians, a few designers and draftsmen, and four-five workshop-managers, and a total number of workers of 150-160.

The two Laub brothers had for a long time become aware that they had some problems in their factory, but they had been too busy with the day-to-day management activities, so they could never had find time to try to analyze the problems. Besides, they were not of the organizer type of engineers, and thus they could not find and state the problems and realize their severity and consequences.

My entering the family circle and as a consequence of their learning about my activities in the Popper factory in the course of our conversations about my job, my technical problems and their solutions: the thought struck them that I would be the suitable professional to deal and solve the slowly developing and worsening problems of their factory. Although they knew my standpoint of not wishing to join the factory on family-member basis, still they reminded me that my present boss: Mr. Popper had been dragging his feet to fulfill his promise to raise my salary to a

Picture 24 – Laub motors being delivered

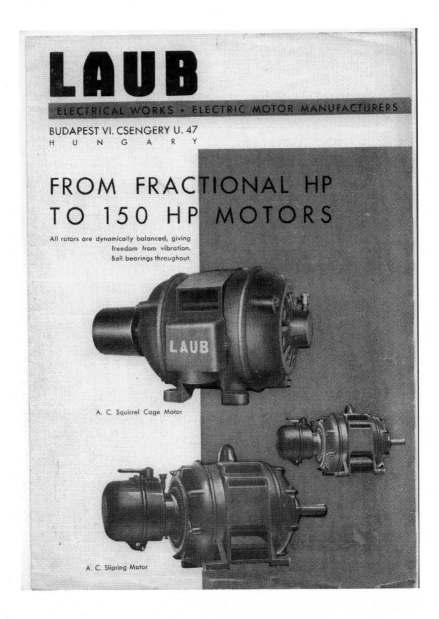

Picture 25 – Laub Factory Catalog page

more-satisfactory level. What they asked me at that time was consulting and joint deliberations on the problems, to which I agreed enthusiastically. We spent many week-ends and even more nights for learning and analyzing the history of the factory's and its product's development, with the goal to properly state the problems at that date and to try to find the best solution for them.

At the end of lengthy and thorough analyses we came to the conclusion that there were two basic problems:

(1) problems pertaining to the catalog-series: motors, dynamos, etc, and

(2) problems connected to mechanical design and production technologies of special, one of a kind, items.

Problem #1 was the more difficult, a multifold and long-range problem, and comprising three main components:

(a) the presently existing products had become a conglomerate of different, incoherent units, designed separately, during a long period, governed by individual ideas and not by any uniform design principle;

(b) the adopted production technologies had not been uniform either, but showed the same historical, individual characteristics of their design-development; and

(c) both design and production technology of the catalog series, had to be modernized and standardized.

Problem #2 was a simpler one to solve, needing a good, intuitive and inventive mechanical design-engineer who could team up with the existing electrical engineers to develop and produce special machines as requested.

The solution to problem (c) was obviously the most difficult to perform, especially considering the fact that standardizing and modernizing both design and production technology, including machine-tools, jigs, tools, etc, would have to be carried out simultaneously with normally running production without - or at least at a minimal amount of - loss of capacity, besides solving a great variety of organizational and marketing problems.

The effects of the historically developed situation, as

described very concisely in problem (1) and (2), were manifested not only in the connecting dimensions, outside appearance and other features of the series, but mainly and most heavily in the low economy of their production, as a consequence of reasons such as: increased variety of components, high inventory costs, high tooling costs, etc.

The time period we had been deliberating on these issues could have been sometime by the end of 1938. In the whole of Europe total uncertainty reigned, a general disarray and confusion on the political level, leaving the peoples totally confused, mainly about what the near future will bring for them. After the Munich agreement in September 1938, and the occupation of the Sudetenland of Czechoslovakia by Germany, the whole atmosphere in Europe seemed characterized by a well orchestrated propaganda campaign, that the Munich agreement will preserve "peace in our time" as Chamberlain declared, and as politicians and newspapers had not ceased to reassure the peoples of Europe about it. In Hungary everybody felt that we will not be involved in the German-French-Great Britain controversy, or in the worst case: only marginally. But everywhere in Europe, and in Hungary as well, many people had a very worrying feeling that something happened that had been contradictory to every normal conventional obligation to fulfill one's duty as solemnly declared in a contract by a country, guaranteeing the safety of its partner when the need arises. We felt that at Munich: France and Great Britain unjustifiably abandoned their ally: Czechoslovakia, with which they had a "mutual-assistance" treaty that they had reneged and treacherously deserted Czechoslovakia.

Needless to say that nobody knew the real reasons for the Munich agreement - except maybe the leaders of the four powers: Germany, Italy, France, and Great Britain. But somehow common men in the streets, even in Hungary, which generally had not sympathized with Czechoslovakia regarded and judged acts of breach of agreement between countries or governments much more seriously than similar acts between people. Thus: many people felt their trust shaken in governments' sovereign authority, similarly to simpletons way of questioning: why do governments enforce people to keep agreements, when they themselves do not keep them?

In the entire Europe a general chaos and confusion existed on the general political level, and superimposed on the general disarray: the fate of the Jews under German controlled countries worsened from day to day.

This situation had a bearing also on our private problem: the opportunity to review the production potential and other connected problems of the Laub factory, because we got information that at government level plans were in preparation to appoint certain factories as "essential for national defense", which was considered in industrial circles as beneficial, in every respect. The Laub factory had already been supplier of various branches of the defense forces, and the Laub brothers considered such an "essential" appointment for their factory very desirable, not only for securing further orders, but mainly because such a status would help in procuring raw materials and other important services that may be curtailed for non-essential enterprises; and - last but not least - it could be hoped that Jews working in such "essential" factories, especially professional people: engineers, technicians, etc, would be exempted from probable further restrictions. This probability had to be considered very seriously in my case, and above all other consideration it seemed very advisable to join the Laub factory as soon as possible, definitely before the factory will get such "essential" assignment.

Based on these considerations: my two brothers-in-law - in addition to their conviction that I was the best man to solve the problems of their factory - asked me to change my strong position of principle of not wanting to join the family factory. At that time the order of the day was to join forces, to help each other for trying to secure a better chance to stand up and overcome our threatening common fate.

During the same few months, as part of our desire to

emigrate from Hungary, I had established a contact by correspondence, with a shoe-machine and accessories factory in England, based on an advertisement in a trade periodical, in which they asked applications for an engineer-manager, with experience in that specific field. I applied for the post; sent a detailed resume, etc, and was invited to visit them, at least for a week, to investigate their plant and prepare a development program. I started the preparations: passport, visa, etc. and I told my two brothers-in-law that - with heavy heart, but - we would prefer to emigrate to England if I succeed at that factory and get an immigration permit from the Home Office. But if I do not succeed in my attempt, then I would join them.

My visit was timed for the first week of April, 1939. On the 15-th of March of the same year Germany overrun the remaining part of Czechoslovakia, after taking over the Sudetenland a half a year earlier. And then there were rumors that Hungary would get back part of Slovakia and Rumania with Hungarian speaking population, and one could only speculate: what recompense will Hungary have to make.

I took two weeks holiday and made the trip to Norwich, to visit the factory. It was bigger than that of Mr. Popper, but their products were outdated, designed a long time ago, that could not enter into competition with the much more modern types used on the continent and those I designed and produced in the Popper factory. During the week that I spent there, I worked out a development plan for both product design and production technology, together with a program for their execution. The boss was much impressed and invited me for a five-o'-clock tea at his home where he gave me a contract, on condition that my immigration- and work-permit will be granted by the Home Office. The next morning he introduced me to the mayor of the city and asked his intervention on my behalf - which was promised. On my way home, I spent a few days in London. My dominant impression was a shock, when I saw posters everywhere: "Your country needs you!", calling people to join the army. I could not believe my eyes,

I was dumbfounded. In April, 1939, three years after the Rhineland invasion, one year after occupation of Austria, half year after occupation of the Sudetenland: Great Britain still had no drafted standing army, or not of sufficient strength. I could not understand it. But if the Government of Great Britain needed to call volunteers to join the army in April, 1939 then something must had been awfully wrong with the whole Government.

Returning home, I told Eva what happened in Norwich, and my general impression on the situation in England. As regards our private future, we had to wait the answers from Australia and England to our applications for immigration permit, and simultaneously we continued in our work. We attained in our life unsurpassable love and total harmony. We lived for each other; we had been thinking the same way; we collected impressions when we were not together for conveying them to the other; we always wanted to do the same thing - there never was the slightest discord, not to speak dispute, about our actions or plans. We lived very modestly - because of the oppressing outside world around us. We tried to build a screen around us, for isolating us as much as possible from the oppressing cares of the situation in general and the frightening future for us, Jews, in particular. We lived very happily, notwithstanding our constant worry about our family and the whole Jewish population.

Our first reactions on the worrisome news and events, our opinions, and conceptions were generally not identical: I was more pessimistic and worried, not only about short-range threats, but in addition about the remote consequences too. I had been a "worrying-type" man and this mental disposition had been considerably worsened by my "engineering mentality", specifically my spontaneous reaction to contemplate every present event as a momentary factor affecting the future process and end of a long-range program. In contrast, Eva was of stronger mental and moral constitution; she visualized short- and long-range threats, but in contrast with me: she rejected to consider single-mindedly only the worst possibilities; she was convinced, she wanted to believe, that -

however grim our future seemed at any given time - future in general is not pre-ordained, many things may happen that could alleviate or even change completely presently grim-looking probabilities. She did not want to give up at the start; she wanted to keep up the faith, to be and remain strong and have self-reliance to fight even if the odds were against us.   By her consistent exemplary attitude, she exerted a strong influence on me, and gave me strength for our common future.

And, sometime by the end of May, 1939, we got the answers form both Australia and England that our immigration application was rejected. Their intention was clear: Jews were undesirables; Australia did not give any reasons for their rejection; England at least justified its rejection by saying that under the circumstances, "East-European" immigrants were unwanted.

Thus our hope for emigrating came to an end. We were sorry for not being able to escape from the threatening dangers, but at the same time we felt relief from our self-accusation to leave behind our families to their fate. Now, we were "re-united" with our families - for better or for worse.

Consequently: I made up my mind to join the Laub factory. Beside all other considerations for this move, here was again a big challenge confronting me, with a double goal: the engineering task for me and the overall, including economic, task for the family.

I notified Mr. Popper about my resignation from my post, effective in two weeks, with the brief explanation that he did not fulfill his promise and obligation to raise my salary, within more than a full year after my marriage.

It was for him a bolt from the blue; he was almost frightened to death. He just stuttered until he recovered some strength, and then he made a long, prolonged reproach, saying among other things that he always behaved decently towards me, etc, etc, and now I am going to bring to ruin his factory, since there is nobody else to replace me in my job, etc. I told him that although I was sorry for him, but reminded him how often did I asked and warned him that one-two engineers and technicians were needed to join me

- but he did not take my repeated strong advice: now he can only blame himself. As regards his "exceptional" behavior towards me: he knew very well that I had always been willing to work day and night, but I definitely was not ready to accept his general tyrannical behavior. By the end of this lengthy confrontation, he told me: "You know, you learned so much in my factory during these five years that you should had to pay me for that excellent opportunity of professional experience!" I flew into a towering rage and told him that nobody else would have designed and produced the more than fifty different types of machines during these five years with the below-minimal necessary prerequisites as I did, and if the factory will get into trouble - the only person to be blamed is he himself. I cannot absolve him from his responsibility for consciously abusing my naive, self-sacrificing, over-zealous work. He tried to pacify me by promising a higher salary, but I refused to discuss it: my decision was final.

During the next two weeks I witnessed as he offered my job to two-three engineers: but he got laughed at when they realized the lack of design facilities and turned down his offer.

When I said good-bye, I told him I was sorry that it happened this way, but he overstrained my very long patience on everything, not only on his unwillingness to keep his word to settle my salary - and so my patience just snapped. In one of the next few days I started working in the Laub factory, with the official assignment of "designer of special machines". The technical staff and I knew each other from my previous few courtesy visits. The fact that for more than one year I did not join the staff, dissolved or at least diminished their antagonism against a third "family-member engineer-boss". What I had and wanted to do was in no way oriented against anyone of the staff members or lessen anybody's authority. They knew that mechanical design of special machines had been a bottle-neck, so they accepted my joining them for this task maybe with a "grain of salt".

I wanted to get familiar with the functioning of the factory, such as organization, design, production, etc, to the last smallest detail. Thus, I spent a few weeks in each one of the departments or workshops, such as: design office, armature sheet metal stamping-, machining-, and assembly-, etc. shops.

Within a few weeks I came to the conclusion that, besides the problems we discussed and approximately defined a few months earlier, an additional and in importance more pressing problem existed that had to be solved simultaneously and in accordance with the others. This serious problem was: organization of the entire functioning of the factory, in all its details. Obviously, there was in existence a certain organization of the successive steps: how procurement of raw materials, production, marketing, etc. had been carried out, but this organization scheme had been developed during the two-three decades of the factory's past and consequently showed the same characteristic features as the engineering design of the products: a conglomerate of separate, incoherent steps, without proper, organic connection among them. After having studied the functioning of the factory for about half-a-year, by direct participation in everyone of its steps, the main task that emerged were to:

(1) design a uniform, modern motor series;
(2) develop the appropriate uniform technology; and
(3) develop the suitable uniform organization scheme.

To complete such a development task would have been the most ardent wish of every ambitious design engineer, and thus it confronted me with a challenge that I took with much happiness, that was even enhanced by severe constrains on the overall task, by the prevailing need to carry out everyone and all its details, with no, or very slight, disturbance of the ongoing current production program.

Consequently, the actual task was very complex. A master plan had to be devised, in its three main components, as outlined earlier, and in addition, the detailed designs had to be drawn up such that their execution should enable smooth transition with minimal losses from the current to the new, uniform, modern motor series' production. Obviously, the master plan had to be devised, showing those steps that could be performed early at the beginning of the program, any time, clearly distinguished from those steps, mainly on the critical path, that had to be programmed, each one separately for ensuring their smooth incorporation in the overall plan.

As it is seen clearly, the carrying out of the master plan made it absolutely essential to re-plan and reschedule it continuously along its total time period. It was an uncommon plan, complex and difficult, that I had to carry out, after my brothers-in-law's agreement, alone and in secrecy - especially at the beginning - from the technical staff. I had to bear the heavy burden of personal responsibility for its ensuing result that made the task increasingly challenging for me. The responsibility was a double one: once that of a conscientious professional and secondly that of a member of the factory's family owners.

This development-cum-reorganization plan was a beautiful, ambitious, and a daring task, even for an electric motor expert with long years experience. It was an even more challenging task for me, with no more expertise in electric motors than how to connect them to the circuit, but a quite extensive experience in programming, designing, and producing machines. This experience, combined with my self-reliance on my sound engineering intuition and inspiration, which directed me in my previous work to success, encouraged me to take up this new challenge with confidence.

The whole ambitious plan of reorganizing the factory and redesigning its products was an ambitious and bold enterprise - but today, in retrospect, I could hardly defend its reasonableness, not to speak about explaining our courage or shortsightedness for embarking in such an enterprise under the then prevailing conditions.

The main menace: anti-Semitism in Hungary had its peak ferocity in 1919-20, after the fall of the short communist regime, during the first year of Horthy's racist atrocities - as it is described in previous chapters. The intensity decreased quite speedily and what remained were a series of restrictions, such as: "numerus clausus" (only 3 percent of the total number of university students was allowed for Jewish students); no Jews were employed in state- and community-offices; and a series of other restrictions. All these measures had not too strong effect on the daily life of the Jewish population, who became conditioned to the restrictions and learned how to overcome the difficulties.

On the economic field a silent agreement evolved: industrial-, financial-, and commercial-enterprises increased the number of non-Jews in their management. Free occupations of all sorts were slightly affected, or ways could be found to live with the system.

This co-existence continued until 1938, when complying with German diplomatic pressure: "Jewish Laws" were introduced in taking stronger measures on Jewish peoples' - mainly economic - activities. Still, the Hungarian Jewish community had not been feeling being seriously threatened in its existence. We felt that we lived in difficult time but strongly hoped that we will overcome the hardships.

We had been anxious about atrocities perpetrated against Jews in Germany, what we learned mainly from rumors and not from newspaper- or newsreel-reports. We got some quite vague information, for instance, that Germany's policy was to get rid of the Jews, they wanted the Jews to leave Germany officially, by emigration, to wherever they could go, and that at the Evian conference they offered to let the German Jews emigrate to any country that would accept them as immigrants - but we had no information on the failure of this Conference.

Notwithstanding our worries about the fate of the German Jews, the general feeling, almost conviction, of Hungary's Jews had been that we would not be affected by Germany's persecutions, since Hungary had been not only an independent state, but in good, friendly relation with Germany and thus what had been happening there, would not necessarily happen here. The Hungarian "Jewish

Laws" started in 1938 and had been much less severe than the German laws. This of our feeling had been prevalent during the thirties, and it is now futile to speculate: what could we had achieved would we had felt differently.

An important comment needs to be made here, without which the story of my - and my family's - life and the narrative of my fellow-Jews of Hungary could not be correctly understood, but would make an absolutely false and misleading perception about the behavior of the entire Hungarian Jewish community.

Information is the input in the control- and regulating-mechanism of every human activity; for instance: information on approaching danger induces man to prepare action of self-defense or flight. The sources of information for us in Hungary during the Thirties were the Hungarian newspapers, a few foreign newspapers, radio-broadcasts, and weekly newsreels. Sometime from the middle of the Thirties, we started to listen to the BBC, which was not very easy to receive in Hungary, because at that time there was only long-wave broadcasting. The news we heard were not too comforting, mainly when they verified German successes. All information we could get from Hungarian sources were heavily censured by the authorities and strongly biased at their origins, mainly by the Germans. This is one of the aspects that has to be considered by the reader when he wants to correctly perceive my narration. The other one is the state of the art of communication at that period, compared with that of today. Due mainly to these two aspects, the reader must not visualize and perceive automatically what I relate here, as if they were today's events. Information service at that time rendered by the totalitarian regimes was highly oriented for achieving their propaganda aims. Besides, its technical level cannot be compared to today's mass-communication (when for instance the whole world could see live war actions occurring anywhere in the world). These main reasons make it very important that the reader shall consciously transmute his perception from today's frame-of-mind to that of the time period of the events narrated here.

As regards the question, raised quite often in the last few decades, why the Jews did not flee the country as long as it was possible: one has to realize the unreasonableness of such a hindsight question, mainly because of the following reasons.

From the end of WWII, the phenomenon of smaller or bigger groups of people forced to flee their home and country and seek refuge in other countries, with increasing cases and numbers, has been compelling a new mentality on the international community of nations and peoples, of first observing, slowly accepting, and trying to solve the problem-complex of mass refugees. A novel "frame-of-mind" has been taking shape, by considering and accepting the notion of people's fleeing their home-country and seeking refuge in another country, and by trying to set up, separately or combined, some sort of legal organization and physical assistance for the refugees. Such a "frame-of-mind" was non-existent before WWII. Thus, one cannot examine and analyze flight concepts and practices of endangered Jews during the years 1936-41, unless one "transmutes" himself from the present "refugee-oriented frame-of-mind" to the then prevailing atmosphere, when to flee one's own country and to seek refuge in another, especially in big groups, was unknown, unusual, unacceptable, and refused by every country. Besides: the Hungarian Jewish community had not been feeling being threatened so fatally that would induce them to take the high risk to flee abroad, leaving behind everything. The overwhelming majority had been trying to pull through the difficult times at home.

The extremely difficult fateful decision to flee from home formed only one of the two-sided processes, where the complementary other side was: to find a country that would let Jewish refugees in. For the majority, this aspect was even more prohibitive than to decide to flee.

The generally established individual, case-by-case approval of immigration, practiced by the leading countries of the world, generally for everyone, not specifically for Jews, was brutally and drastically changed at the Evian Conference, where not one single place was made available for the many thousands of German Jews. So, this was the unanimous answer to the question of the Hungarian Jews too: where to go.

Of course, there was a relatively small number of people, engaged mainly in finance, commerce, free profession, etc, who either had financial bases and good connections abroad and at home, and so they could rescue all or part of their wealth when fleeing, and from their relatives and connections abroad could build a new existence. A very small group could get away individually with some luck: scientists, artists, etc, with world-known name. Another small group consisted of people active in export-import, or black market, with foreign contacts, whose economic basis had been mobile, liquid, so they could move their existence easily, any time. All these people, who had been making steps in their resolve to get away, had been preparing and making their steps in the extreme secrecy possible. Consequently, the possibility and modality of fleeing could not have been the subject of discussion among the majority of Jews.

But, the biggest portion of the Hungarian Jews belonged to the middle- and lower-middle-class, engaged in small trade, crafts, commerce, industry, etc, and employed as blue- and white-collar workers, who would had no problems how to transfer their wealth when fleeing: they had no transferable wealth, Thus, generally, they could not even start pondering on the otherwise very difficult dilemma: to remain or flee.

Those people who could manage to transfer their wealth and succeeded to reach some other country and establish there a new existence, could do it, more or less legally. But there was one more group, who had no money to transfer and practically no foreign connections - and still decided to flee and succeeded to reach some haven, the members of which were smart, clever, dexterous people, who had no fears and extremely courageously managed to find ways and means, more or less illegal, in order to overcome regulations, bureaucracy, etc, and they gambled a very high, maybe the highest, stake.

Returning now to our family: Mama, Fred, Paul, and their wives, Erno and Oly and their son George, Eva and myself, what did we think and do as regards the fateful question?

Starting with ourselves, we really wanted to emigrate (as it is mentioned above), without any financial backing and with no relatives or friends abroad, but were refused both by England and Australia. All other members of the family were well established, owned the two factories and other properties. As long as a way could have been found to sell the factories and properties and manage somehow to get emigrant passports and transfer, even a small portion of their money, and get from somewhere immigration entry-visas: they had not felt any hazard approaching, and so they - together with the majority of the Jews - had not considered the need to liquidate their entire well-established past and present, and immigrate to some foreign country. Moreover, one has to consider that then, in those years, a Jew could have felt himself fortunate if he could sell his property for a fraction of its real value. And later, when the situation became more and more serious and frightening - it was already too late, and no Jew could leave Hungary legally.

One disturbing question has to be mentioned here, in connection to the Hungarian Jews' behavior. Until after end of WWII, we, the Jews in Hungary, didn't know the facts on the fate of the Jews of the German occupied countries. The Germans didn't conceal the Jewish Laws and other actions they made against Germany's Jews, on the contrary: they made proclamations on them. But from 1939, the Germans hadn't announced the persecutions perpetrated against the occupied countries' Jews. There had been rumors, but no reliable information had been available for us, Hungarian Jews, during the years 1939-1944. It is almost inconceivable to suppose that information about, some or all, horrible persecutions perpetrated against the Jews hadn't been reached the outside world. The disturbing question is: how could it had happened that, one or more, Jewish, Zionist, and non-Jewish anti-Fascist, anti-Nazi, and human-right organizations, world wide, didn't shout at the top of their voices, to the whole world, about these persecutions. Would they had done so, maybe, just maybe, at least part of those persecutions would had been stopped or lessened; but definitely their information would have served a severe warning to the Jews of still non-occupied countries, among them Hungary. This embarrassing question hasn't been answered to this day.

In the meantime, after 1938, the pace of events in Europe accelerated. On March 23 1939, Lithuania had surrendered to the Germans. It was exactly one week after Prague's fall; thereby another provision of the Versailles Treaty had been torn up. There was a fear that it will be the turn of Danzig and the Corridor, based on German troop movements adjacent to Danzig. Time after time, in 1936 when the Germans marched into the demilitarized Rhineland in 1938. When they took Austria and grabbed Czechoslovakia: Great Britain and France, backed by Russia, could have taken action to stop Hitler at very little cost to themselves. But they had done nothing. It was a sudden surprise when, by the end of August, 1939, Germany and Russia signed a non-aggression treaty. On September 1 1939, the German armies poured across the Polish frontier, in spite of the fact that Great Britain and France declared their guarantee to Poland to come to the aid when she was attacked. So, on Sunday, September 3, 1939, Great Britain and France declared war on Germany. Almost all of Poland was overrun within two weeks. On September 17, the USSR invaded Poland and captured the Eastern half of it. In the West nothing much happened and it was called the "sit-down war".

We tried but couldn't understand what was happening - and nobody could. We felt as being in the center of a tornado - even worse than that for us, the Jews, because we were doubly threatened.

THE   WORLD   AS   I   KNEW   IT   DISAPPEARS   -
1940 - 1945

Then after a lull, on April 9 1940, Germany sent ultimatum to
Norway and Denmark, and on May 10 to Belgium and Holland,
and within a few weeks they conquered their countries. Germany
attacked France through them and thereby outflanking the
"Maginot-line, the utmost folly of the French who built it as an
impenetrable border fortification, and Paris fell on June 14. At the
beginning of September the Germans started a big air offensive
against England.

Although Hungary was not directly involved in the war, still
there were a series of restrictions, shortages of supplies, etc. A few
additional Jewish laws were issued; one of them, which affected all
Jews of military age, obliged them to do "forced military labor
service", instead of regular military service. Nobody knew how
this law will be put into practice. The concept of it was novel and
unique: the invention of the Hungarian Government and the Army
General Staff, on the model of their rival fascist state: Rumania.

Thus, beginning from 1940, all Jewish men, in the age group
18-50 years, were called up for forced military labor service,
within various military groups, sometimes for a few months,
sometimes for unlimited terms. Fred, Paul, and I served about
three-four months in 1940, attached to sapper companies. I was
called up in September, 1940, and I had to present myself in a
small town in East Hungary (Picture 26 & 27). We had to take with
us clothing, toilet articles, etc, because we were going to get only a
soldier's cap, a yellow armband, but no uniform; feeding by a
field-kitchen, and some sort of billeting - nothing else. Some 200
of us formed a labor company, and were sent to the old Hungarian-
Rumanian border. A few months earlier Hungary got back that
region from Rumania that until the end of WWI was a province of
Hungary: Erdely, with a mixed, Hungarian-Rumanian population.
As part of the Versaille peace treaty, Erdely was one of four
provinces that were detached from Hungary and handed over to

Picture 26 – Jewish forced labor camp ID card

Picture 27 – Jewish forced labor camp ID card picture

Rumania, and in 1940, by a declaration of Hitler, was re-attached to Hungary. Consequently, the border was moved to the east, and the heavy border fortifications: bunkers, barbed-wire fences, etc, built by Rumania and remained intact, had to be moved to the new border line and build there new fortifications. The task of our military labor company was to carry out the dirty and very heavy work of winding off the barbed wire fences and wind up on wooden barrels for transporting it to the new border line. It was a very heavy work and on the first days not one single hand remained unscratched. Once or twice a week we got some scanty medical service, otherwise we were on our own.

We were billeted in a few empty cow-sheds and barns that we cleaned out and spread out straw for bedding. The cow-sheds and barns , in a tiny hamlet, with almost no people, were some three-four kilometer distance from the border site where we worked, all day long, with one hour interval, when the field-kitchen brought us some food, with bread for the day; morning and evening we got what was called coffee and a piece of bacon. It was allowed to send us parcels, with food and clothing, and correspondence too. We were attached to a company of sappers. One officer and a few soldiers shared out our work, but we distributed the tasks between ourselves, and they checked the progress only once a week. The relation to our officer and soldiers was cool but quite correct. As an example: on Rosh Hashana and Yom Kippur we were free and we arranged open-air service, with one of our fellow leading the prayers, - and the officer in charge came and spent a few minutes listening to the prayer service.

Once, at the morning order-assignment, engineers were asked to step forward. I was the only engineer and an officer of the sappers took me and explained that the concrete bunkers that had to be blown up, first had to be charted, and asked me to do the job; gave me measuring tape, papers, etc, and showed me a number of bunkers to be charted. It was not an easy work, but I was not pressed.

We were taken once to a well-known health resort: Felix spa, what we enjoyed very much. Otherwise we used the well in the yard of the cow-sheds. Our service ended after three months. After a day long march we were taken by train, in freight-cars, to Budapest - and released.

Our encounter with forced military labor service life made mingled feelings on our company-fellows. As always: there were optimists and pessimists, as regards the future, but the overwhelming feeling was helplessness.

Returning home, we were very happy to be able to continue our family life, although we two, together with our family, were very much depressed because of the creeping worsening situation of the Jews in Hungary, and imagined sorrowfully how happy we could live in normal circumstances. Eva continued working as in the past and I continued in my work in our factory. Both of us, partly consciously, were burying ourselves in work and in our spare time we took advantage of the special situation of the whole family living together in the same building. In the evenings we spent the time among us, and the few family friends. We went rarely to the movies, concerts, or to the Opera.

In the factory, work proceeded quite well, not only the regular work, but the reorganization steps I started the previous year. Electric motors and all other equipment were in great demand, mainly by the military industry. The material contents of these products have an extremely high copper intensity. Copper, on the other hand, was one of the most important war materials in general. Thus, procurement of copper for our products was extremely difficult, causing delays in delivery.

This was one of the reasons, why we could achieve, sometime in 1941 that our factory was assigned officially as "war factory". Such assignment meant not only preferential treatment in raw material procurements, but - what was at the beginning important, but became extremely so later on - our workers got the official assignment of "essential military-industry workers". Such status meant exemption from military service, including military labor service of Jews.

Copper was one of the raw materials totally imported; thus, "war factory" or not, shortages in supply happened and increased. For trying to appease copper hunger in our factory, I started speculating, how copper could be replaced by some other material. Copper is used in electric motors as conductor of electric current. There are metals that conduct electric current better than copper: gold and silver for instance, but because of the huge quantity needed in the electrical industry on the one side, and the very great price difference between gold and silver versus copper on the other: the use of them as substitute is out of the question. There is still one metal: aluminum, the ore form of which: bauxite, is available in huge quantities, almost all over the world. Due to its many advantageous features, aluminum use and production increased immensely during the Twenties and Thirties, with a concurrent decrease of its price - and vice-versa. Almost all physical properties of aluminum are equal to - or in some cases even better than - those of copper, except one: electric conductivity, which is about 64 % of that of copper. This was the main big problem to be solved when considering its use as a substitute for copper. One other difficulty was that copper can easily be bonded together, mechanically and electrically, by soldering, which cannot be done with aluminum.

Alternating current electric motors, the main bulk item of our production line, uses copper conductor in two forms: wire - insulated winding material in the stator, and drawn profile rods in the rotor. Aluminum as conductor material could be conceived to be a substitute material in the rotor - provided the problem of its lesser conductivity could somehow be compensated for.

By proper redesigning of the rotors, both mechanically and electrically, we came to a solution which not only made the substitution possible, but rendered their production less expensive than that with copper rods - by casting melted aluminum in the slots of the rotor-body. We set up an aluminum foundry workshop; designed and built an electrically heated melting machine, with graphite crucible. Automatic control provided the melting during the night and casting the aluminum into the rotor was made during the day-time.

It was a complete success. We were the first in Hungary who applied this method. We did not know whether or not such a method was used elsewhere; we could not get information during those years.

Reorganization of the factory and redesigning all products into a new uniform series progressed nicely, and the novel aluminum-rotor solution would have made me quite satisfied and a little proud - were the situation not so depressing.

It was for us a surprise when at a new twist of the war, after the defeat of the Italian army in Greece, the Germans attacked Yugoslavia, on April, 6. 1941, overrun it within three weeks, and captured Greece also.

So far the war raged far away from us, and now suddenly it turned to the east and we had a fear that we couldn't avoid being involved in it. There were rumors that Rumania and Bulgaria were occupied by the Germans, but - strange as it sounds - we didn't know what the actual situation of Hungary was. No German soldiers could be seen and no sudden change happened, beyond the creeping war restrictions.

But the biggest surprise - not only for us, but for the whole world - came when in the morning of Sunday, June 22 1941, the German army attacked the USSR. News was spread by the newspapers and the radio and verified by the BBC - that the Russians were not prepared and so they were overrun before they could organize resistance. It seemed like the Polish campaign all over again. By December, one German Army was at the gate of Moscow, another headed for Leningrad, and a third for Stalingrad.

Understandably, we were very depressed by the news what we read and heard. It was very strange that we didn't know when and how we joined the war against the USSR, but there were call-ups of soldiers and Jews were called up also for forced military labor service, but otherwise no war atmosphere could be felt in Hungary. Later, sometime in the fall, one night we were awakened by air-raid sirens, for which we were absolutely not prepared, so much so, that we went out to the corridor to have a look for what was happening. Flare bombs were falling on Budapest which was in full, normal illumination. After a few minutes a few bomb detonations could be heard; one quite near to our house. We didn't go down to the air-raid shelter, because no one was prepared. It didn't last long and after a while the city lights went out. We felt that we entered a new phase which promised nothing good.

I was called up for military labor service, but thanks to our "war factory" assignment, and personally as "essential military-industry worker", I was reoriented to do military labor service in our factory. This gave us some relief, and we hoped that this arrangement will last.

Rationing was introduced, but the supply of foodstuffs was quite satisfactory, although there were shortages of clothing and all luxury items. General black-out was ordered, which made daily life quite uncomfortable, not only in traffic, but mainly because of the harsh prosecutions in cases when even a slight light was perceived by the many supervisors walking the streets.

Very strict orders were introduced to build air-raid shelters in every dwelling-house, or modify existing buildings to accommodate appropriate shelters. We had a complete reconstruction made comprising new heavy steel columns and beams, covered by heavy gauge steel plates, and necessary equipment. Air-raid shelters of adjacent buildings had to have connecting openings, so that one could crawl over an entire street length.

A Hungarian army group was sent to the Russian front, to man a section of the front line, together with Rumanian and Italian forces. Jewish men were attached to soldiers as forced military labor companies.

The direct involvement of Hungary in the actual war caused - among other things - a significant shift and increased intensity in our state-of-mind, our contemplation, and our philosophizing about geopolitical happenings around us. Recalling my childhood's memories of the WWI, the revolutions at its end, the Versaille- and Trianon-treaty, irredentism in Germany and Hungary, the devastating economic situation, joblessness and inflation, political movements all over Europe, the two adversaries: communism and fascism, Hitler and his early bluffs, the follies of the Western Powers, etc, etc, and the concomitant anti-Semitism everywhere: made us, the family and close friends, recollect and revive our concurrent perceptions and philosophizing about the world around us, the various trends and their possible effects on our lives. Such "discussing politics" among us had been going on all the time, on two interwoven levels: one, the political events and issues per se, and two, the Jewish projection of them. Our "discussing politics" had been based on the very limited information available, mainly from German sources, strongly propaganda oriented, and their ready Hungarian servants. Listening to the BBC became not only more difficult, because of jamming, but more dangerous: it was prohibited to listen to it and declared "enemy's propaganda" and people caught at listening were prosecuted. Our evaluations and predictions had been proven not too successful; events quite often followed contrary to our intellectual-logical notions.

Since Hungary's entry into the war, we were getting more and more direct information on the war in Russia, by soldiers coming and going between home and front-line, the difficulties and sufferings of our Jewish forced military labor companies, and consequently we became quite depressed. The German war machine seemed to us being victorious on all fronts. We grow pessimistic, on both levels: the general geopolitical situation and the fate of us, the Jews.

And then something happened, unforeseeable and unforeseen by the whole world: Japanese bombers attacked Pearl Harbor, USA, unprovoked, on Sunday, December 7 1941. On December 11 Germany declared war on the USA.

This was the first glimmer of hope in our depressed mood. All of Europe under the heels of German soldiers; the attacks in Russia although halted, but still menacing - and in North-Africa their thrust clearly aiming to the Caucasus: the prospect was very worrying. We hoped that the mighty potentials of the USA will turn round the German military advances and will eventually defeat the Axis powers.

By the end of the first half of 1942, Hitler seemed to be on top of the world. German U-boats were sinking many hundred-thousands tons of British-American shipping a month in the Atlantic; the Mediterranean had become an Axis lake; in North-Africa German troops stood sixty miles of the Nile; and they reached the Volga north of Stalingrad.

Day-by-day life was difficult for everybody, in a country in war; men were called up for front-line duty and so were the Jews called up for military labor service work. I was called up twice during the year, but fortunately was sent back to my permanent forced labor work in our factory. Paul was called up too, and, by bad luck, was not sent back but drawn into a company and sent to the Russian front. We were doubly broken down, first because of his bad luck, and second because his case showed that our "essential worker" status in a "war factory" proved to be subject of refusal. We were very worried because extremely bad, distressing information were circulating among the families of forced labor workers, about brutal treatment, inhuman conditions, barbarous, bestial behavior of the soldiers toward the Jews, very bad and meager food, etc.

A very threatening event happened to me. One afternoon, after work, both of us wanted to take a walk on the Margaret Island. We had to change tramway line at the Danube promenade, when at the stopping place a man stopped me and curtly asked for my documents. I showed him my "essential worker" document, but he, without any comment, wrote my name and other data in his note-book, at the end of a long list. All other men were asked for documents, by two-three men in civilian clothes - but not all names were listed. I immediately had very bad misgivings; we turned back and went home, very worried, because I had a feeling that the listing of not all but only selected peoples' names meant some malevolent action against Jews: probably sending them to the front as forced military service workers.   We went home, very depressed, and called one of the family-friends, a lawyer, and a defense-counsel, who had connections with the police, and asked him to help me by trying to cancel my name on the list on the basis of my "essential worker" status. By next morning he called us and told only that he succeeded to beat extreme difficulties for releasing me. As it turned out, a number of Jews were called up the next day and sent immediately to the Russian front, in the clothing as they were, as a special forced military labor service company: the "Promenade Company". Only a very few people survived and returned home to relate inconceivable tortures and inhuman cruelties what the Hungarian soldiers perpetrated on them.

Understandably we lived a very solitary life, burying ourselves in work and spent the evenings at home with the family and close friends, discussing politics, following with great attention - and holding back our breath - the macabre "Dance of Death. Our newspapers and the radio blared the great victories of the German armies, and even the BBC news, to which we listened behind locked doors and in complete black-out, couldn't give us any solace.

By the end of October, 1942, another gleam of hope appeared on the horizon: the British army, with Montgomery in command, stopped the menacing Germans, commanded by Rommel, and within a very few weeks repelled them to several hundred miles along the coastline. At the same time, by the beginning of November: a large Anglo-American Army landed in Africa, with Eisenhower in command, occupying Algeria and Morocco within days.

After so many years of continuous German victories, the first big defeat of them lifted our faith that we were not doomed. Then we learned that by the end of November Stalingrad was surrounded and a big Russian offensive broke through the German line at the Don river. Our morale was raised high when at the beginning of February, 1943, the German army surrendered at Stalingrad. One wouldn't need to be a great strategist to guess the fateful importance of these Allied victories. We felt how the BBC's signal of "pa-pa-pa-paa" became really the signal of destiny.

Work in the factory had been progressing satisfactorily; somehow everybody, who was not called up for military service, was quite happy to be able to work in the factory. We had plenty of orders, and beside the serial motors, special equipment were in demand that had to be specially designed. We had good success e.g. in designing and producing big galvanizing dynamos; special middle frequency (150 Hz) generators; miniature single-rotor motor-generators with permanent magnet stator, for converting DC to AC current; etc. My big program of the uniform motor series was almost completed, with considerable success. Was it not under the war situation in general and the perilous Jewish situation in particular: we would have been very happy with the technical progress and success of our factory. By the way; about one year after my joining the factory, I became the real "Technical Director" of the factory; not by official appointment, but as a result of my continuous directing and participating in every technical activity with indisputable achievements.

By the time we were married about five years, my beloved dearest wife told me one night, with some charming self-esteem, that she was pregnant. In normal circumstances I would had been a very happy and proud man, but at that date, in March, 1943, I couldn't conceal on my face that I was worried - although very-very happy. I felt that she was disappointed as a woman but then she admitted that she was worried too. But we concurred that, trusting in God, we shall do everything to give the child the best loving care and upbringing possible, and hope for the best common future.

During the summer of 1943, we lived an even restrained life, spending our free time within the family circle, closely following the world situation, with growing optimism. We spent the week-ends on the Hill (Swab Hill), in the family villa or in the Hotel Mirabelle, which was, at that time, a novel apartment-hotel establishment, initiated by Erno. The Mirabelle was adjacent to the elegant Majestic Hotel, and above the hillside of the family villa.

Sometime in July, 1943, we got the highly encouraging news that American forces landed in South-Italy; Italy jumped out of the Axis, restored the king and arrested Mussolini. Unfortunately, our hope of a total retreat of the German forces from Italy didn't follow.

A few times during 1943, we got messages from Paul, by soldiers returning from the front-line at the Don river, that he was, together with all the Jewish slave labor comrades, in a terrible situation, lacking warm clothes, food, etc. His brother Fred, I and one more of our old friends from Brunn, also an engineer, employed in the factory, decided to attempt to have him exempted and transferred to do the labor service group in the factory. The three of us feverishly designed a new electrical apparatus, a servo-mechanism, for moving anti-aircraft guns, controlled by electric signals instead of cumbersome mechanical device. We entered a patent application in his name, and sent an application to the proper military authority, asking to redirect him to the factory, for finishing the device. We couldn't find out whether or not to this application, but Paul was returned sometime in September. He was one of the very few military labor service Jews, retreating after the Don defeat, abandoned by the Hungarian army, going on foot, in small groups, in -30 - -40 C cold, the distance of 1300-1400 kilometers, until they reached the infamous so-called hospital at Doroshits, where he suffered spotted fever, together with more than thousand comrades, with no medicament, nothing at all. He miraculously recovered and arrived home.

By the end of 1943, a few more Jews returned from the Russian front and then we heard somewhat more about the mad, inhuman, barbarous crimes to which they had been exposed. One of them called themselves "slaves condemned to death". Perpetrators were groups of the Hungarian army soldiers and officers; they competed with each other in putting the Jews to suffer unimaginable cruelties, Gone were the days of 1940, when the first such companies served, when, besides humiliating treatment, some useful work for the army had been gained from them. The purpose changed in 1942-44 to deliberately wipe out the service companies' members, by subjugating them to inconceivable, barbaric, savage deeds, causing their slow and horrifying death. Characteristic cases of these crimes: In 1942, during the march to the front-line, when war materials, mainly ammunitions, were transported in horse-drawn carts: the officers and soldiers let the horses jog along by the roadside and put instead nine men to each cart to haul them for hundreds of kilometers. Blind hate and the urge to commit cruelty overruled war expediency. In 1943, when the Russian army broke through the Don front-line, the Hungarian army, in its hasty retreat, abandoned completely the Jewish military labor servicemen, so they had to flee on foot, in small groups, drugging themselves along on snow-covered terrain, in extreme cold, with no warm clothing - and when sometimes they found a peasant allowing them to rest at the fireside - Hungarian soldiers chased them away. Many of them froze to death, and whoever reached the so-called hospitals at Doroshits or Kiev succumbed there to spotted fever and died. An estimated 5% survived that "military labor service" campaign - done much "honor" to the Hungarian Government that had invented it.

In the second half of 1943, there were air bombings in Hungary, mainly at railway junctions, refineries, and heavy industrial targets. A few times we had to go down to our air-raid shelter and we had to equip it with all necessary arrangements.

Eva ceased to work, partly because of new restrictions on Jews in higher positions, and partly because of her expectancy. She had been well all the time and had been busying herself with all necessary preparations for our baby. On September 26 she felt labor pains, so we brought her to a private sanitarium to the obstetrician doctor, one of the family's old friends. The same evening our baby was born: a boy Robert, named after the hero of the book Winnie the Pooh, which Eva was reading during her pregnancy (The Hungarian translation of the book has the hero's name as Robert, not as Robin in the original English version). Both were doing well, and after a few days we went home where everything was already nicely prepared. I adored our dearest Mamika even more than before, for her wonderful talent, from a new angle as a new mother managing everything beautifully with the baby.

Due to the air bombing threat, the whole family thought it advisable to go up to the villa on the Hill, but after a week or so we returned because shopping on the Hill was too difficult.

Our whole life was centered on our sweet little boy - Robi; (Picture 27) we tried to live and devote all our attention and love on him, as if nothing as terrible as the raging war and cruel killings of Jews would surround us; hoping that by some miracle we would overcome.

By the end of 1943, the "war factory" assignment of our factory was strengthened by appointing an army captain, a professional soldier, a middle-aged man, as commander of the factory. We had to provide an office room for him and one of our women clerks as his secretary. He was a fair, correct man and as it turned out: he considered it as his duty to further the interests of the factory and provide it with every help necessary for its functioning.

By the middle of March, 1944, due to probable air bombings of Budapest, the big banks permitted to their old-standing clients to place one big wooden crate in their underground store-room, containing personal belongings, for safekeeping.

On Sunday morning, March 19, we started to pack in one big crate those personal things we thought would be necessary in case our home would be bombed out: one or two set of clothing, kitchen utensils, bed-clothes, etc, silver and porcelain tableware, etc. We barely started to pack, when unexpectedly my brother arrived. He seemed very troubled when he told us that he came to inform us that from the early morning hours the Germans have been occupying the whole country, in complete silence; taking all

Picture 27 – Robi is born

government buildings, offices, radio station, etc.; taking many people by prepared list of prominent people, etc, and extremely serious orders will be given soon, according to information he received from someone. It hit us as a bolt from the blue; we became numbed with fear and it took some time until we could start somehow to think about what to do. My brother told us furthermore that only men were taken, but no women. He was worried about the four of us: Erno, Fred, Paul, and myself; he was only a public accountant - he didn't think he was involved. We phoned Erno, Fred, and Paul, but all we could decide was to wait till next morning and ask our commander: what to do. We embraced and tried to embolden each-other - and he left. We finished the packing and pampered our baby, and enjoyed his giggles.

We felt that very hard times lie ahead of us, but we were powerless. On that same day in the afternoon, we got a verification of my brother's information: a very saddening one. The foster-daughter, Fodor Evi, of our sister-in-law: Oly, had been staying with them for the last few weeks. She was about eighteen, lived in Hatvan with her father, who was a lawyer and an old-time Zionist. He was due to arrive in Budapest that same morning to visit her. When he didn't show up in the afternoon, intensive search was made by his daughter, resulting with the information that his father, together with a few other men, was identity-checked at arrival on the railway station and taken away.

Next day, Monday, we were told by our commander that we have to wait for instructions and until then we have to continue working in the factory as usual.

Some announcement was issued by the Government about the need to strengthen war effort and to follow regulations and instructions to be issued. Great uncertainty reigned among the general population, but especially among the Jews. I cannot recall the dates and sequence of regulations referring to the Jews, that were issued from day to day, sometimes several in a day. One of the first and most important rules ordered the establishment of

Jewish Boards ("Judenrat") to take care of the requirements of the Jewish population. This was the code-name, but within a few days we had to learn that the actual task of these Boards were to carry out the regulations and instructions given to them by the authorities.

The orders given with respect the Jews were far beyond the Jewish laws of Germany, as we knew about them. These were seemingly supplemented by the experiences they gained in the occupied countries, as we could only guess, because no information reached us, beyond sometimes contradictory rumors. The whirlwind of rapid orders, each of which separately made us desperate, and made our life unbearable, We had no strength of mind to analyze and define those orders: we found them inhumane, as we were called and considered as "not human beings".

A few of the orders - as examples only: Every Jewish man, woman, and child had to wear a yellow star, of a given size, on the left breast (Picture 28). Travel on train was forbidden. Houses were assigned for Jews only, where they had to move within a few days from their residence, three-four families in each apartment; the outside door marked by a yellow star. Except a few hours in the morning, Jews were forbidden to walk on the streets. Jews were forbidden to employ household employees, Automobiles, bicycles, radios, etc, jewelry, silverware, etc, have to be handed over to collecting offices; and hundreds more.

These things refer only to Budapest; we had almost no information what was happening in the countryside during April.

Understandably, big confusion was prevailing in Budapest: Jews running around to move to Jewish houses from their present residence; and in general: to carry out the orders issued by the authorities and by the Jewish Boards. Jewish employees were uncertain whether they will be kept by their employers and how could they commute to and from their work places due to the go-out prohibition. Morale was at its lowest ebb; raging rumors were rampant.

We were really very fortunate that we were allowed to

Picture 28 – Evi's yellow star that all Jews had to wear outdoors

continue working in the factory as military labor service company members. Moreover, since the factory got many new orders, our commander permitted to hire additional workers, among them Jewish apprentices (one of them was my brother), who were then attached to the military labor service company. Furthermore, because of the go-out prohibition, we were allowed to lodge the entire military labor service company within the factory building compound. Permit was given to build bunks for the company, on the second floor of the factory building that was vacated by closing down the Relief textile factory, owned by our brother-in-law Erno.

I knew of very few cases in Budapest, similar to ours, where military labor service company members were allowed to work and be lodged within a war factory.

We knew that we had been very lucky. The five women of the family: Mama, Oly, Katharina, Agnes, and Eva cared for the household, prepared food - not only for the family but for the labor service comrades too. We adapted ourselves to the go-out prohibition. In the square-shaped building complex of factory and dwelling house, there was an inside corridor to the courtyard, on the first floor, and one Sunday afternoon we, the entire family sat there and looked at the bulkhead of the adjacent building and reflected about the question: how long will we be allowed to look at this bulkhead.

My beloved dearest wife Eva amazed me more than before by her wonderful bravery and self-control, at that mortally perilous situation, by doing all the joined household work, taking marvelous care of our baby boy, of eight months, and uphold the spirit of the family.

Our family, on both sides, had a few members living at various cities in Hungary. During the first weeks of April we heard nothing from them, but by the beginning of June, we received small notes, brought by country-men, saying that they were taken to the brick factories of their town, and they will be transported away for work. Other Jews in Budapest got similar information; thus it became clear to us that all the Jews of Hungary were destined to be transferred; where to and what for: we were terrified to think over it. Once we got a postcard, with a uniform text, that gave rise to suspicion ,that they were well, got everything they need, and soon will be assigned to work-places - and a familiar signature. Location of dispatch - Waldsee. When more such cards arrived to other people: it became clear that Jews on the countryside were taken away from their homes, gathered together at the town's brick factory, and then taken to the railway station by armed gendarmes and pushed into freight-cars, 80-100 people in each one, locked the cars, and set the train off: as we could reconstruct from a few benevolent eye-witnesses' reports. They related moreover that the population of the villages could hardly wait for entering the homes left behind and taking over the houses and belongings, without any intervention of the gendarmes.

It was impossible to believe what we learned, but repeated reports corroborated each other. At that time we still didn't know about the existence of extermination camps, but we knew about millions of people's slave laboring in Germany, from reports of the BBC. Our sole reliable information were the broadcasts of the BBC, what we followed carefully, hoping that some mention will be made about the Hungarian Jews. But there weren't any.

That we were able to listen to the BBC at that time - was almost a miracle. We had to hand in our radio receivers. But the commander of the factory had a radio in his office, that we entered secretly in the night and - although it was very risky - we listened every night to the broadcasts.

The news of the war had been our daily "vitamin tablets" that sustained us and gave us hope that the end came nearer every day. We learned from somebody that the SS made their headquarters on the Hill, in the hotels Majestic, Mirabelle, and in our family villa, and that the top commander of the whole Jewish affair in Hungary is somebody called Adolf Eichman.

In spite of our permanent assignment as military labor service workers in the Laub factory, I got a call-up order to a distant town in the north, for June 3. On my travel to that town, at one station an old Jewish couple, with yellow stars, was escorted and pushed up to the carriage by two gendarmes, with bayoneted guns, taking them probably to some concentration place. They were old people, with cane and some small bundles; seemingly they were even not aware of what was happening with them. They were treated harshly by their guards, but obviously it was out of the question to speak to them, especially not for me, with my distinctive mark of yellow armband and a soldier's cap of the military labor service companies. Had they wanted to detain me: nobody could rescue me from the clutches; theirs was the highest, non-appealable authority at the countryside.

After two days nervous waiting, three of us from the few hundreds Jews were dismissed and sent back to our permanent places. At the railway station a few freight cars were assigned to us, partly occupied by similar Jewish military labor servicemen. I climbed into the next to the last car. At the next station of Hatvan, some arrangements were made and cars were bumped into the car behind us. After a while the car behind us started to move away from us, in the direction we came from, pulled away by a long train, so our car became the last one of the train we had been traveling to Hatvan. We stayed for a while and then our train set off in the direction to Budapest. When we arrived to Budapest, a railroad worker told us that the long train, to which the car from behind us was attached, was carrying Jews from a brick factory to unknown destination.

Arriving home, we heard the BBC announcing the successful landing of the Allied forces at Normandy. This news compensated somewhat for the previous three days' events and for Eva's anxiety.

An eventful journey on June 6 1944.

Sometime by the end of June, our girl guest: Eva Fodor got a message that the group of selected Jews, was going to leave, end destination: Palestine, on one of the next days and she had to rush to the Columbus street gathering place. She knew about the plan, but still it seemed to be a very happy occasion that some hopeless, unprecedented secrete deal was miraculously kept. Nobody knew how that "deal" had been made and by whom, but there were rumors that some other "deals" were being prepared secretly, between the Germans and certain Jews, to rescue larger groups of Jews. We couldn't find out details. Only once did we get wind of such an operation, when one night a certain Dr. Kastler came to Fred, in secrecy, and pleaded for contribution to Jewish rescue operation. Fred complied willingly with a handsome sum.

Hungarian newspapers and radio broadcasts made no mention of the concentrations and railroad transportation of the Jews from the countryside. Jews in general had continually been depicted as enemies of the state and mankind, and who should be evicted altogether. On the war: Allied victories had been described as "flexible rearrangements". Despite all huge propaganda efforts, people couldn't avoid to make their own conclusion from the names of rivers and towns mentioned along the rearrangements. The fate of Hungarian army at the Don bend had not been mentioned at all, but from returning soldiers' tales reality couldn't be glossed over any more.

As a consequence of our seclusion, we had had almost no direct contact with people on the whole, so we could only guess their reactions to everything happening. Still, some information reached us by speaking with a few of our workers, whom we had known for many years and whom could be relied on, being old-time social-democrats, even communists. Slowly we got to know the common lot of the countryside's Jews.

Our military labor service company was a few times commanded to do some irregular work. One Sunday morning we were taken, together with a few other comrades, to the Danube quay, where we had to ship huge copper plates into a big barge. Each plate could weigh at least 120-150 kilos. Six people formed a gang that had to pick up one plate, bring to the plank leading from quay to the inside of the barge. It was an awfully heavy work, on a very hot day; we sweated heavily. I drank too much water and got very ill.

On our way, I kept close watch on the people on the streets.

They could not had miss to identify us as Jews, due to our yellow armband and military cap. They pretended not to see us, and made no remarks.

During June-July we became aware that a ghetto was being set up in Budapest, in the old, central district of the city, with old houses and streets, where, from old times, almost all Jewish institutions had been located, including the large synagogue of Dohany street. The Jews of Budapest had to converge into the vacated houses, district by district, two-three, even more, families into one apartment. Some streets were sealed off and at the others police guards were stationed. Uncertainty leapt to unprecedented heights; some Jews got information that this meant a permanent arrangement; others feared that this concentration was the step before transportation, as it had been done from the brick factories. My parents had to move in too; they were 77 and 68 years old. We could not help them in any way. Due to our lucky special arrangement - we were not affected personally but it caused big anxiety for the future of all of us.

I felt that I had to do something: I had the vague idea that some hide-out should be made, for at least a short stay, for a few days, if not for more. I went over every square-centimeter of our building's cellars; there were a few; all rooms, and the attics. At the middle of the second story, a high atelier had been built originally, that was later finished with a false ceiling. This resulted in a normal room inside, but on the attic this rearrangement was not readily noticeable. There I found a useable hide-out: removed a few bricks at the lowest point where the sloping roofing met the attic's flooring: this was the entrance that could be closed by placing back the removable few bricks. In fullest secrecy we furnished this hide-out room with three mattresses, many blankets, sheets, towels, etc, wash-basin, soaps, etc.; a big quantity of canned foods, crackers, biscuits, sweets, etc. I installed electricity and telephone connection also. Without additional supply this could serve a good place for a few days, for three-four people; with re-supply even longer.

There had been air-raids, mostly at nights, with increasing frequency. Factories, refineries, railway-junctions, etc. were the targets. Our prepared air-raid shelter proved to be satisfactory. We were not afraid: we became to the standpoint that every bomb on the Axis territory brings nearer the end, and if we have to die: it will be best to be hit by a bomb than to be transported away. We still had no knowledge about the fate of the Hungarian Jews transported away, but we lost all hope.

On a Sunday in August, we were taken for work and brought to the Csepel Island, to Hungary's biggest machine factory: the "Weiss Manfred Works", to clear away rubble, after a heavy bombing raid. Several companies were converging on the site, where we saw heavy damage. All of us were eventually led to a big open space and there we had to wait for our work assignment. We waited for a long time, and by 2 p.m. we got some food - but still had to wait. There were all sorts of rumors, and slowly we got a very strange feeling, a mistrust that something was not in order. After more waiting, by sundown, all of us were taken back to Budapest. After two-three days we learned from several sources that on that Sunday an attempt was made by the gendarmerie - who was in charge all over the countryside outside Budapest - who wanted to take all of us for deportation, since the site of the factory was out of Budapest's city limits. The military authorities, to whom we belonged, resisted that attempt and somehow got the upper hand - and so we were saved. This event showed us, not for the first time, how doubtful and perilous was our status and existence.

During the summer months we became more and more aware of the growing power of the Hungarian fascist movement, the "arrow-cross" party. Arrow-cross was an imitation of the German swastika: a cross with arrow at each tip. They had several members in the Parliament, but their real power expressed itself to view by their green-shirted, para-military uniformed groups, with arrow-cross arm-bands, flags, weapons, and other paraphernalia. They called themselves "race-defenders", another name for Nazism. They grew rapidly to one of the most ferocious member of the power hierarchy: police, Hungarian army, gendarmerie, arrow-cross groups, German army, and SS. Their main activity was to hunt down Jews living in hiding.

On one Sunday morning, by late August or beginning of September, the American air force made a heavy carpet-bombing raid on the vicinity of the City Park (Varosliget) . Air raid sirens had been howling and we went down to our shelter, but when the air started to vibrate with a low growling sound: I went outside to have a look. As far as I could see: a huge number of small silver spots were moving, seemingly very slowly, at great altitude. There was no anti-aircraft gunning; they flow beyond target distance. Then suddenly one airplane descended sharply, flew in a big circle, leaving a smoke ring, into which the high-flying aircraft threw a big number of bombs. I went inside, closed the steel door and then we felt the earth trembling and we were deafened by strong noises of repeated explosions. The raid lasted an hour or even more. After "all clear" we went out, but couldn't see anything, it was almost night-time darkness and we couldn't breath: the air was filled with dust. Much damage was done, with many casualties.

On the following days rumors spread around that the raid was a severe warning to the Hungarian government and especially to regent Horthy: not to let the Jews of Budapest, already concentrated in its ghetto, be deported. The rumors even retailed that Horthy was notified by diplomatic channels. Whether those rumors were true or not: we couldn't confirm - but the fact was that the Jews from the Budapest ghetto were not deported.

Meanwhile, we had kept fingers crossed for the Allies' further victories on all four fronts, preferring the Russian front. By the end of August Rumania and Bulgaria were occupied by the Russians, after Rumania withdrew from the Axis. During September and October Russian forces had been advancing along the entire front-line. Maybe this was the reason, more than others that prompted Regent Horthy to his decision to leave the Axis. He made a radio announcement on October 15 as it turned out later - without any diplomatic and military preparation, as a consequence of which the Germans arrested him within a quarter-of-an-hour after his announcement, and took over the whole country.

The effect of his radio announcement on the Jews in Budapest was tragic: most Jews fell into euphoria, believing that the war and the Jews' predicament in Budapest were over; many of them tore off the yellow stars and started to go up-and-down the streets, etc. We, of course, were more skeptical and feared very much some heavy back-set. We didn't let anybody from our military labor service company to leave the premises, but couldn't contact our commander for further instructions. We had been very worried, but tried to get at some solution to the question: what to do, how to behave in order to overcome the prospective reaction of the Germans and the arrow-cross groups. In the afternoon submachine-gun fires could be heard, and small groups of people had been running around.

One entrance led to the premises of factory and dwelling house, with a heavy, solid, two-winged wooden gate. A name-plate on it proclaimed: "Laub Electrical Works - War Factory - Ministry of Defense and a number". There were two French-balconies on the first floor, at both sides of the entrance, with lead-glass window-panes. Opening slightly these windows, we could look and see the street in front of the house - without being seen from below.

We had been watching all afternoon, although we could see our street only. In the next block, at the corner house of our street and the Andrassy Avenue, was the Headquarter of the arrow-cross party. We saw groups of arrow-cross bandits coming and going, sometime leading groups of people, obviously Jews, with their hands on their head. A few hours after nightfall, a group of some 8-10 arrow-cross members, led by a woman, with submachine guns, entered our street and went into the house adjacent to ours. After a few minutes, shots and shouting were heard, and some 10-12 people, with hands on their head, were led away. We saw among them a man, a relative of the family.

This was the crisis. We hold our breath and waited. If they

had entered the house: our fate would have been sealed, either by killing us all on the spot, or taking us away and handing over to the SS - but not to the Hungarian Army, because the arrow-cross party was jockeying to snatch Jews away from the Hungarian army. The woman, leading the party, put her hand on the metal door-handle, then she had scrutinized the name plate, waived her hand and they turned away. The momentary danger was over - and we breathed a sigh.

But this had been the beginning of our ordeal only. The group proceeded on their way in our street. One house, obliquely to ours, on the opposite side, was a yellow-stared Jewish house. They entered the house and within seconds we heard shots, spine-chilling shrieks, rattles in the throats of the victims, shouting, vulgar cursing, and by the end: deadly silence. It took some ten minutes, but for us it was an eternity. As it turned out: they went from one door to the next, and shot everybody: men, women, and children. Few if anybody survived.

They tumbled into the street, proceeded to the next Jewish house, bawling in excitement. There were a few more Jewish houses along the street, further away. Fog blanketed the October night. It was black-out, but the arrow-cross bandits had powerful torches, crisscrossing the nightly street.

We were standing on the balcony, became paralyzed with terror, for a long time. Then went to bed, without a word, but couldn't fall asleep.

A harrowing, horrifying remembrance that won't ever go away.

Next day we went down to the factory. Only half of the workers showed up; everybody was confused. The commander ordered the factory to continue producing, but we were absorbed in thoughts: how to escape. We considered that during the day we were more secure than in the night.

Eva's and my main concern was about our son. We found out that there were two-three Red Cross hospitals for children, and succeeded in getting Eva and Robi accepted in one of them. Every one of our family members was looking around for a place of refuge, one sort or another. Rumors were circulating that Swedish "safe-houses" were set up, where Jews, having Swedish passport or similar document, would be accommodated. These houses had a Swedish flag flying above the entrance and a notice on the gate declaring the house Swedish property, having ex-territorial status. Similar houses were set up by the Swiss embassy. Rumors had it that the Swedish, Swiss, and Spanish embassy were issuing "Safe conduct" (Schutzpass) passes, declaring the holder of these passes Swedish, etc. citizens, out of the jurisdiction of Hungarian authorities.

We learned furthermore that the Swedish passes were handled by an office managed by a special Swedish diplomat: Raoul Wallenberg. This Wallenberg-office issued not only the passes, but, by his staff, rendered all sorts of help to Jews: housing in the Swedish safe houses, foods, etc. The three of us: Fred, Paul, and I, filed requests for passes, based on our old-established commercial dealings with big Swedish companies, and got registry numbers.

Hunting down Jews by the arrow-cross gangs had been going on incessantly. Sometimes they didn't care about diplomatic immunity and took away Jews from Red Cross hospitals and other such places. They prowled the streets, checked people of Jewish looks by leading them to the next doorway, pulled down the trousers - and herded them away. At night-time they took the Jews to the Danube-quay and shot them into the river.

Eva got identity papers from the Christian wife of one of the family friends. Since the Red Cross hospital, where they had been staying, was threatened to be evacuated, she decided to lease a furnished room. I must not live with them, because that would have put all of us in immediate life-danger.

By the middle of November all of us from the factory, the entire company, were taken to a big empty office-building, where many more military service companies were already concentrated. From the family we were four of us: my brother, Fred, Paul, and I.

We had very bad foreboding. On November 21, all the assembled men, maybe some thousand people, were taken, by soldiers' escort to one of the freight depots (Jozsefvarosi goods station), where a long freight train had been waiting; which meant: deportation. We understood that the Gendarmerie got the upper hand.

Then suddenly a group of young people arrived, put up a table, and the gendarmerie officer in charge of the train station announced that those who had Swedish safe conduct pass could go to the table for verification - but whoever steps out without having the safe conduct pass : will be shot on the spot. Two of us: Paul and I had only registry number of our request for a pass, still decided to try - and went to the table. (Fred was not with us at the station: he escaped a day earlier from the concentration point.) Wallenberg, the Swedish special diplomat, took our piece of paper, leafed a large book in front of him, and gave both of us endorsement. While waiting, I saw my brother walking with the others to the train.

Some ten people, who had Swedish endorsements, were then taken to a Swedish safe-house. We got some food, sat down on the floor, and tried to make up our mind - what to do now, after having been saved by Wallenberg from deportation, on that day. But what about the next day. We were distrustful of the safety of the house and decided to go home, to our prepared attic chamber. We exposed ourselves to a very great danger of walking all the way on the street to our house at some 2 kilometers distance, with huge rucksacks, but of course without the yellow armband. But we wanted to hear about our family and make arrangements together for the next future.

We arrived home where Fred had already been waiting for us. We learned with the help of the telephone, that I installed, that everybody was OK and, for the time being, had some arrangement. We learned that an arrow-cross group had taken over the factory, as we heard them talking in our office when we went up to our safe place. We had been staying there for three-four days, during which stay we once made a very grave mistake. During the night we climbed out and used the toilet in one of the empty apartments on the second floor. The next day we heard steps and people talking, and realized that our janitor and two more people were checking the attic and obviously were looking for us. They didn't find us; but we then realized that the janitor, who lived on the ground floor, just below the flat we used the night, must have heard water running down the drain-pipe, although nobody lived in the house, so he became suspicious.

It became too dangerous to stay there any longer; we had to find new hiding places. Fred went away first; the next night Paul, and the following night I left the place, carrying a small suitcase with a very few clothes in it. Went down the staircase and heard people talking in our office on the first floor. Through our air-raid shelter I passed through the shelter of the adjacent building and went up to the street. As I planned during my solitude in the safe-place: I went to a nearby house where one of our old-time workers lived alone, and asked him to allow me to stay one or two nights in his apartment. He agreed. Next morning I traveled by the underground to the City Park's public bath. Returning to the city, I walked the street, up and down, where I knew that one of the workers of the Relief factory, a Jew of about 30-35, had a small shop, and that he was in contact with my brother-in-law: Erno. As by magic: I recognized him as he walked toward me, although in military uniform. We walked together onward, and he told me that the uniform was a disguise: this way he could go around in the city. He told me about his activity in helping Jews; he had contact with people who made forged documents, etc. By a fortunate accident, he mentioned that somebody, a genuine disabled soldier, who was on sick-leave, needed money and was looking for somebody who would be interested in buying his papers and his two crutches. I didn't believe what I heard: it was tailor-made for me. He told me to meet them in the afternoon at a certain address, for closing the deal. I paid a handsome price and stepped out to the street on two crutches and military papers on his (my) war wound and sick-leave permit till December 15. My acquired name was:

Zoltan Kovacs.

A gift from the heaven!

As a disabled soldier I succeeded to rent a room. I realized only late that the room was in Buda, on the west-side of the Danube whereas we lived in the eastern part: Pest. But it was difficult to get a room and I needed one urgently. The room was on the ground floor of a three-storied building; the owner of the apartment was an old widowed woman. The first few days passed uneventful: I stayed in my room, went out only once for a one-course meal that was sometimes available. Then air raids became more frequent, day and night, and so we had to go down into the shelter. Some thirty people lived in the house, mostly elderly, and as it turned out, they were old-time reactionaries: government- and municipality- high officials from the beginning of the Horthy regime that is old time anti-Semites. There were bunks prepared in the shelter for all of us, and within a few days we had to spend the nights in the shelter, and most the day-time too.

I knew that I had to be very careful to secure my status as a war invalid and a good Christian. I found it quite early: how difficult it was for a "fugitive" to live 24 hours a day among thirty detectives. Beside my personal peril, my main concern was for Eva and Robi. Two days before Christmas I ventured to visit them. I found them in comparatively good condition: my dearest wife proved anew her superb courage and persistence. We said good-bye to each-other with heavy heart, not knowing whether we would see each-other again.

Next night the Germans blow up all the bridges across the Danube in Budapest, thus our connection was cut. The Russians had been converging on Pest, and they approached on the west side of the Danube from the south too, and arrived to the railway line near to the house we lived in. Bombardment had been continuous, day and night, from the air, by heavy guns, and mortars; we had been living almost continuously in the shelter. Food supply had been non-existent, only at few occasions could we get some corn, bread, and bacon. Starvation had been extremely hard to endure. It is deeply engraved in my memory how I felt when after three-four days starving, I went around the shelter and tried to eat wood-shavings from the wooden dividing walls.

One afternoon all tenants of the house had been sitting in the shelter, when a patrol of two policemen, two soldiers, and two arrow-cross men entered the shelter for identity checking men of military age. A lieutenant in uniform, a steady resident of the house had been sitting in the first cubicle of the shelter. He showed his documents about his leave of absence from his unit. The arrow-cross man called him a deserter, beat him, and told him to go with them to the command post. I sat in the next cubicle and heard everything; took out of my pocket my papers and handed them to the arrow-cross man. Drops of thawed snow fell from his steel helmet on my paper in his hands, and I felt relieved because thereby my forging of the limit date was smeared over. Still, he told me to come with them to the command post - and went to the next cubicle.

I sat there and felt that this was the end. An investigation at their command post would immediately reveal that I was a Jew: I would be tortured and shot. With some unconscious equanimity, I started to mumble, in the air, of how could I go in the snow on the ground, on my two crutches, to the distant command post, and why should I go there anyway, I have here my certificates, I had been wounded on the front; and a few more words. One of the policemen, who lagged behind, stepped near me, looked at my papers and at the crutches and said to me: "It is in order, you don't have to come to the command post, and you can stay." It was the first glimmer of hope; and when they left, taking with them the lieutenant, I breathed a big sigh, deep inside, gratefully.

I had been living there in the shelter, together with the elderly tenants, day in day out, but not one day went by without some greater or smaller danger overhanging me, beyond the dangers of war threatening everybody.

There were quiet days, with no shootings and explosions in our neighborhood; when all the other people in the shelter could calm down and breathe somewhat freely - except me, because of my continuous anxiety about Eva and Robi. My overwhelming emotion, gaining strength day by day, had been the strong desire, resolution, and hope to survive our ordeal, to live to see the end of our anguish; that we already survived so far, and when the escape was so near: we were surrounded by the Russians, we could even see them.

The population had been ordered to dig anti-tank ditches; only disabled persons had been exempted. One day, sometime at the beginning of February, the patrol announced that during the next three days everybody requesting exemption must go to the command post. Doing this would be a suicide for me, but I couldn't remain behind when the others go out to dig. A very difficult predicament it was: my brain worked in high gear, day and night, to find a solution.

Next day was quiet; some people stepped out of the house to breathe in fresh air. Suddenly a rocket struck nearby and two boys were hit. One died immediately, the other was wounded by splinters at a few points at his body. We took him down to the shelter where one of our people, a nurse, treated him. This accident bestowed me an idea, the details of which I worked out mentally, till my plan seemed to me a good, although dangerous, solution of my predicament. I announced to my fellows that the coming day, first thing in the morning, I shall go to the command post for exemption.

Early next morning I stepped out from the shelter, with my crutches, went up to the gateway, waited a few minutes, listened attentively. Silence. With resolute fast movements I took off my winter coat, jacket, sweater, and shirt-sleeve, cut a few holes in them with a prepared razor-blade, tore them at a few spots, especially at the left sleeve below the elbow. Then came the crucial phase: I propped up my left arm on the wall, palm toward the wall, and, with the teeth clenched and a deep breath, made two-three incisions, criss-cross, on the back of my forearm, cutting out a small piece, until it bled profusely. I was worried only from falling down in a faint, but I was determined to endure the pain - otherwise I would be doomed. The thought that I was fighting for my life and for seeing my family again, in those last writhing of that bloody war, and that it would be a pity to get myself get killed in the last minutes: kept me strong. I stood there, breathing deeply for a short while, grinding my teeth; then I put on my clothes, caring about staining them with blood, went down the stairs, stumbled through the door of the shelter, and shouted for help. They came running and I stutteringly told them my story of having been wounded by an exploding rocket and showed my torn coat and the blood seeping down on my hand. The nurse removed the clothes, bandaged the wound, and those who looked on pointed out that I had been very lucky having been hit only at one spot, although several splinters went through my winter coat. I was laid down. The person responsible for the shelter said that I won't have to go out for work: he will take care of it. Obviously, I won't be able to go to the command post either, with only one arm capable to hold one crutch.

That was it exactly what I had intended to achieve - at least for the time being. I breathed a big sigh. During the next few days the front came nearer to our house; air bombing stopped, only tank guns and machine guns thundered on the street. The digging work stopped. The trick with my self-inflicted injury was very timely and saved my life.

A few more days.

On February, 10, Russian soldiers advanced on our street and entered the house. A few of them checked the empty apartments, and others entered the shelter, with weapons on the ready. They put us up to the wall, facing forward, and made a body-search. One quite young soldier stopped in front of me, looked at me and searched me only superficially. He noticed a small slide-rule sticking out the upper pocket of my jacket, pulled it out and looked at me questioningly.

I pointed my finger at me and said: "engineer". He laughed and said something that sounded to me as saying that he was an engineer too. Anyway, he took my slide-rule.

We heard earlier horror stories about the Russian soldiers being crazy about wrist-watches. I had no watch on me, so I was safe. They didn't shout much; the whole affair ended without a hitch. That first search groups left, but during the day a few more soldiers stepped in. looked around, and went away. One group put on the table 2-3 loaves of black bread and a large piece of bacon: a friendly act, they guessed that we had been starved. They had even offered bottles of vodka. The only people among us who were terrified were the women; they tried to camouflage themselves by smearing their faces with dust.

Two soldiers stayed in the shelter for the night; they drank some vodka, sang for a while, and went to sleep.

I lay down, and only then did I suddenly realize that in the hubbub of the day: the arrow-cross terror and the war - was over! Except for my anxiety for Eva-Robi.

Then, like a bolt from the blue, I conceived that with the war's end in Budapest: a chance was being given to me to try to find my loved-ones and the family. I sat up and started to plan my strategy program, starting from event one, followed by actions, step by step, leading to successive events, carefully selected and planned.

The principal goal was to find Eva-Robi in good health; and the primary target: to get through to our house in the Csengery street.   We knew that Pest, the eastern part of Budapest, had been taken by the Russians by January, 17, but because the Germans blew up all bridges in Budapest, by Christmas, there was no possibility of connection and communication between the two parts.

In the following days after the Russians entered the western part: Buda, a few people ventured to come up from the shelters to the streets. Heavy traffic filled the streets, Russian heavy military trucks and soldiers, on foot and on carriers, tanks, etc. Civilian population was generally not disturbed; on the contrary: some provisional administration started a big propaganda campaign, on posters and handbills, calling people to come up from the shelters to breath fresh air - and freedom. I was maybe the first from our house who went up, keeping the crutches, for looking around and trying to enter into conversation with as many people as possible, inquiring mainly for information on getting across to Pest. During the first two days all I learned was that somewhere south of Budapest the Russians built a military pontoon-bridge, but people who wanted to cross it had been chased away. On the third day I went to the center of the district and there I found bustling traffic, even the district office of municipality started operating. To my inquiry they told me that a ferry-boat started operating, an unofficial, private venture, and north of Budapest. During the next few days I learned more about the ferry-boat; I met even a man who came over from Pest by that boat. He told me that the boat-operator charged a high sum for a crossing, which was moreover quite dangerous, due to heavy ice-drift. The crossings were random, depending on the Russian soldiers on duty on both banks. The place was some 9-10 kilometers away from the house I had been staying. Sniper fires had been still happening on the section between these two points. It would be a doubtful venture to set out for such an uncertain and perilous attempt but compared with the events I had gone through: it seemed to me still worth-while to go.

I took my real personal documents, money, and a gold wrist-watch from the hide-out place where I had put them in my rented room the first day I entered it. I kept the crutches which served me very well, not only during the time I had been lying in hiding, but during the last week, when able-bodied men were taken from the streets by Russian soldiers for a "little work". Besides, I didn't want to uncover myself to the people in the house.

Never in my life did I want to succeed more in doing something than to get through to our home and to find my loved ones, Eva and Robi, and the family. I set out, very early on February 18 on the first step of my new strategic plan.

I could advance quite speedily on my crutches, as I learned how to put in front of me both crutches at the same time and swing my body forward. The streets were full of debris; some buildings still smoldering; bodies of dead soldiers lying around - otherwise dead silence. A few times I had to make detours where heap of ruins closed the way. I met nobody on my way. By the northern edge of what seemed to me the previous city limit, I watched carefully the river's bank, to find the landing place of the ferry-boat. After a while I noticed a few people standing at the bank - and saw the boat. Luckily I found the ferry-boat: event two in my program.

As it turned out, the people standing around, had been waiting for the next crossing, but there were more people there than the capacity of the boat. I joined them in waiting for the second crossing. It took a long time till the boat returned from the first crossing. We watched anxiously as the boat made its way among the huge chunks of drift-ice, sometimes piling up and threatening to crush the boat. I was the last in the queue; gave the boat-man more money than he asked for - and climbed in the boat: event three in the program.

It was noon-time. As we crossed, the feeling in that roller-coaster boat was much worse than that we guessed from the bank. As we reached the other bank, a Russian soldier stood there. Our boat-man stepped out, they exchanged a few words, and the soldier turned around and went away. We stepped out, and my excitement increased - I arrived at Pest: event four.

I turned south and in great haste started to run on my crutches, as in a hurdle race. I advanced easier than on the other side, the streets were partly cleared. As I neared our neighborhood, my excitement grew more and more; I vigorously hoped to find Eva-Robi sound and well - and didn't dare to consider the opposite. Turned the corner of Csengery street and as I neared our house, I saw a Russian military truck in front of it - and standing on it: Paul. He didn't recognize me until I called his name, and he almost fell from the truck. His first words were: "All the family is well, at home!" I stepped in the house, threw away the crutches, flew up the stairs, burst the door and saw people around in the room - but I had eyes only for Eva and Robi. She came, Robi followed toddling. We embraced tightly, kissed, trembled, and wept. No words came for a long time as we stood there. Then came Robi, our son: a big boy of one-and-a-half; he kissed me, seemingly he sensed that I was kind to his mother. Then the other members of the family. They were tears too. Everybody was all right, except my brother: there was no information about him. My parents were already at home; well.

For a while I was completely confused - maybe not only I was so; no one of us was inclined to mention even anything about all of us went through since we last seen each other. We were in a trance, we just looked at each other, smiling and weeping at the same time. Eva and I sat side-by-side, clasping each other happily. Something loomed in my mind about the fifth event in a program, but - thank God - I found Eva, Robi, and the family, alive and well.

After a while, we perceived that the Nazi-fascist persecutions were over, at least for the few of us, in Budapest; but leaving us with much fear over the fate of those dragged away.

SECTION 4 - FASCISM TO COMMUNISM

HOPES OF RECOVERY AFTER THE WAR – 1945 - 1948

The survival of the 13 members of our close family was near-miraculous, in particular because almost all of us had been exposed to many perils during the last year (Picture 29). We refrained from narrating bygone events - except now and then some specific episode - a peculiar psychical phenomenon, found later as almost generally characteristic. Gathered together again in our previous house, we tried to build anew our family lives. The other family members had three-four weeks lead-off on me, so they helped me to make myself familiar with the situation in general and the home in particular.

Little if anything was left behind in our apartments - except big pieces of furniture and odds-and-ends of no use for other people. Losses of our belongings resulted from three actions and categories: the first, when we had to hand in things like cars, radios, jewelry, etc, the second, when during our absence the homes had been plundered by people unknown to us, and the third, the deception and fraud committed by a few acquaintances to whom we gave valuables for safe-keeping - that were not returned by them on pretext of "taken by the Russians". This third category was the most painful to accept. Still, the family had succeeded to furnish the apartments of each family, although only with the most necessary items, mainly with bedroom furniture and bed-clothes. We returned to our previous arrangement to eat together - whatever could be acquired. Next in importance to housing: food. No food-supply was in existence, in a regular, customary way in the entire city, partly because hardly one single shop was intact and partly because no supply organization was in existence. The principal supplier of foodstuff to Budapest was the Russian Army. Nobody cared whether it was the duty of an occupying power to care for food supply or it was the generosity of the "Glorious Liberating Red Army" (as it had to be called): when potato, bread, sugar, or

Picture 29 – The Laub family that survived the war

lard, etc, was distributed, free of charge, on street corners from Russian army vehicles.

Besides, most foodstuffs were supplied by peasants from the countryside. The majority of the farms remained intact, and they wanted to sell their produce. They brought it on horse-drawn carriages to Budapest and sold on street corners; first for money, later on barter basis, for tools, clothes, furniture, jewels, gold, etc. Consequently, we generally had one-two sort of foodstuffs; but not a variety of them: and we ate what we got. Once we got a sack of flour: Mama prepared a big dinner of vermicelli with poppy-seed; I enjoyed it very much, ate a huge portion and became very sick.

Regarding municipal services: it is simpler to list items that were supplied than those that were not. Water supply had been almost uninterrupted, to most part of the city - and nothing else was available for many months in 1945; no electricity - except where emergency generators were available -; no public transport; no telephone; no gas; briefly nothing. The two parts of the city were separated, and traffic started only later when first a pontoon-bridge, and later the first, provisional bridge was built.

Municipality administration started functioning already in January, under the first mayor of Mr. Vas Zoltan, an old-time communist leader, who spent 16 years in Hungarian imprisonment, then released and exchanged to the USSR, and returned with the Russian Army. He performed a superb job: he had very good contacts with the highest Russian military authorities and succeeded to acquire exceptional help in rebuilding the city's life.

When my two brothers-in-law returned to home by mid-January, they found the house and the factory unimpaired by bombs; the machine-tools undamaged; cast-iron motor houses, steel rods, and steel plates on stock - but all other raw materials of greater value and useable for other than motor production purposes, such as copper, aluminum, silver, tin, etc.: all gone. So had been taken hand tools, driving straps, measuring equipment, typewriters, calculating machines, etc.; together with every stock item: small motors, switches, permanent magnets, in short: every stock item was gone. It seemed to be almost hopeless to start the factory; still a few old-time workers returning - they started to clean up the workshops and mainly to make an inventory. A very few days after the fight stopped in Pest, the Russian Army took over the factory from the Hungarian Army's designation as a "war factory", and put a guard-group on the premises, of three soldiers, for whom living quarters had to be arranged. As it turned out, it was a blessing in disguise. Almost every day, one-three Russian Army groups came to the factory, on trucks, bringing electric motors, generators, etc, for repair. They wanted everything fixed at once, on the spot. Since we didn't know Russian, the conversation went on merely with gestures, but generally very friendly. The officers were understanding; when we showed them that we were in want of something needed for the repair job: they asked us to show the place where the needed items could be found; they took us on their truck, and when we found what we wanted: they just took it, the soldiers put it on the truck and brought back to our factory. This way, we made the repair: they were happy; paid the price we asked, and didn't care about surplus material. By the end of March, we succeeded to persuade one high-ranking officer that it was extremely difficult - if not impossible - to repair his equipment without electricity to drive machine tools. He took us to a few places until we found an emergency diesel generator what he gave us as payment for the job we made for him. Until then: lathes, boring machines, etc. had been driven by hand: a very exhausting work. We noticed that Russian army groups, that ordered repairs, almost never came back once more, and sometimes didn't show up for taking their repaired equipment; they must had been on the move in the war. Similarly we noticed that every high-ranking officer acted independently of any higher authority; quite arbitrarily taking what they needed without considering other similar group's previous orders. But still a war was going on and the Red Army progressed westwards speedily.

By April 4, on their way to Berlin, they pushed out the Germans from Hungary. This date became a Hungarian national holiday, called the "Liberation Day".

The Russian guard-group stayed with us further on, consisting of three soldiers of some far eastern province of the USSR; with Achmed their commander, brandishing a huge curved sword, but actually quite amicable. They took the room that previously had been Eva's room, with beautiful parquet with wooden intarsia - and they made open fire on it for cooking and frying. But actually that was a small price to pay for the benefit we gained in rebuilding our factory.

Each of us received a Russian Army identification card, with a huge red "sickle and hammer" stamp, which proved beneficial a few times - but not always. Once I had to go to the Municipality; on foot of course, since there was still no public transport. Crossing the Octogon square, a Russian soldier shoved me to step in a burnt-out shop, where a few people had already been waiting. I presented to him my Russian identity card which he rejected by a wave of the hand - and pushed me in the room. When the room became full, we were lined up and led through the streets to some unknown place. In a school-yard a few hundred people had already been assembled; and after some waiting, we were lined up and an officer and two soldiers made identity checks. With a wave of the hand he rejected my Russian identity card, but on my insistence he looked at my Hungarian military labor service card, with a distinctive "Jewish" stamp on it: and released me by showing the gate. One of the soldiers gave me a kick - but I never was more delighted at a kick than at that time. I saw, among the people gathered there, one of our workers. He showed up again about two years afterwards: they were taken for a "little work" - in Siberia. Whoever survived - was returned after two years. This was another example of their arbitrary cruelties.

Hungarian state administration had been started by establishing a provisory Hungarian government already in early January. One of its tasks was to liquidate previous arrow-cross administration and round up their leaders. In March-April special tribunals were set up for trial of the leaders and perpetrators of fascist killings. The leader of the arrow-cross bandits: Szallasi had been captured, together with a few other ringleaders; sentenced and executed. I attended a few sessions and was disgusted by their cowardice.

During March-April: orders - mainly repairs - were coming in and the factory slowly began producing. As a consequence of the loss of almost all casting forms, they were replaced with new ones, in compliance with the modern, uniform series, as designed previously, in 1939-40. At the beginning, money was used as the legal tender, but within a few weeks inflation started and increased, first day-by-day, later hour-by-hour, and exponentially. The entire economy switched over to barter trading, using gold for payment.

Life was very difficult during February-April, with no electricity and gas, and very little fuel material - wood and coal - for heating. We were relatively fortunate; for instance, we had car-batteries for lighting and made a simple device for gasifying kerosene for heating.

On May 7 1945 the Germans surrendered and so the European war was over. We were awakened the night by persistent rifle-fire in the streets: the Russian soldiers celebrated their victory.

We, the family, hoped for better times. Spring was coming and a few of the family members, including the three of us, made up our mind to have a look at what had once been our villa and the hotel Mirabelle, on the Hill. We knew that the buildings had already been cleaned out, so we wanted to spend a few days there, taking a rest. With still no public transport: we went on foot up to the Hill. Buildings were undamaged, furniture almost intact, but bunkers and tunnels had been built by the Germans. A few rooms had been turned into small laboratories, libraries, etc. Eva, Robi, and I settled in a room in the Mirabelle - and tried not to think on the memory of the bitter past. The second day Eva felt unwell and had fever. After long running-around we found a doctor, who came and prescribed aspirin tablets and diagnosed a cold. It was not easy to get aspirin tablets, but we got them. Next day she felt worse and weakness. The third day she could not move the left leg, could not step off the bed. All of us were very worried, but especially her sister Oly, but she didn't tell us the reason. She went down to the city and through doctor friends contacted the best physician-Professor and both came to the Hill the same day. The Professor diagnosed infantile paralysis; extracted some fluid from the spinal column by a syringe, and the next morning confirmed the diagnosis. No words could described what we felt, especially she. Neither of us was familiar with that illness; we believed it a children's disease, not that of adults. The Professor explained that the disease kills nerves, which cannot be restored.

It was a disaster; we were struck down; I was more dead than alive. It would have been a common reaction to sorrow about the cruel, blind fate - but she didn't succumb to such passive attitude. She was broke down at first, wept when couldn't go alone to the bath-room, but recovered emotionally. She hated a situation surrendering herself to other people's help. What worried her was not her condition, her main concern was: how she could take care of her child, nursing him, and bringing him up. I had been well aware of her superb self-confidence, self-devotion, and self-sacrifice - but she surpassed all her previous achievements. She did not despair, had hope against hope that she will recover. The best physio-therapist woman-doctor treated her, three times a week: the goal was to achieve that another nerve in her leg should replace the dead one, by constant gymnastic exercises. Nothing was too difficult for her, she pressed on exercising relentlessly: she wanted first of all to be able to use her left leg, to walk around, even with the help of a cane, and be again self-reliant, independent. And by her strong will and determination: she succeeded, slowly but perceptibly. She exercised untiringly and intuitively devised all sorts of exercises and helping means for speeding up her recovery. I was amazed by her moral greatness which not only helped her to recover, but gave me strength in my grief and torment about the cruel stroke of fate. She was in high spirits; took Robi into her bed every morning, told him tales and poems of her own composition; they played with toys, mainly with puppets she made out of textile pieces. Besides unceasing exercises and nursing Robi: she learned English, listened to classical music, and participated in the family's and friend's company, at evenings, at Oly and Erno's apartment. Any two of us: Fred, Paul, and Erno took her down from the second floor to the first - and up again - on our arms: she couldn't move on stairs. It made my heart bleed about her misfortune; I was living in protracted depression and was working in the factory burying myself in strenuous activity.

Life in general had been slowly improving; services slowly returned. Factory orders started to pick up; and I continued to deal with the uniform motor series; mainly with the problems of technology and production organization. One feature of a uniform series is that its components are of the same shape, only dimensions are different. Consequently, drawings of the various components were made blank, only on the copies were the dimensions inserted. This advantageous feature made possible to devise a component list of all mechanical components of any particular member of the uniform series. A three-digit number identified each particular member. In our uniform series each member was composed of 12 mechanical components, each of them of the same shape. I drew up a long-shaped printed component-list form; up at the head a rubric for the three-digit identification number, and below it 12 slips, divided by perforation, one for each of the 12 mechanical components. One or two number had to be added to each slip, for identifying the dimension of the particular component and the quantity of the order. Fill out a form took a few seconds. These component-lists for each order were passed over to the procurement office. The slips were then torn off from the component-list form and put into an appropriate slot for collecting the slips. This was the memory bank of the material procurement office. From time to time, the boxes were emptied, and the quantities summed up for procurement. Ancestor of a modern computerized material procurement administration - many years before computers.

A Jewish organization was established for providing

information on concentration-camps' survivors; their arrival in Budapest, etc. I requested information on my brother. Sometime in August I was advised of his arrival, by train, to a certain railway station. I waited anxiously until a freight train arrived and many people got down, and were helped off, the freight cars, and they lay or sat down on the platform. They were in rags, dirty, and exhausted. I checked, in a flutter, from the first to the last - but I didn't find him. At a second - I found him. He was almost a skeleton: nothing than skin and bone; without glasses, covered with coal dust, in a big blanket, with a huge cane - but alive and home! Their home was quite near, so we walked slowly, almost without a word, only I wept silently. Zsofi, his wife, didn't know that he was going to arrive home. He was extremely weak, spoke very little; drank some tea, and then a bath was given to him; was put to bed - my God, the first time after some nine months. A doctor, a friend of him, was called to see him the next morning. He told his wife and me the bad news that my brother was very ill, with tuberculosis. With the joint help of a few friends of them, doctors and pharmacists, we succeeded to get the necessary medicament, a Swiss product, for a big sum in gold (Napoleon coins of 10 French franks). It took a few months until he recovered. He spoke very little about his sufferings in the Mauthausen extermination camp, as was usual with almost all other survivors.

As we learned, a few survivors slowly arrived home to the countryside; who similarly didn't speak much about their pain, terror, hunger, unimaginable hardships; we could rather sense from their eyes, empty or focused to some infinite target. Not one single soul survived from our families from the countryside. Besides, we ourselves were overburdened by our own sadness, especially I, by my special worry about Eva.

Life in Budapest was slowly restored, first at stages electricity supply and tramway service. The factory was receiving more and more orders, partly form factories producing machines for Russian reparation deliveries. Besides the uniform series of alternating current motors nearing completion, orders were increasing for small: 0.1 - 1.0 kW motors. These small motors had been produced not with cast-iron housing, but using standard steel-pipes, cut to length, and machined the inside to fit the diameter of the steel lamination. This cylindrical inside machining and the subsequent fixing of the lamination inside the pipe was quite cumbersome; thus some novel solution was needed. I designed an original, novel series of small motors, having steel pipe housing, without the need to machine to precision the inside of the pipe. On the outside diameter of the lamination small double-grooves were punched at equal, 120 degree intervals. Bundles of lamination were then compressed together and spring-steel clamps were inserted in the double-grooves. The spring-steel clamps, pre-bent to a double-arch form, had two tasks: first, to keep the compressed lamination-bundles together, and second, to hold the lamination-bundles in position after their insertion by pressure in the un-machined pipe-housing by the spring-pressure of the three clamps. It was a success: production cost decreased and quality increased. Patent was applied for.

During 1946, life was slowly returning to a semblance of normal, except a number of difficulties. One of them was inflation, increasing exponentially to height exceeding that in Germany and Hungary after WWI. Everyday shopping was generally done by using broken pieces of gold chain for payment. Every - even the smallest - shop had small laboratory-scales and pincers. As an example of such everyday shopping: once we entered an ice-bar and ordered two cones of ice, gave a piece of gold chain; she nipped off a piece, weighed it and said: it is the equivalent of two-and-a-half cones of ice - here you have an additional half-cone.

Car for a private person was a luxury even before the war, but these years after it was practically unavailable. We needed a car, mainly for running errands, hunt after raw materials, etc. One of our workers was a garage-mechanics who knew about places where war-damaged junks were available. We bought components and slowly assembled two cars. It was very timely for Eva, whose condition improved, as a consequence of her self-discipline and determination to recover, and to this goal she did two-three hours a day gymnastics, and a series of things she invented herself by her superb inspiration and inventiveness. We were told that a physiotherapist doctor had been treating polio-stricken children in a clinic. I took Eva there and she was received by a very likable person: Dr. Peto, who immediately started treating her. After an hour treatment Eva was enthusiastic, and they agreed to have treatment twice a week. He was a genius; his method was physiotherapy cum psychology, and Eva was a congenial patient. I took her twice a week for treatment, and she told me every time what new element they found for enhancing her treatment - and recovery. At about the second half of 1946, she already was able to go around the apartment, with the help of a cane; climbing stairways was still for the future. She was happy: primarily because she could spend more and more time with Robi. Beside the household-help, a very pleasant young girl, a school-teacher was employed in caring with Robi.

Work in the factory was increasing and expanding; additionally to series motors, special equipment was ordered. One of them needs special mention. The equipment in question was not of our invention: it was patented and we bought the license for production and marketing. The basic idea of its functioning was so brilliant, surpassing all other inventions I encountered so far. A serious problem had been worrying the live-stock breeding community. It had been long known that animals sometimes heave - and die of it; and the cause had also been known: the fodder had been poisoned by a parasitic species of plants, the seed of which not-discernible with the unaided eye from that of the healthy ones. The seeds are longish, of the size about 1 by 0.8 mm. Magnifying glass reveals that parasitic seeds are hairy, whereas healthy seeds are smooth, drupe. The problem had been therefore: how to separate them. Size, color, shape, weight, etc, being the same: no known separation process had been seen appropriate. Somebody might had thought of pulling a needle out of a heap of rice, or something similar; and the parasitic seeds had not been out of iron which would had been attracted by a magnet. So how could the seed's physical properties be turned into the magnetic characteristics of iron, in order to be attracted to a magnet. It might have happened in a flash of inspiration to invent the solution, which is as follows. Seed grains, in bulk, containing healthy and parasitic seeds, are to be blended with finest grained iron powder, in a rotating mixing drum, by spraying it with a trifle of water. This way the parasitic seed's hairy surface kept tight hold of the wet iron powder, whereas the healthy seeds remain clean. The "Magnetoclean" machine is composed of two powerful electro-magnets, in the form of shallow cups, fixed on a heavy steel shaft, so that the circular edges of the two cups face each-other with a gap of some 10 mm in between. In the inner volume of the two cups a spool of copper wire generates a strong magnetic field between the edges when energized by direct current electricity. The cylindrical cups are placed into a copper cylinder, with a small gap between them, so that the copper cylinder can be rotated around the magnets. The whole assembly is placed horizontally. When the magnets are energized, the magnetic field across the edges protrudes the rotating copper cylinder and thereby forming a circular strip of magnetic field. Letting the mixture of healthy and iron powder-covered parasitic seeds to flow, through a chute, at the top of the rotating copper cylinder, the healthy seeds will freely fall down perpendicularly, whereas the iron powder-covered seeds will be attracted and pulled strongly to the rotating copper cylinder and brought to its lowest point, where the magnets are cut away. Thus: two streams of seeds fall away from the copper cylinder - at distant points: one stream consisting only healthy seeds and another of parasitic seeds. Complete separation is accomplished.

We produced a fair number of "Magnetoclean" assemblies; almost all Hungarian seed - grain traders and silos had been using them; and we even exported them to a few foreign countries: England, Poland, Italy, USA, Canada, etc.

During the years 1946-47, public administration was

restored, together with - seemingly - democratic political activities. At the first parliamentary election several political parties participated, such as: social-democratic-, small land-owner-, communist-, progressive-, etc. parties. Later the communist- and social-democratic- parties merged into a "workers-party". The communist party made strenuous propaganda efforts, with success. From the early days after the war, when factories and offices started to awaken: "works-committees" were initiated, first to deal with problems of wage-payments in the raging inflation, later to protect workers' interests. Simultaneously, the communist party launched its overall propaganda campaign, one part of which was setting up local(factory, workshop, office. etc.) party organizations. One amazing triumph of the government was when on a certain day they stopped inflation, after having stored up large quantities of supplies: foodstuff, clothing, cigarettes, etc. - and from one day to the other everything was available at low prices. The best example: cigarettes had earlier been available only at the black market, at high prices; but the day when the new system was introduced, cigarettes could be bought, at low price, The price on the black market suddenly dropped below the official level.

During 1947, three of the four brothers-in-low families: Fred's, Paul's, and ourselves moved from the family house to new apartments. The main reason of our move was the need to live on the ground floor to make movement for Eva easy. We found a beautiful baroque villa, on the Rose-Hill, a one-story house, where the ground floor had been damaged slightly during the war. We bought the ground floor, had repaired it and newly furnished. It had a big living-room, at one end an elliptical double-door directly to the garden; on the opposite end a big dining-room, separated from the living-room by a circular arch, with a fire-place and mantelpiece. It was built in real Baroque stile; e.g. all doors and windows were circular at top. There were two bed-rooms, a step-in wardrobe, a huge bath-room, vestibule, and kitchen; a separate room and bath-room plus toilet for the domestic aid. We had central heating, a garage, and a very large garden with several flower-beds. It was a dream-house, but its true benefit was attained to Eva, who could easily move around the home and could enjoy the many beautiful flowers in the garden she loved so much. Her health had been improving, slowly but steadily; she continued exercising, at home and with Dr. Peto, and she even took delight in doing so. We had with us the school-teacher girl and a house-keeper woman. The entire Rose-Hill was a big garden city; almost built up by villas and surrounding gardens. We found there a few friends, but generally we didn't want to get in social contact with old-time residents; we suspected most of them as - at least - passive supporters of the previous fascist regime.

As a consequence of Eva's improvement, I took more and more delight in my work at the factory. I started anew to look for challenges, not only in actual design work but on the scientific field too. There was a scientific-technical association: the "Hungarian Electrotechnical Association" (Magyar Electrotechnikai Egyesulet: MEE) in existence since 1898, established by Eva's late father. Fred and Paul had been active members, and I joined in its work already in 1938. The MEE, like similar scientific societies abroad, had been engaged in studying problems of electric sciences and technology, in several ways. One was by writing articles and discussing problems in the monthly periodical of the MEE:"Electrotechnics"; another: treatise some concrete problem in a small working committee; another one: lectures on treatises of specific scientific questions; yearly congresses; conferences on timely problems of the Hungarian electrical industry; Bi-yearly general assemblies when the board of staff-members were elected: president, general secretary, board of directors, etc. Office holders had been on honorary basis. The MEE had some 1500 members: scientists, engineers, and technicians, who paid membership fees. I had been participating in several such working committees, and in 1947, I was elected as responsible secretary of all working committees.

The "Relief" textile printing factory: Erno's and Oly's business, was not reopened after the war; they, together with a few experts in the field, set up a cooperative enterprise. Sometime during the summer of 1947, Erno's brother, who emigrated from Hungary to the USA in the early thirties, came to visit the family, and most probably he persuaded Erno and Oly to join him in the States (he was a well-to-do bachelor). Actually they decided to make a visit to the States, and leave open the question: to stay there or return. Their apartment was kept unused and intact, and the three of them - with their son: George, eighteen at that time - left the family, in an optimistic mood, for them and for us too. One day, by the end of 1946, an event of great importance happened. By the end of the war many properties had been abandoned by their previous owners, and an Authority was established to deal with these properties, mainly buildings, that were to be sold on auction at very low prices. We also laid claim to a factory building, because our old building was too worn out and jam-packed. We were offered one factory building, in the North of Budapest - but we had to decide within 24 hours to accept or turn down the offer - with no possibility of further participation in the auctions. The building was quite new, but only slightly larger than our existing building. On that basis I was against it - but my standpoint was overruled by my two brothers-in-law. Thus: nothing was left to me but to take the challenge and design a good arrangement for our new factory. The mark was very high - and so was my responsibility too.

To design a factory is a complex and difficult mission, necessitating a wide range of professional knowledge and a fair amount of inspiration cum intuition of the engineer in charge of the design. Only a very few engineers, who possess all required qualities, have the luck to meet such a challenging task of designing a factory. After thorough consideration, I concluded: first that I was competent to design the factory in general, and second that nobody else was more suitable for designing the new factory than I was, above all because I knew to the last detail all of our products - since I designed the new uniform series - and moreover because I designed not only the products, but the new production technology too. In addition to these two basic prerequisites, I knew - because I made it - the long-term development program, for both design and technology, for future product extension and production increase. Furthermore, I had a long time ago made a plan to detach store-rooms of cast-iron motor housings, shields, etc, from our present factory building, because these store-rooms constituted the largest single portion of the total factory area, with no need for almost any of the expensive supplies (electricity, gas, etc,) and equipment of other areas of the factory building. This was my reserve area, which when pre-planned, could at the proper time be set free for production area. Based on these primary reasons, I set about doing the design with gusto.

The basic, the ideal way to design a factory is to do it from the inside out, which is to design the building to suite the requirements of the factory's functions. In our case I had to do the design by adhering to the factory's requirements and modify the building accordingly. Complete description of the design work cannot be the task of this narration; rather a few aspects will be described here, where problems had to be defined and solved ("a problem properly defined - is half solved"); technical and economic problems had to be worked out, etc. etc.

The factory was designed for simultaneous, returning, individual and small series production of our uniform motor series; special machines, and equipment. Machine tools and equipment were arranged in an appropriate pattern, although allowing maximal flexibility of easy rearrangement by a large number of supply points: electricity, compressed air, gas, etc, in floor conduits and overhead mains. A few anchor points were arranged with less flexibility, such as: raw material- and semi-finished products' storage areas, test-stand, heavy stamping machines, etc. Only minor changes were needed in the building. Component- and finished product production program was introduced, similar to the raw material requisition system (described earlier), with the double aim to keep semi-finished products on stock, and larger than actually ordered component production, for better cost-efficiency.

Monorails were equipped for transporting components and products.

For achieving arrangement's flexibility, machine tools had to have individual drives. A number of our machine tools: lathes, milling machines, planers, etc, were still old-fashioned models with transmission drives. I started to modernize them some time ago, by attaching to them an automobile change-speed gear box, with three speed ratios, driven directly by an Dahlander-type electric motor with four revolutions: 470, 930, 1400, and 2800 rpm. Selection of spindle speed was made by the combination of the electric motor switch plus the change-speed gear box's handle bar. We ordered a few new machine tools, e.g. a modern copying-lathe, etc, which were already equipped with individual drives.

Other equipment needed modernization too. The motor stators windings had to be insulated in such a way that they should compose a solid block with the laminations. The wiring inside the slots of laminations had to be insulated; for this purpose a liquid insulation substance was used, which had to penetrate inside the slots and between the wiring, and then the stator-winding, embedded in the insulation material, had to be dried completely until it became a solid block. We observed that sometimes this process didn't work out as required. I cut two-three stators lengthwise and crosswise and fined out two faults. One: there were a few cavities where the insulation substance didn't reach; and two: on both heads of the coils a hard crust had been formed, with the inside still wet. For solving both problems, we built a big steel chamber with gas-tight door, an inlet for the insulation liquid, and another for connection to a vacuum pump. The stator with the windings was put in the vacuum chamber, the air pumped out, and then the insulation liquid let in to flood the stator with the winding, thereby ensuring full penetration; air let in and the stator removed. In the following step the stator had to be dried out, that is the solvent of the insulation liquid be vaporized by heating, and sucked off. Another big steel chamber was built, heat isolated, with a number of pipes through the walls for blowing in hot air, and a few outlets to pump out evaporation gases. Heating was electrical, regulated and controlled by process programming equipment which could be set to control temperature and time, for any required sequence, set on a control panel. The proper sequence was found: slow heating for vaporizing the total amount of solvent at such temperature that didn't bake a hard impenetrable crust on the heads of the windings. Then a fast heating at higher temperature and total evaporation to finish the process. Instruments on the control panel showed the program and actual values of temperature, suction, and level of solvent in the exhaust. The equipment was operated at night. It was a success.

A common feature of every machine workshop is a quite high level of noise, which makes communication by audio paging devices almost impossible. I devised a visual paging system for calling and instructing, from a command point, people moving around in workshops. On the walls of every workshop, high up for good visibility, two signaling display panels were installed; each one divided into four equal squares, of about 200 by 200 mm. The squares were made of glass plates, behind them an electric lamp, and in front an opal glass plate. One of the two signaling panels served for calling certain people, and the other for instructing them what to do. The four squares of the calling display panel had different colors: red, yellow, blue, and violet: the same position-arrangement on every one of them. The instruction display-panel's four squares had the signs: M, CE, a phone apparatus, and a writing desk. 15 people could be called by combinations of the four colored squares: four singles, six doubles, four trebles, and one quartet. To each of fifteen people, appointed to be paged, one specific combination was assigned. Each single square of the instruction panel gave advice to the person called on the calling panel: what to do: 1.) go to the management office; 2.) go to the chief engineer, 3.) call the phone central from the nearest phone; and 4.) go to your office-room. A control panel was installed in the phone central room, and had nineteen push-buttons and one main switch. Each one of the fifteen push-buttons for each one of the fifteen people, by name; and the other four push-buttons for the four different advices. The electrical circuits were interlocked, so that no double-signal was possible. As an example: Mr. A goes down to the factory and gets a phone-call. Phone central presses the button "A" and the button with the phone apparatus. Mr. A catches sight of his combination on the calling panel (for instance the simultaneous lighted colors of red + blue + violet), and the lighted square on the instruction panel: the phone apparatus. He walks to the nearest phone, calls the central and is contacted to the caller. (An important remark: no transistorized beepers, etc, were in existence or available in Hungary at that time.)

It was efficient and spectacular organization-helping equipment in our new factory. The factory was equipped with modern hygienic installations: wash rooms, etc, and a nice, spick-and-span dining room.

Machine tools and all other installations, equipment, etc, were transferred to the new factory, according to a program for minimizing production drop-outs. By the end of 1947, the entire factory functioned in the new place, perfectly, beyond all optimistic expectations.

1948 was the golden-jubilee year of the Laub Electrical Works that had been established by the late Leopold Laub, in 1898. A "50 years jubilee" catalogue was issued, containing the entire range of our products, with all technical specifications. Based on a respectable past, complemented with the new factory with its new, uniform motor series and appropriate technology - we expected, with good reason, a successful future.

Besides designing and equipping the new factory, production of series motors and special equipment were progressing. As an example only: one of the Hungarian research institutes ordered from us some very special equipment. Two motor-generators were needed, for providing middle-frequency (150 Hz) alternating current; one of 30 kW, the other of 15 kW output. Two very stringent requirements were added; one, that the generators must supply voltages of accurate sine-line, and two, that when both generators working in parallel - the two sine-lines should match each-other without the slightest deviation. We accepted the order and designed the machines that the other electric motor factories could not produce. We succeeded splendidly; so much so that when they came, with their own electroscopes, to test the machines, we started them and they looked and measured the sine curve - and found it acceptable. Then they asked to start the second generator too, synchronized with the other one for checking the second sine-curve - and when we said that both generators were running in synchrony and the seemingly one sine-curve was the common curve of both machines: they could only compliment on our success.

Meanwhile, in the course of general consolidation, parliamentary election was held; the communist party won the majority, and formed a new government. Life went on with no particular event.

One day, on March, 28, we had a meeting in the MEE, in the afternoon. During the meeting somebody, not of our staff-members, went up to the stage, whispered something to the chairman, who stopped the meeting for an urgent and important announcement: the government nationalized all factories employing 100 and more people, valid as of 5 pm that day. It took one-two seconds until I grasped the meaning of that announcement: our factory was taken away, it was no longer ours. I called Fred at the factory and wanted to tell him the news, what he already knew, because at five-o-clock one of our young engineers came to see him in his office and informed him about the government's decision, and showed him his credentials to take over the factory. Fred had to hand over the keys to the safe, check-books, keys to the building and offices, etc. Detailed directions would follow.

"In appreciation of 50 years' good work!"

RESCUERS TURN INTO SLAVE-MASTERS - 1948 - 1956

It was a heavy blow - and it was swift.

I didn't know how it was with other factory owners, but for me the factory had been not only a building with machines in it, or the place where I had earned my living - our new factory was my baby.

Everything went with the factory's nationalization: three cars - because these were registered on the name of the factory, for tax benefit - the buildings - both the old and the new one -, etc, and we remained there with as much money we had in our pocket. Compensation - nil.

The three of us didn't speak too much that night; we were preoccupied with our future, mainly with the professional, and only marginally with the monetary one.

Next morning we went to the factory. It was quite awkward - but not for us. It was rather for the workers, colleagues, and clerks: they didn't know how to behave. Most of them were old-time employees, some of them from the time of my late father-in-low. During the last twenty years Fred and Paul - and somewhat later I - had been the "engineers" rather than the "bosses" - and now we had to be thrown out. Most of them couldn't look us straight in the eyes. We handed over our spheres of activity to our colleagues, together with information on works in progress. After two days, the director, appointed by the Ministry of Heavy Industry, presented himself; we had a friendly conference, showed around the factory, and gave as much information as was possible. We continued the transfer the next day too. At that time Fred and Paul informed him about their intention to leave the factory, because they were invited by scientific institutions: Fred by the Research Institute of Electricity Production and Paul by the Standard Institution. He asked me to remain with the factory as chief engineer - and I consented. None of us had any doubt about finding a new job, as Fred and Paul got within two days, since the three of us had good professional reputation, but I decided to remain with our former factory as an employee than to go to any other factory.

As I went back to my previous office and continued in my job, in the next few weeks I noticed that I behaved more strictly than ever before; maybe this was an unconscious compensation for my changed role.

After a week or so, the director told me that the factory was marvelous, a real "jewel-box". "You are telling me?" - I answered.

At the time of the nationalization we didn't know how in that new situation professional people could get employment. The three of us got within days, but at very many cases professionals - whether previous factory owners or not - had just to wait, weeks and months, and then sent by the relevant ministries to a new employment somewhere at the countryside - a sort of deportation. It took some time until I perceived that work-force "distribution" was being done the same way as everything else was collected and distributed as constituent elements of a comprehensive, overall plan. "Plan" became the leading notion; everything was planned: consumption, production, services, etc.; per day, per month, year, and period of five years. We had to learn how to get along in a "planned economy".

Everything went smoothly in the factory - until one day in September I was called to the communist party center. They were polite and friendly; they told me that they knew everything about me: my previous job, my relationship with the Laub family, my professional reputation, etc. - and on that basis they offered me a leading post in the Heavy Electrical Industrial Center (Erosaramu Ipari Kozpont) in planning. The Center was intended to be the central management of 27 nationalized factories, and they offered me the post of technical director for development, organization, and planning. At that time I already knew that one mustn't refuse a party center's offer of a job without exposing me to the danger of waiting long months and getting a store-keeper's job somewhere in a small village - and the job offered to me was a highly challenging one that I couldn't refuse. I had to start in two days time, attending the first meeting of the Center's management.

It was new to us, but became characteristic to that time that basic decisions were made in the party center, which were then executed by the relevant ministries.   The Center's task was to centrally manage on the higher level all nationalized factories of the heavy electrical industry, whereas day-by-day management were to be carried out by the staff of the individual factories. Moreover, central planning of the factories' activities was the duty of the Center, joint and individual, in all its details; to merge two or more smaller factories into one larger one for better efficiency; to distribute plans of production, raw material needs, financial transactions, manpower, business management, etc.

It was a very high task. The first step was to organize ourselves. At the first meeting of the Center's management, five department heads, inclusive of me, took part. The general manager was a young man, who had previously been a technician of one of the factories: a good cadre. Luckily, he was an intelligent man, with commonsense and no self-conceit. We made a preliminary plan for the Center's activities, and started to work. Two floors of an office building were allocated to us. Our Center was one of three divisions belonging in one section of the Ministry of Heavy Industry. I set up my department with five engineers, five technicians, and one secretary. First, I coordinated our activities with our supervisory section on our first task: to make an inventory-listing on every aspect of our factories. We prepared a questionnaire to be filled in by the factories and then we visited every one of them, checking and correcting the data. This became the basis for the next year's plan concerning all activities of the factories. The plan's deadline was December 31. I requisitioned ten technicians and ten typewriters from our factories to work a night shift in our offices, for two weeks, in order to finish the summary plan of our department. As I later learned, our plan was the best among all the divisions.

During the next year, the main activities of my department were centered on the problem: which two or more factories were to merge into a bigger one; where to locate it; and how to implement such mergers and reorganizations with minimal loss of production. As if fate had wanted to play joke with me: our former factory was among them under our control, and this situation made its management wary in their reports they had to send to my office: they had to be cautious since I knew better everything with respect of the factory than they did. Current new management, including technical and financial staff, of the nationalized factories were not all too enthusiastic about our Center's supervisory role, they didn't like to be called to account. But it was exactly the duty of our Center to size up capacities of the individual factories and their current efficiencies, determine their plans, and check their performances. Production plan was the predominant factor, all other plans were the functions of it and had to serve production plans' fulfillment. My department spent much effort to persuade the factories' management, together with the staff of our Center, about the necessity of properly determining plans, based on objective criteria and standards and I succeeded in it quite well. Almost every one of the factories was set in motion, in merging with one or more others, and part of them to move to new premises. Detailed programs had to be prepared by the factories involved, checked and authorized by me. As regards merger, I knew all the while that it was the right thing to do - but not sufficient. For achieving better efficiency: not only the production means had to function together, but the products themselves had to be made uniform. For instance: if before nationalization two factories had produced electricity meters, each one of its own design: some improvement in efficiency could be achieved by merging the two factories and producing both types simultaneously. Obviously, better efficiency could be achieved by producing one type only - either one of the previously produced two types, or a newly designed, uniform type. This of my standpoint and contention didn't find immediate and unanimous acquiescence: the technical staff of the merging factories fought for their own old product, for the sheer sake of their own conservatism. Strenuous effort was needed to persuade them to design and produce a new uniform product - none of them would lose face at such solution. The Center held weekly management meetings when activities of the departments were reported and discussed, together with reports on progress in fulfillment of factories' plans and needs of their modifications. The Center gained appreciation from both the Ministry and the factories' management.

At home everything went well. Eva could move freely and happily in the house and the garden, caring and bringing up Robi, who was nearing school-age and an extremely intelligent, inquisitive boy (Picture 30). We had to cut down on our living standard; dismissed the schoolteacher girl who had been caring for Robi.

Almost imperceptibly everything became controlled by the "Party" (there was only one). Party groups were established in every factory, office, establishment, organization, etc, headed by a secretary who held constant two-way contact with a district office, and so forth, on the hierarchy's steps. Everything was measured on a "Marxist-Leninist" scale; non-conformity could bring on dangerous consequences, some day, somehow. Factory, office, etc, meetings took people to task on such charges, and at the best, they had to perform self-criticism. Nobody was exempt, and the higher the post he held - the more severe the judgment. An annoying side-manifestation of the Marxist regime was that the "Jewish" aspect was completely removed from the agenda on the fascist past of Hungary, as if Jewish persecutions and extermination of some 600,000 Hungarian Jews by the fascists did not happen. Fascism was exposed as adversary to Marxism and the working class alone; Jews were eliminated from among the adversaries. Seemingly nobody cared about who was a Jew - and Jews did not make effort to ostentation.

From time to time, when from among us: government personnel or professional people, etc, some people just did not show up at their work places - nobody even dared to inquire: what

Pictire 30 – with Robi

happened and why. A few of my colleagues, at high or medium posts, were lost to view - and we knew nothing about them. The head of the section in the Ministry to which our Center belonged, disappeared one day and was replaced by somebody else. Only rumors had it that he was accused of taking bribe from a foreign company when nationalized and compensated. No open trial was held and he was executed. People went around in his and our offices speechless for a long time.

One day when I worked late night in my office, the head of the Center called me in his office, offered me a coffee, we sat down and he told me what had happened that evening at the Party-Center. The director of the Laub factory brought a charge against me for not letting him to move machine tools from the present to the new location of the factory as a step of its merge with two other factories, and accused me of sabotage, with the intention to keep the factory intact until I could get back "my property". My boss defended me by explaining that I had not allowed to move machine tools until all supply connections were ready, so that the machines could immediately be put in operation with minimal loss of time. He told furthermore that he knew about the details of the moving, since I reported them at the Center's weekly meetings - and he approved my decision not to allow moving until necessary preparations completed at the new site. The Party Center repudiated the charges.

I didn't say a word about this disquieting occurrence to Eva, I didn't want to cause anxiety. I pondered over this event for a long time. I knew the man as a trouble-maker, a rabid accuser of every intellectual for being enemies of Marxism-Leninism - but this was only small comfort for me. Of higher concern was the thought: what would had happened wasn't my director present at that meeting. Nobody would investigated the case - and I easily could had got the same verdict as my colleague or could had got a one-way ticket to some distant place.

It was a severe warning to me - and I had to find a good escape (Picture 31).

Pictire 30 – photography

First: I had to change my place of work to another, as far away from production as possible. At that time it was out of the question to ask for a transfer - and where to anyway. After a while it occurred to me that I had to fight more resolutely and forcefully for acceptance of my previous idea to design new, uniform products, for the many reorganized factories, to be produced instead of their two, three, or more, old, outdated products simultaneously. Such an endeavor would be at least as important and profitable as merging several smaller factories into bigger units. Furthermore: One feature of almost all products of the heavy electrical industry is that they are constituents only of an end-product and not an end-product by themselves. For instance: an electric motor won't be used in itself, but always coupled to some machine, driving it to perform work. Consequently, uniformity of connection-dimensions will provide overall efficiency-increases higher than those achievable in production of uniform models.

I then decided to prepare a persuasive report, with examples and calculations of possible efficiency improvements, concluding in a proposal to establish a central institute for designing such novel uniform products, instead of old ones, for merged factories. Nobody else knew all data referring to the relevant products as I did, so I could present my proposal based on actual values, not only on general deliberations.

Simultaneously with my work at the Center, I worked a second shift in the evening hours at the Electrotechnical Association (MEE), as leader of the work committees' group. An average of 30 committees was dealing with scientific and technical problems of the heavy electrical industry. I established a very close cooperation between the Association and our Center, and the relevant section of the Ministry - by farming out specific problems of the industry to work committees of the MEE, to be discussed and the results reported back. Such cooperation proved to be quite beneficial for both partners. By the end of 1949, at the general meeting of the MEE, I was elected General Secretary.

By February, 1950, I finished my proposal for establishing a central development institute to design novel, uniform products for the heavy electrical industry. I had a dual goal; first: to set up such an institute, because it was needed; and second: I very much wanted to be engaged in its envisaged activity. It was handed in our Ministry and in the Planning Authority. The Planning Authority was the top organization, surpassing all ministries in matters of plans, investments, establishment of new undertakings, etc.

No official reflection was issued, but I got wind of strong opposition at the Electrical Section of our Ministry, by its people who had been almost without exception employed previously by the relevant factories. Mistaken and erroneous loyalty to their previous workplaces led them to their opposition. In the middle of April, a few of these colleagues were visiting our Center on business, when they informed me ☐unofficially - that the Ministry will reject my proposal at the Council of Ministers meeting. Two days afterwards I got a call from the Planning Authority, saying that the Chairman of the Authority wanted to see me next day. The Chairman was Vas Zoltan, who had been the first Mayor of Budapest at the end of the war. He told me that my proposal had been approved by the Council and an institute will be set up immediately. Next day the Minister of Heavy Industry called me to his office, notified me about their decision, and handed me the document on my appointment as director of the "Design Office for Electrical Machinery" (Villamos Forgogep Tervezo Iroda = VIFOTI), effective May 1, 1950.

That was "tailor-made". I was impatient to start working. But the road to this was predicted to be long and difficult, because no professional people - especially good ones - were looking around for jobs; they were allocated through the manpower departments of the various ministries. I explained to our Ministry's manpower department my special problem and asked their help in acquiring a number of engineers, technicians, and clerks. From another department of the Ministry, my Office in "status nascence", got, by coincidence, a huge office space, in the inner city. My previous work place, the Center, looked favorably on the whole affair and they approved even the transfer of my secretary to my new enterprise. Beyond expectation, the factories' managers came to see me to congratulate and offered every help they could give to my new Office. Within two weeks we were some fifteen people, two of them engineers who were going to retire and were happy to get an opportunity to continue in their field of expertise: electric motor computation. I took two-three young electrical engineers fresh from the University and a few draftsmen. As news got around about the scope of the VIFOTI, more and more people offered themselves for employment, and what is more: a few managers from the Center's factories came and offered to transfer to my Office engineers and technicians and asked me to take their problems in our plans, saying that they now understand the correctness of my standpoint to design novel, uniform products to replace two-three old ones. I didn't care too much about the fact that their offer to help was not completely unselfish; namely they received monthly salary-wage premiums based on over fulfillment of the plans - and uniform products offered them better efficiency - and higher premiums. By the end of the first month we already were about thirty people - and started designing earnestly. We received ample budget allocation, so I could equip the Office with everything necessary. A car with driver was allocated for me.

Preliminarily, the following scopes were set:
* electric motors,
* manual and magnetic switches,
* electric household appliances,
* electric installation equipment,
* lighting equipment,
* electric heat technology, and
* production technology.

For proper functioning, two clerks were assigned to administration, one each to finance and personnel. I attached great importance to set up a good documentation department, with many handbooks and a big number of professional periodicals from the field, and trade journals. A small workshop was set up for producing prototypes. I extended the goals for our uniform products' design to include requirements of exportability. For this purpose not only relevant periodicals were needed but actual products, produced abroad, that we should be able to scrutinize and good ideas adopt in our design work. For all these activities, budget allocation was necessary. I motivated all my budget requests properly - and everything was approved.

One day I got an offer from the Planning Authority to visit the next International Trade Fair, in Prague (Czechoslovakia). Needless to say that I accepted the offer and went to take a good look at it. As it turned out, a small group of engineers got the same offer, from various industrial branches. I spent there weeks or so and enjoyed very much, not only the many exhibits, but the beautiful city of Prague, which had had a miraculous escape from the damages of the war. I collected a huge amount of prospects, not only of products of my field, but about everything I found as novel, of interest, etc. Returning home, I prepared and presented to the Planning Authority a quite extensive report on the trip, evaluations on products, and proposals to transfer the prospects to relevant factories and people.

After having organized ourselves, I had to perform the very difficult task to put into practice my own novel "creative engineering design" theory, by transferring it to my design engineers and technicians for adaptation in our work. My staff of engineers and technicians was not top quality people, besides they carried with them conservatism and old-fashioned, non-scientific design traditions imprinted on their mind. But that was the staff I could get at that time, and since I wanted my Office to succeed in its work - I had to reeducate them. And the surest and quickest way for achieving this goal was through actual design work, defined, directed, and controlled by me. I wanted my design engineers to use their own inventiveness in liberty in their work - but I constantly checked their progress and made changes when necessary, by persuasion and agreement. I spent most of my time in the design offices; I knew about every single line they drew, and I noticed how, day-by-day, they accepted and adopted my creative design principles. My overall motto was that the new uniform products should be of high quality, built-in the products. However, quality cannot be built-in unless it is first designed-in. This was a novel idea at that time; creative engineering design-education had been non-existent or undervalued or neglected.

One day a conference was called together by Vas Zoltan, the Planning Authority's head, on the problem of some small accessory, product of the heavy electrical industry that caused work-delay in the biggest steel plant. I attended at this conference, and after having listened to a few participants' excuses, I properly exposed the problem as one of the consequences of merging factories producing two or more old models that were not-interchangeable. Next day the Chief Engineer of the Planning Authority wanted to see me, and told me that his boss: Vas Zoltan had been much impressed by my comments and wanted me to join in the Authority's staff. I could hardly persuade him - and Vas Zoltan personally - that I was unsuitable to administrative job and promised them that the first thing I was going to do next day to check the situation on the spot, and we shall immediately design a new uniform product to remedy the situation.

Soon after that I was called by our Ministry and offered me to go to visit the International Industrial Fair at Bari (Italy), in the company of another engineer. I gladly accepted the offer; duly visited the Fair and wrote an elaborate report. I knew that my companion's task was not to report on the Fair, but to see to it that I shouldn't slip away. Generally, people were not allowed to travel abroad alone, and in particular not accompanied by wife and child. (In spite of his vigilance, I still contacted from Rome my brother- and sister-in-low in New York.) I handed in "our" report to both the Ministry and the Planning Authority, which was received very appreciatively.

In February 1951 my father died. He was 84, and only in the last few months felt weakness. One night he felt unwell; an ambulance brought him to a hospital where he was treated. In a few days he died at night. Asking the doctors about the cause of his death, they answered simply: "He was 84, what more can anybody expect." That was customary there and then.

By May 1 a Progress Report was compiled on the Office's work in its first year; designs completed and delivered to factories, and presented it to the Ministry and the Planning Authority.

The Electrotechnical Association had customarily held yearly general meetings when - among other things - scientific and technical problems had also been discussed. I extended the Association's activities to include yearly national conferences, discussing one or two currently prevailing problems of the electrical industry and electricity generation and distribution. Problems to be discussed were defined in cooperation with relevant ministries. Conferences of this novel sort were to be alternatively held at assorted locations. Already the first such conference caused wide interest and was approved not only by the members, but the ministries as well. Beginning from the second such conference, ministers and chief engineers of the ministries also attended the conferences, and the resolutions were seriously considered and implemented. Our Association gained significant appreciation among principal experts of ministries, the Planning Authority, and factories. Without noticing it, my work-load increased; not only in my Office, but in our Association too in the evening hours - but I found much delight in working at both places, promoting thereby my favorite subject: creative engineering design.

Thanks to Eva's supreme resoluteness, both physical and psychical, in improving her health condition: she started to work again, as a designer of woven fabrics.

One day, the Chief Engineer of the Planning Authority paid a visit on our Office, and told me about the request of his boss to set up an ad-hoc committee of experts to look into an urgent and very important problem and present advice on steps to be taken by his Authority. He entrusted me with organizing and heading this committee. He explained what the problem was, and I asked 24 hours to prepare and present my proposal. Five experts by name: chief engineers of factories involved in the matter plus me proposed as members of the committee, described our work procedure, and undertook to present our recommendation within one month. Next day Vas Zoltan called me to his office, commended on the procedure proposed, and asked to complete our work within three weeks. I conceded to his request, and ventured to mention something which - at least to my knowledge - nobody else dared to raise before. I explained that the six of us had to work in my Office, six days a week, every time at least five-six hours, after our daily work. I proposed he should agree offering them sandwiches, coffee, cakes, cigarettes - and furthermore some reward if and when our proposal is accepted. He welcomed my frankness, accepted my proposal, and asked me to propose percentages for each committee member of the total reward sum he will determine. I informed the five people about our task, conditions, and promised reward. Everybody agreed and we started the following day. We were on the job, full speed, completed in 20 days and presented to the Authority. Needless to say that I didn't include myself in the premium list. In a few days Vas Zoltan called me in, complemented on our excellent work, and informed me about the reward sum he already sent to each of us. I received the highest percent, but the others got sums equaling about two months salary. The committee members came to a closing session - and offered their services further on. A nice reward for a good work.

There were some twenty-odd scientific- and technical-associations in Hungary at that time, and they established a "Federation of Technical- and Natural-Science Associations". I was elected a Council member, which meant - besides the honor - additional obligation and work.

By year's end an "Order of Merit" decoration was awarded to me for professional achievements. Being appreciated gave me a good feeling.

Work at my Office progressed well; more good engineers and technicians joined the Office, and as a consequence of nice work-progress and an increase in the number of people: a slow but consistent reorganization was carried out. Senior engineers were appointed department-heads; held weekly department-heads' meetings with planned agenda, and so the progress of every single work got scrutinized in turn. Moreover, our office space became too crowded and so we had to look after some new, spacious office accommodation plus floor space, suitable for our workshop that had to be increased too. After a short while, one three-floor factory building became vacant due to its merge and move to a new site. This building was too big for our Office alone; so I proposed to our Ministry to allocate one part of the building to the Electrotechnical Association's Electric Standards Testing Station. They approved this proposal and thus we moved to two floors of a big building, with a large workshop space on the ground floor. Accidentally, a few days before a meeting was arranged to discuss our request with the Deputy Minister: he was replaced by the chief engineer of one of the factories of our Center - where I had been his boss. When we sat down, I saw that he felt a little embarrassed, and lastly he told me he knew that I should sit at his desk; I deserved it - but it had not been his intention to get this appointment, and he would gladly change posts with me any moment. I declined his "offer" laughingly.

Some cooperation had been developing among the countries: Hungary, Czechoslovakia, and East-Germany, in the field of development of heavy electrical products. I was asked to lead a small delegation to the next meeting, in Prague (Czechoslovakia). I was glad, on two counts. First: the subject was really in my domain; and second: I just loved trips to foreign countries, which I could otherwise not attained (as no common citizen could had got passport and travel abroad during those years).

Another request of the Planning Authority came for establishing an ad-hoc advisory committee. The subject to deal with was complex and urgent action was needed. One bigger and two smaller factories, producing household appliances: electric ranges, cooking plates, etc, had been merged and relocated to a city far away from Budapest. After about half-a-year operation at the new site, they realized that a high percentage of steel-plate components that had to be sent for enameling to Budapest, were chipped of when returned to the factory. The ad-hoc committee had the task to find the proper solution to this problem. An additional practical difficulty had to be solved too: the factory had been timed to be inaugurated by the Minister in six months time: it was a show-case. I called the chief engineers of the two enameling plants in Budapest, plus two more engineers, and set to work. It took almost no time to reach the conclusion : the only reasonable solution was to equip a modern, electric-heated, automatic enameling workshop as integral part of the existing factory. On the basis of our advice, we were asked to convert our committee to a construction management team. The dead-line was of essence; cost made no difference. I farmed out necessary design and production of equipment, etc, recruited technicians and construction workers, etc, and directed the entire construction work. The then most modern enameling plant was set up, and in time. Appreciation and reward was generous.

I was delegated to two more trips to visit trade fairs: to Milan (Italy) and Zurich (Switzerland) during the year. These times I could make the trip alone, with no "escort". The trip to Italy already was my fourth, including those before the war. I enjoyed seeing Milan, Rome, and Venice, where I made a side-jump on a week-end; regretted only that Eva was not allowed to come with me.

My official trips made me the target of envy of many of my colleagues - what I could understand under the circumstances when trips to abroad had only been a dream of common men. And lately a mischievous gossip had been circulating among our colleagues, saying that "Balla writes the instructions and the Ministry rubber-stamps them". The fact was that people from the

Ministry came to me, from time to time, for consultation on current problems of the electrical industry. Such consultations and advising had been an inherent part of my Office's duty, promoting mainly the overall importance of proper design of products, enhancing built-in quality achievable only when designed-in. Assuring designed-in and built-in quality of electrical products had been not only the basic task, but the firm resolution, of my Office. This endeavor had had a series of side-effects. One of them was the realization that electrical products could be marketed, especially for export, only by expert professionals. Thus, for properly scrutinizing the issue, I set up a work-committee in the Electrotechnical Association. Further, the need for a special "Foreign Trade Company for Electrical Products" was included as one important subject in the next yearly conference of the Association. Our proposal for establishing such a new Company was unanimously confirmed. The Planning Authority consented to our Association's resolution - and set up the "Transelectric Foreign Trade Co.". The head of the Authority called me to his office, announced his decision, and told me that I had been nominated for general director of this new company. Only with great difficulty could I dissuade him from offering that position to me, until, at last, he agreed that in my present post I can do the most benefit to our industry.

By the middle of December 1952, I, together with one colleague from the Ministry, went to Prague for the yearly meeting on cooperation. For the Christmas holidays I went to the Tatra Mountains, took the cable-railway to the highest peak: Lomnitz. After lunch the weather took a change for the worse, snow was falling and very strong wind started blowing. The cable-railway stopped running. All of us stranded up at the peak were given accommodation for the night in the nice tourist hostel. At nightfall the wind got extremely strong; we felt the mountain top quacking, we couldn't sleep. I met there a Hungarian-speaking person, about my age, who as it turned out was a Jew. Somehow we entered into conversation and slowly, as if initiated by the hellish weather, he started to tell the narrative of his personal experiences of the extermination camp of Auschwitz. He had been there a member of a team, called the "Musulmans", whose task had been to drag the dead bodies from the gas chambers to the furnaces, to pull out gold teeth, cremate the bodies, and dispense ashes. Such teams had, from time to time, been executed; but he had been lucky to hide from the SS at the last hours before being liberated, by the end of January, 1945. A sad remembrance to the six million Jewish victims, including our relatives.

At one meeting of the Electrotechnical Association, dealing with questions on heavy electrical products, the Deputy Minister, Biro Ferenc, of the Heavy Industry, participated too. A lively discussion ensued, and among other aspects, exportability of some products was dealt with. The Deputy Minister entered into the debate too, and made an outburst against a coffee-making machine, that our Office designed, mainly for export purposes. This coffee-maker was an electric type that automatically switched off the heating when the coffee was ready, and stored the coffee hot for unlimited time. He raised the objection that the machine was made out of copper, an expensive raw-material and of short supply. He called the designers - meaning my Office and myself as indifferent to national interest, people "sitting on the Olympus", devoid of understanding the real problems of industry. Obviously enough he had been given a tendentious and malicious, partial information and he drew an erroneous inference, without first requesting information from us. The charge was serious, because he was not only the Deputy Minister of Heavy Industry, but a Professor at the Technical University - and last but not least - he was the brother of Rakosi, the General Secretary of the Communist Party and Prime Minister. I was not present at that meeting, so I couldn't answer the charge on the spot. I sent him a report, explaining that an automatic coffee-maker had been designed by my Office, based partly on a specific order for it by the producer and partly because we had been informed by the Foreign Trade Corporation for Machinery that they had received request for such an appliance. We searched the European market for existing coffee-makers and found several products - mainly Italian ones -, ordered one as specimen, took it to pieces and studied its functioning. A coffee-maker to be exportable and competitive had to have artistic appearance besides functional perfection. Moreover, it had to be lightweight, shiny, and nicely curved. Consequently, it could be made only out of copper sheet, pressed to form, soldered together, and nickel-plated. Having been aware of the copper shortage: simultaneously with the copper design, we started a research for a method of aluminum soldering that had not been in existence anywhere. We reached some preliminary result, but so far it was not reliably good enough. If and when a proper aluminum soldering method and device is completed: the copper-design could be used for aluminum too. A full technical description of the aluminum soldering research in progress was added to the report.

The most assiduous effort had been spent on the development of the national uniform alternating current asynchronous motor series. Considering the fact that these motors were destined for driving practically all machines in every branch of the national economy: a great number of sometimes contradictory - requirements had to be stated for the development work. For achieving the highest overall efficiency in both production and application: the then most advanced theories and computation methods had been adopted; for instance the Renard system for power outputs, etc. 144 prototype motors had been produced and put to rigorous testing and on the basis of conclusions: adequate changes had been introduced in the design. Performance data had consistently been collected and analyzed. To put an end to the previously general situation where electric motors had been accepted as good when they performed their nominal power output: we started investigating how the motors performed when driving machines, on a long-time basis, continually. Preliminary results had already shown that medium motors, less than 10 kW power, had rarely been used to their nominal maximal power, and even then only for short periods. Another important result had been reached on small motors, up to about 2 kW power, used mainly in the light industrial branch: textile factories, etc. Those small motors had been utilized only up to 70 - 75 percent of their nominal powers; consequently their so-called power factors had a value of 0.5 - 0.6, compared to 0.8 at nominal load. Owing to this lower than nominal value of the power factor, a certain amount of the electric current, generated and transmitted to the motor, had not been converted into actual work. I made a computation for the money- or kilowatt-hour-value of each percentage-point decrease of the power factor, and concluded that it would be a paying proposition to exchange the selected old motors for new ones, free of charge, because the present-worth value of a new motor would equal the annuity (the yearly saving in power cost due to higher power factor) over a time of 1.5 - 2 years, at a normal interest rate.

Due to the uncommon, novel nature of my proposal, I didn't want to hand in to the Electrotechnical Association, for preventing an accusation of incompatibility, so I presented it to the Hungarian Academy of Sciences, where I was a member of two Work Committees. Despite the fact that nobody could prove the incorrectness of my computation: still my proposition was sentenced to collect dust in a drawer.

One day, colleagues in the Ministry, who felt themselves indebted to me, told me that the Deputy Minister, Mr. Biro, intends to close down our Office, at his visit the next morning. He arrived, escorted by three officials. We sat down, and after preliminary politeness, he asked me to show him around. We went to every single room; from desk to desk; and he put questions to every one of the people: what he was doing, etc. But I didn't let my people to answer, first I answered his question, explaining their current work, to the last detail. At one workplace a technician was ironing a long piece of linen. To his questioning eyes, I explained that it would be easy to design an electric steam-iron, but to ensure that high quality had been designed-in, we test a few prototypes to see uniform heat distribution on the entire bottom surface, checking temperature changes, functioning of the thermostat, no burn-out spots, etc. In the motor department, I showed a few foreign-made motors we ordered, and dissected them for close investigation. In the household appliance department, washing machines, ranges, and refrigerators, foreign-makes and home-industry prototypes, were under investigation. Magnetic switches made strong noise by rattling, and I explained that we were on the right track in developing a new type of magnetic switch with practically "no-prall", which will eliminate oscillating electrical contact-making. I showed him our library with a large number of foreign periodicals, scientific and technical journals, and trade magazines.

The round-tour took about three hours; I was explaining everything in detail. Besides a few questions, he was silent all the time. He had cold, inquiring gray eyes in a bald head, stubby stature, reticent; on the whole - frightful and menacing. He was known as peremptory and ruthless, saturating everybody with fear. But I was absolutely calm and collected; even I myself was impressed by the superb activity and performance of our Office, summed up into one comprehensive picture. I knew he was a professional engineer, demanding and imperative - but felt that I was of the same kind. I fought for my professional principles of creative engineering design, demonstrated by facts along our round-tour.

When we returned to my office, we sat around the conference table, he opposite to me. Cookies, cigarettes, and coffee were served; the coffee in the controversial coffee-maker of our design. I started the conversation by giving a brief address. I told him I knew that there were some people who didn't sympathize with our activity; they liked the customary, conservative method. But what were needed at that junction were new, uniform, quality products; the high quality built-in and designed-in by adopting novel creative design principles. Prominence of our design and products was amply demonstrated on our round-tour, and thus I was convinced that he comprehends and approves our activity.

He remained silent for a few more seconds and then said - more to his aids - which he had been maliciously misinformed and he was glad he experienced the truth. He appreciated and approved our superb method of creative design - and added: he will order that design engineers from relevant factories should work for six-month periods in our office for perfecting themselves in design practice.

I couldn't have received better praise.

Our Office organized a technical exhibition, at an Exhibition Hall in the center of Budapest, of products designed and developed by our Office, because I felt that it was not enough to practice our method: it had to be propagated. The exhibition aroused the interest of many professional people.

Along with the steady good progress of the uniform AC motor series, we started developing a variant of it, namely the same series only with aluminum-wire winding, for alleviating copper shortage. This development was the second step in substituting aluminum for copper as had been done in the Laub factory in the rotors, at the beginning of the forties. Furthermore, direct current (DC) series was included in our program, despite their specific complexities.

At the beginning of March, 1953 I received a telegram, notifying me that I was awarded the National "Kossuth Prize". (Kossuth had lived in the nineteenth century and had started the Hungarian war of independence against the Austrian Empire, in March, 15. 1848.) This highest non-military order was awarded, once a year, on March 15 to a small number of people with prominent achievements: artists, scientists, and of all walk of life, including farmers, factory-workers, etc. The awarding ceremony was held in the beautiful festive dome-hall of the Parliament building, on March, 15. 1953.

Concurrently, two colleagues of mine received Kossuth Prizes: one was the President, and the other the Deputy-President of the Electrotechnical Association. An unprecedented occasion: the three highest office-holders of our Association were awarded the Kossuth Prize, to each one for his prominence in his individual field of activity. Nevertheless, this triple decoration reflected great credit on the Association. I regarded my Kossuth Prize just as much an appreciation of my personal achievements as an establishment of the respectability of creative engineering design as prestigious among the disciplines of engineering.

Actually, my Kossuth Prize should have been awarded to two of us: Eva and Imre Balla. Never could I perform what I had done without her active participation in my efforts. Creative scientific work is said ten percent inspiration and ninety percent perspiration. I always told her my problems and ideas for solving them, as well as details of day-by-day work. She, with her congenial perception, had always found the right direction how to proceed, in the inspiration phases, and had continuously given me encouragement along the long perspiration periods.

After my father's death, their apartment was given to the Jewish religious community for receiving our mother into one of their old-age homes. She read in the newspapers about my Kossuth Prize and was very proud of me, and together with her companions celebrated when I next visited her.

By the beginning of May, I got an invitation to participate in a joint reconnaissance mission to India (Picture 1). This was going to be a joint mission of the Ministries of the Heavy Industry and the Foreign Trade, with a dual purpose: first to investigate if and how the Hungarian electrical products could find a market in India, and second to start promoting our products by making proper people acquainted with our potential. Actually, this purpose was nothing else than the reiteration of my previous contention that exporting heavy electrical products needs special expertise. Their invitation meant their acceptance of my view-point.

We discussed our program in detail, the duration was scheduled for three months. My partner, a high official, Dr. Konrad from the Ministry of Foreign Trade, already went ahead and I was to join him in Bombay. We had to go to the four main centers: Bombay, New-Delhi, Calcutta, and Madras. My partner had already been in India the previous year, so I won't need to start from scratch.

Again, not the first time, a challenge was confronting me: needless to say, I accepted it, in spite - or because - of the fact that it was a difficult task. Another reason - if it had been needed - was the exceptional opportunity to see India; not one in a million Hungarian person could go there in that time - and I will be even paid for it. Not even the difficulties that were to be overcome in carrying out our mission could suppress the anticipated pleasure to see India. Waiting for my flight in Rome, one gentleman reassured me that the weather in India is either hot or hotter; but he could not spoil my liking for going ahead.

Hungary had an Embassy in New-Delhi and a Consulate in Bombay. From both these places we received the necessary diplomatic and organizational support we requested, so we visited many factories, met a number of high officials in ministries - even ministers, trade societies, etc, collected information, checked them; told them about our potential in producing and supplying heavy electrical products, etc, etc. We went to all four main cities, stayed for a while and returned to Bombay when necessary.

India, a huge sub-continent, comprised 27 countries, of some 500 million people. They gained independence in 1947 and were still at the beginning phase of development. That India was a completely different world from what I knew in Europe: left its mark on us. Nothing was urgent for them; in the scale of transmigration of souls: one day or week made no difference for them. One of my strongest impressions was to see the incredible wealth and splendor versus gruesome poverty. Sitting in the very elegant dining room of the Hotel Taj Mahal, in Bombay (entrance in evening dress only), all we heard from the adjacent tables were "yes, your Highness"; "yes, your Majesty". And when we stepped out of the hotel, we had to watch our steps otherwise we stepped into the belly of people sleeping on the sidewalk, their only lodging.

They had an excellent flight service: Air India, international and domestic. Daytime flights among the five main cities, including Nagpur, in the center of the country, were frequent; but besides these flights, they arranged nightly, so-called mail-flights. It was an ingenious arrangement. Planes from Bombay, New Delhi, Calcutta, and Madras took off to Nagpur by nightfall, to arrive at Nagpur by about 2 am, at five minutes intervals. After about half-an-hour, the four planes took off to the four peripheral cities. By this arrangement, nightly flights were accomplished among the five cities by four airplanes, which otherwise could had been made by using twenty planes.

One cannot consider daily life - especially that of European visitors - as independent of the weather, particularly in the summer months. Monsoon, the wind system that influences large climatic regions, specifically dry and wet seasons in India, starts the rains regularly by the middle of June and lasts three months. The total yearly quantity of rain pours down during the three months, causing floods, epidemics, deaths - besides.

While consciously doing our work, we still managed to visit and enjoy the many wonders of India. The most enduring impression placed on me was the sight of the Taj Mahal: the perfect beauty incarnate.

In August we returned home, compiled a comprehensive report on our findings, including proposals for future steps to be taken. We handed in our report to the two Ministries. I returned to my family and my Office. I was away for a long time, but we exchanged letters almost daily. I brought nice gifts for them; Robi got two sets of "Meccano", large number of various machine components: bolts, nuts, screws, rods, cog-wheels, etc, etc. He was ten years of age, very intelligent, inquiring, and very good at school - but first of all had an exceptional talent for everything "technical". One evening he showed me his five models of automobile's "differential drives" he figured out and assembled - and I was amazed. I was considered by a few as a good design engineer, but I thought: I couldn't have done it. And I was even more proud of him.

Sometime in 1954, the party's district secretary joined in a periodical workers meeting of our Office. He listened attentively to the procedure: I summarized the work-progress in the last two months, criticized a few shortcomings, gave a preview of additional tasks, answered questions, etc. By the end of the meeting, he addressed the assembly, praising the workers for the achievements of the Office and my leading role - and in recognition of my good work: he handed me a membership-card, emphasizing how much the Party respected the technical intelligentsia.

I could only speculate whether this distinction was allotted to me as an individual - or to enable the Party to boast of how large a percentage of the leaders of scientific and technical institutions were party members.

Work was progressing nicely in the Office; we already were some 150 people. Since we started four years ago on a wide front of problems, there was an overload of "inspiration" needs, and with passing time we arrived to the period of more "perspiration" needs in our work. For the fifth anniversary of our Office's establishment, we prepared a detailed report: "Five years of the VIFOTI", a quite voluminous book of a few hundred pages. It was "confidential", due to a number of subjects of that nature, so only five copies were issued and handed in to the Planning Authority and three relevant Ministries. One of the confidential subjects was that of the atomic energy; we were involved in it by doing some development work for the Central Research Institute for Physics.

I myself wrote a few papers on timely problems of heavy electrical products, electricity generation and transmission industry, and their relation. These problems were continuously discussed by the Electrotechnical Association, both in Working Groups and at the yearly Conferences. By the way, at the General Meeting I was reelected, for the second time, as General Secretary. During the years, the problem of interconnection and interdependence of the two branches: electricity-generation and transmission vs. heavy electrical products came into prominence: one Conference of the Association was entirely devoted to this problem, and adopted a resolution, by common consent, of the necessity to establish a new "Electric Ministry".

By September, 1955, Mr. Biro, the Deputy Minister of Heavy Industry asked me in his office and told me that the "Old Man" (referring to Mr. Rakosi) wanted him to head a small government delegation to India and Burma, to start negotiating scientific- and technical-cooperation. He wanted me to join him, together with my partner of the previous trip there, plus Professor Gillemaux, the Rector of the Technical University, and two more people from other ministries. He outlined the goal of the mission, referring to a few points we made in our previous report. I duly accepted his invitation. We set out sometime in September, to Bombay. Our headquarters was put up in New-Delhi, where the Embassy arranged meetings and visits, and from where we traveled to Calcutta, Madras, Bengalore, and a few more places. We had a series of conversations with Chief Ministers (the Prime Ministers of the individual countries) and their staffs; interviews and discussions at universities, visits to big industrial plants, discussions with scientific- and technical associations, etc. Before proceeding to Burma, we were invited to the big reception at the USSR Embassy on the November 7 anniversary of the revolution in 1917. Next night Mr. Biro gave a festive dinner, and handed me a telegram from Budapest, informing that a medal was awarded to me.

He sent home the other members of the delegation, only the three of us: he and the two of us from the previous India-mission, proceeded to Burma. By the middle of December he returned home, from Calcutta. Before he boarded the plane, he asked us to prepare a report on our mission; we assured him that the report was already being worked on. A week or so after our return, we presented Mr. Biro with our draft of the report. I got a phone call from Mr. Biro, telling me that the "Old Man" was very satisfied with our work, and invited the two of us to a dinner at the Matthias Cellar, the elegant old-standing restaurant.

"Kossuth Club", a social organization of artists, scientists, writers, etc, invited me to join them. Once. I gave a lecture in the

Club, the story of my travel-experiences in India and Burma, with some 150 color slides.

Beginning from 1955, a sort of commotion could be felt, primarily on the social level. Journalists and writers started to speak out cautiously but more freely than earlier, demanding freedom of expression, in literature, music, fine arts, etc. New literary magazines were published, recital evenings were held, etc, an indefinable vibrating of the whole atmosphere could be felt. No sharp opposition was manifested by the party and government; on the contrary: some sort of appeasement was apparent.

At the first sign of a thaw in the political atmosphere: anti-Semitic symptoms started to appear. The Jewish question had been suppressed since 1948, but it didn't disappear, it had been boiling under the surface. At first, after the war and the Nazi-fascist persecutions, all those people who, in some way or other, benefited from the deportation of the Jews, hated all Jews more than previously, as a sort of compensation for their guilty conscience. Besides, fact was that a few of the communists' leaders were Jewish: thus Jews, in their totality were then blamed for everything reprehensible in the communist system. Party members were anti-Semitic, beyond the average level, because "Jews made bad name for the Party". Some Jews were among the writers too, who started to speak out for democracy - thus communists hated the Jews because "they were anti-communists". Many Jews didn't like their Jewishness, they didn't like to be hated, for everything, forever. Jews were again in a quandary situation: "heads - you win, tails - we lose" was the writing on the wall.

One night after business closure, a few of us, the leaders of the Electrotechnical Association, chatted about problems of the Association, among others: what percentage of the membership was active, etc. Somehow the question arose: how many of the office-holders were Jews. A short, scanty inventory revealed that: the President of the Association, one Deputy-President, the General Secretary, the Secretary, a great part of the Department-Heads, and a large percentage of the Working-Committees' Heads were Jews. All these offices were honorary, voluntary; office holders were elected by the members; they worked hard and long night-hours, for months and years - with no recompense. Everybody could take upon himself such work that had interest in doing theoretical scientific and technical work - for no pay. What was wrong with that that more Jews than non-Jews volunteered and worked successfully. The question was obscure and obtuse; we couldn't and didn't want to scrutinize it, we sensed only the simple but frightful answer: anti-Semitism. Again - and forever.

The "Federation of Technical-and-Natural-Science Associations", that could be considered as some sort of representative body of the technical- and scientific-intelligentsia, organized a festive ball, with the State Opera's orchestra and dance-group performing; guests in evening dress dancing through the night. It was maybe a bold act, but certainly it wasn't a counter-revolutionary manifestation - although it wasn't exactly a Marxist-Leninist standard action. It was not reprehended.

In August, I was asked to make a trip to Egypt. An electric power plant was being built there by Hungarian companies and I was given the task to promote Hungarian made heavy electrical products, not on the conventional commercial level, but by contacts, discussions, etc, on the higher scientific and technical plane. I gave lectures on benefits of modern, uniform electrical products.

I was quite busy, still I could manage to visit a few places in and around Cairo. The pyramids, temples, and other gigantic buildings rise admiration in everybody, but wonder and admiration is excited in the technical mind: how could people build such complex and huge structures, some 4000 years ago. The latest excavations that started in 1950 were at Qattara, south of Cairo, near to a long line of stepped pyramids. Among other sites we were shown by the experts the latest findings, a burial place of sacred oxen. A huge, rectangular tunnel had been carved out, about 30 meters underground, with large chambers on both sides of the tunnel. In the center of each chamber one big sarcophagus had been placed, containing the cadaver of one ox, sacred in the ancient Egypt. The sarcophagi had been made out of very hard black or porphiritic stone: a large through, of about 3.5x2.5x1.5 m, cut out of a solid block, with a cover plate of 0.3 m thickness. The outside surfaces were as smooth and shiny as the best mirror. The mystery of how the ancient Egyptians could bring down and place in the middle of the chambers these huge and very heavy sarcophagi was solved by the archeologists. First, a long sloping tunnel had been built and at proper depth continued in a rectangular tunnel with chambers on both sides. The lay-out had been marked on the ground above. When a sarcophagus had had to be buried: it had been placed on the proper location on the ground, directly above the designated burial chamber. Then, they had dug out the sand from the ceiling of the chamber, had brought it up to the ground and put on the top of the sarcophagus. This way, the heavy sarcophagus had sunk slowly, deeper and deeper. One of the many ingenious technical methods invented by them.

At the saddening message of our dearest little Mother's death, I returned home, on October, 12. She was 80; had cancer, but died peacefully, without pain. We mourned for her, she sacrificed her whole life for us, had been so proud of both of us: her sons.

SECTION 5 – AFTER THE REVOLUTION

ESCAPE FROM COMMUNISM - 1956 - 1957

During the month of October more and more "literary papers" started to write specifics of their previous general terms' demands for freedom and independence; they were against the USSR military's presence in Hungary. People became being under an illusion that withdrawal of Russian troops and stopping to drag away national wealth as reparation payments would solve all the problems. Discontent started during the previous months were fomented and supported by broadcasts of "Voice of America" and "Free Europe". People misunderstood the propaganda campaign by believing that beyond encouragement, real help - even military would assist them if they revolt. Fluster and commotion increased, but no single person was known as the leader, and no threat by the government was felt. A strange phenomenon appeared in the streets, as if characterizing the benign nature of the discontent: big barrels were placed on the pavement, with posters calling for donations - but no specifics. Passers-by filled up the barrels with banknote, and with no guards - nobody stole a single piece.

One night the Council of the "Federation of Technical-and-Natural-Science Associations" held a special meeting, where I participated too, considering to draw up a manifesto "What is demanded by the technical intelligentsia?". Suddenly, the secretary of the chairman came in and whispered something in his ear. He interrupted the session, saying that Mr. Gero, one of the leaders of the Communist Party will be on the air with an important announcement, and we should better listen to it - and switched on the radio set. We heard him referring to some "mob" making an assault on the radio station, and he threatened with counter-measures. We stopped the meeting and left the building to have a look at what was happening. All our cars and drivers were missing; we were told by passers-by that a big demonstration was taking place in the City Garden and during the mass action the huge Stalin statue was pulled down by a big crowd, and shootings were going on at various locations in the city. Public transports stopped, trucks carrying soldiers were running, in both directions in the streets. Some of the soldiers had flower in the gun barrel. I went home on foot. Tanks stood at both ends of the Margaret Bridge, the guns directed to the streets leading to it that were filled with people, by commotion.

I told Eva what I knew about the situation, and we listened to the radio. Reports were confused, and after a while a new announcer reported that the radio station was taken over by "nationalist" forces. Among the announcements was one of lasting importance, referring to all broadcasts of the previous years, saying: "...we lied during the day, lied during the night, lied on all wave-lengths...". A later report told about the "freeing of Cardinal Mindszenthy, the primate of the Roman Catholic Church" who had been convicted a few years earlier but he spent his time in political asylum at the US Embassy for years. He spoke on the radio how they would "...take over the inheritance of the bankrupt regime...". A cold shiver ran down our spine on the thought what his vengeful fascist reactionaries followers would do if they could come to power. We had the misfortune of being in want of a middle-of-the-road democratic political organization or personalities.

Within hours a full-fledged revolution broke out. Entire military units attached themselves to either sides of the divide, there were skirmishes. Revolutionary Committees were set up in every factory, office, institution, etc.; a sort of workers' tribunals. Many workers went on strike, mainly miners. Many managers were thrown out, some bodily. Police stations were attacked by armed groups and a few officers of the dreadful and hated AVO (the Hungarian KGB) were hanged. There was sporadic shelling and complete chaos reigned.

A three-member Revolutionary Committee was set up in our Office too, and a workers meeting was called together. Despite the warning of a few friends - I went to the meeting. Excitement filled the air. The Committee's head opened the meeting with the words:

"Ladies and Gentlemen" - instead of the "Dear Colleagues and Comrades" used till then. Then he said: "Our Office had been an island in the ocean of fear...", and moved to endorse my status as Director of the Office. He was an engineer, the son of a Horthy-regime colonel, who had been displaced to the countryside together with many other high-ranking officers, but whom I employed as a good engineer who finished his university studies with distinction.

By the end of October a new Government was formed with Mr. Nagy Imre, an old-time communist, as prime minister. He pleaded and persuaded the USSR to withdraw its forces, mainly the tanks, from Hungary. Indeed, tanks were ostentatively moved out of Budapest in the direction of Russia, to the satisfaction of the populace. A few days later he made a radio announcement to the world about the Government's decision to become independent and appealed to the world for help. The reaction was swift: large tank- and other forces approached Budapest, shooting on their way, irrespective of resistance or no. It sounded strange to us when Russian soldiers called the Danube the Suez Canal. Only later did we learn that they had been sent from Russia to the Suez Canal - and then redirected to Hungary. Many parts of the city were more heavily damaged than during the war. Public buildings were occupied; the Government arrested, except those who managed to run away and got asylum in neighboring countries. A new radio station at Szeged, a city south of Budapest, started regular broadcasting in the name of a new, legitimate government of the country, calling for order and resisting the counter-revolution. The leader was Mr. Kadar, an old-time communist, who had been imprisoned by the Rakosi regime. Newspapers were scanty, rumors abundant. None or little fighting occurred between Hungarian and Russian forces, but some parts of the Hungarian military were against the Russians. Civil administration was partly restored, but almost no public transport could be re-established. No one knew what was happening, and what to do. The "Voice of America" radio station announced that refugees were welcome at the Austrian border. An extraordinary situation evolved at the western border: Hungarian guards were on duty one day - and off for the next days, irregularly. Opportunity presented itself, for the first time in twenty-odd years, to flee from Hungary: simply by walking a few kilometers through the border region, in snow and mud. Sometimes, when border-guards were on duty: they shot at the people.

We tried to continue working in the Office, although we didn't know whether or not money will be available for salaries, Our people came to work irregularly, due to many reasons: traffic-, shopping-, etc. problems. A number of our colleagues took to the road westwards. General uncertainty reigned. Our Ministry started to reorganize itself. One day the Ministry's party secretary came to a visit, inquiring about general atmosphere at our Office, and asked me to prepare a list of our workers who were "active" during the "counter-revolutionary" period. I was shocked by his request. It was a vast difference between people who didn't like the communist system - and the actual fascists, and I didn't want to label people as members of either one of these groups and by no means wanted to become an informer. I told him that no one of our workers could be considered a "counter-revolutionary", not even those few who had already gone.

According to "Free Europe"- broadcasts, tens of thousands of people arrived in Austria, where they were received with all sorts of help, donated by countries from all over the world.

The new Kadar government tried to appease workers still on strike, mainly miners, and to consolidate its power, but they were essentially distrusted by the population due to more than one reason: old-time communists leaders, ministers of the previous government were detained or run away, among them Mr. Vas Zoltan. The prevailing opinion had it that the new government - after an intermediate consolidating period will inevitably become much more intransigent than the previous communist regime, due partly to Russian pressures.

No information - not to speak about reliable ones - was available about many people: politicians, party leaders, writers, etc.

Rumors were circulating, among them one about Mr. Nagy, the former prime minister, that he was executed. No announcement was made regarding the previous politics and leaders, their shortcomings or faults - and nothing about a new trend, improvements, difference between "new communism" versus "old one". A large number of friends and colleagues fled the country through the on-off border to Austria, wading through the snow-covered field at the border area. My brother-in-law Paul went too, with his wife and two small children; they wanted to go to Australia, where the brother of Agnes lived. Eva's cousin: Laub Juci, her husband: Somogyi Laszlo, the chief conductor of the Hungarian Symphonic Orchestra (a Kossuth Prize laureate) and their son went to Switzerland; two best friends of Eva with husband and children went to Brazil; and many others. Everybody escaped in secret, as in the days of 1944.

Many changes of high level people were made, in the Ministries and the Planning Authority; as well as directors of research institutes were replaced. The whole society and mainly industry - my domain - was in ferment. The more a person was gray, the lower rung he occupied - the less was he endangered in the change-over of the guards. I had already been pondering, in the last few weeks, that unfortunately, with no ambition and no intention of mine, I reached a position too high, a reputation accepted by many, in brief: overexposed and therefore too vulnerable by aspiring careerists, to usurp my position. After talking it over with Eva, I came to the conclusion that the proper thing to do was to resign from the post of General Secretary of the Association, by the end of the year.

One day, one of my colleagues, a high-up official told in all confidence an inside information that plans were being made to reshape the government and to establish two more ministries, one an Electrical Ministry - and I was the nominee for the post. I was shocked. Even under normal, stable circumstances I would not wanted to have such a political appointment, but under the current situation the hazard would be suicidal. I still didn't forget the accusation of sabotage, in 1949, when my fate hung by a single hair, that my boss had been present and could save me. Under no circumstances was I willing to expose myself to such a hazardous target in the current situation. And in general: I did not want to be a member of any communist government or any other authority; to work as a professional under the regime was not by choice but by necessity, and that was the end. I lost heart, mainly because in the communist system it was out of the question to decline whatever assignment by the Party. We talked about it with Eva, night after night, but couldn't find a solution. In the meantime several acquaintances left the country; the atmosphere was panicky.

Then, one day, by the middle of December, we got a phone call from a German-speaking person, who referred to our brother-in-law, the Goda's, in New York, and wanted to visit us for talking about an important matter. Two gentlemen came by car, and told us that they were from Vienna (Austria), active in helping Hungarian refugees, and they received a commission from the Goda's to smuggle us through the border by a car to Vienna. We were in a perplexing situation, in a strait; we couldn't decide on the spot, so we agreed that they would come the next day and we should phone our relatives the night. The Goda's confirmed their commission, they deposited some 2000 dollars, and encouraged us to come to the States - it was the last chance. We deliberated with Eva through the night and day until they came again. We concluded in a number of pros for leaving: hazards because of my current plus the prospective position; fear of increasing intolerance; probability that some new cure for Eva would be attained; an advanced education and bright prospects for Robi; to live in freedom that we knew from literature but never experienced; and the last chance of escaping. Cons: heart-ache to leave everything behind. We selected the hopefully safer and better future - attainable albeit through difficulties, and give up our hardly achieved life-standard - against the constant fear while staying.

They came again, and we agreed that they take us on

December, 25. They asked for a quite big sum of money, for bribing border guards; what we gave them. We explained everything to Robi, who took it very intelligently. He knew that it had to be kept secret.

The days following were grueling: to select the few things we could take with us, to dispose the others. We tried to sell our apartment to a few reliable people - with no result: everybody was afraid. We were sitting on our suitcases; came December 25, then 26 but they didn't show up. We called them on phone and they said: sorry, the commission was canceled - they won't come. We called the Goda's and they confirmed that due to some disquieting information about unreliability of the people involved - they canceled the commission; hoping for a new opportunity. We were struck down, and bewildered. But the die was cast - and I had to try to find another solution, and fast. In the meantime more friends and colleagues left, and I got further worrying news from our Ministry about my coming prospect. Our nerves were overstrained, especially those of mine. Eva was indescribably courageous, collected, and self-restrained. We needed much self-restraint for overcoming amassing difficulties. Once we decided we had to go ahead and we wanted to. Border-guards were restored, fleeing people were shot at and thus many of them returned from the border. Anyway, this route was out of the question for us: Eva could not go on foot and wade across the snow-covered fields at the border, so we had to find a way to secure a passport for crossing the border in the normal way. I had to be extremely careful for preventing official sources getting scent of my intention.

One day one of my good friends told me that in a few days he will leave; he succeeded to acquire a passport for a big sum of money, arranged by a go-between. We got in touch and in a few days he told me that he could get for us an authentic emigration passport for giving up our apartment, intact. The scalpers took advantage of the situation, and we had no other choice - so we assented. On my cautious inquiry, the US Consulate refused to grant us an immigration permit: with emigration passport we were not refugees. The gates banged on our noses. Now we could get out - but couldn't get nowhere in. I tried Switzerland and Sweden, on basis of the business connections with the Laub factory with no success.

We could hardly bear up under the stress; in the ups and downs we found ourselves very deep down. Then, suddenly, an agent of the Israeli Embassy contacted me and invited for a meeting. Next thing in the morning I went to the Embassy, was received by a Hungarian-speaking secretary, and we had a long conversation - while a radio receiver was set to high loud volume, for preventing probable tapping. One of my old-time colleagues from our common university Zionist association, who immigrated to Israel a short time earlier, called their attention to me. At that juncture of circumstances he offered me all the help of the Embassy to facilitate our immigration to Israel. He was quite well informed about me. He used no sentimentalism; stressed two points: Israel's need of professionals like me, and that time is ripe now, maybe never to return again.

I wanted to discuss it with Eva. Although we knew that life in Israel was still in the pioneer stage, hard, difficult - but free of the omnipresent Jewish problem elsewhere in the world: we consented to go to Israel. The concomitant devastating suicidal feeling of leaving behind our life we couldn't put into words, we suffered silently, and Eva was the stronger.

The day when it was due to get our passport: the middle-man told us that I deceived them by not mentioning my Kossuth Prize. To overcome this difficulty, the person in question requested more requital. We knew this was blackmail - but time was running out and so we consented to give him our apartment, intact, with everything in it: paintings, carpets, etc, plus more money, jewelry, etc. I had to run around for transit visas: Yugoslavia and Italy. We agreed that the person in question would come February, 6, at 5 p.m. to take over the apartment. They came, sharp; nodded and without words, we handed over the keys and left our dream-villa we lived in for the last ten years, not looking back, only our heart bleeding.

In the previous days we visited the graves of my parents, Eva's father's; said good-by to Mama, Fred and family; knowing that we won't see each-other again. On our way to the railway station we took leave of my brother and his wife Zsofi. We wept silently - but we had to hurry to reach the train. We could take three suitcases, a limited small amount of jewels; four more packages were allowed to send as slow-goods, by ship. We arrived at night to the border station and after lengthy passport- and custom-examination: our train pulled out of the station, for Belgrade (Yugoslavia). On February 7 1957 we crossed the border never to return.

This was the third time that our life went into thin air.

We resolved to build it anew.

START   LIFE   ONCE   AGAIN   IN   FREEDOM-
1957 - 1969

We arrived in Belgrade (Yugoslavia) in the morning, more dead than alive, due to the strain of the previous weeks. Continued to Genoa (Italy), via Venice, by train, where from by ship to Haifa (Israel). Venice, even from the train, was a sad reminiscent of our two visits there, almost twenty years earlier. We had to spend a few days in Genoa, waiting for our ship. Eva called the Goda's in New York and reported concisely the sequence of events that brought us to Italy on our way to Israel. They said they were glad that we were "out" - but they did not even hint at any suggestion of help or assistance. Eva had always been a very self-respecting person - and I consented to keep silent on the whole matter; so we took notice that we were on our own.

I bid farewell to my Office and the Association, by a short letter, thanking for their work and cooperation.

We took a walk in the city and as if by magic - I noticed on a billboard in big capital letters the name: SOMOGYI LASZLO DIRIGENT. It was a poster of a concert, to be conducted by the husband of Eva's cousin, in one of the next days. We know that they fled to Switzerland, still it was a happy coincidence that we could now meet in Genoa. I immediately went to the concert hall where I supposed they were rehearsing, and we really met there. We were very happy to see each other; we told them our intent to go to Israel. It was amazing to learn that their next stop will be in Tel Aviv (Israel), where he will be conducting a few concerts in the next weeks. They will be staying in the Hotel Tel Aviv, so we agreed that we will call them there when we arrive.

In a few days we set sail for Haifa (Israel); the voyage was bearable, in spite of the season. We were told one day that the next morning we could see the coast at Haifa. We saw the mountain range, not too high, right at the sea-shore; the city Haifa climbing up the mountain, and about at the middle a beautiful golden dome that was, against expectation, the temple of the Bahai faith, and not a Jewish synagogue. We set foot on the port in the afternoon, February, 17. 1957. Since Fodor Eva, the foster-daughter of Oly, arrived in Israel together with the Kastner group, we had been in contact, by correspondence now and then. She was the only person whom we informed about our immigration, and called her from Genoa on our arrival date. Her husband came to meet us. During our voyage, a committee interviewed every immigrant, apportioning everybody to an absorption location, taking into account their occupation, etc. Eva as a textile designer and I as an engineer were directed to a new locality, by the name: Kiryat Gat, where, they said, a big textile factory was being built. Some twenty-odd people were taken by a bus, arriving by nightfall. We were lead to rows of small houses, standing on sand, with no pavement, no electric lighting. The houses were actually sheds, built out of a sort of cardboard, uniform in design: two rooms, kitchen, and bath-room. A number of people, who had arrived a few days earlier, came to receive us, very warmly, trying to soothe our shock by explaining that the actual situation was only temporary, a huge settlement program was being carried out that we can see the next day. Everybody got a bed, bedspread, pillows, etc., a kerosene stove and heater, basic kitchen utensils, etc. It was already late at night; we were dead tired. We put Robi to bed; and tried to accommodate ourselves for the night. It was raining heavily. Eva went to bed, I was standing at the window, looking into the blackness of the night - and of my soul. I blamed myself for taking Eva and Robi into such disaster, and were it not for them I would have drown the ultimate conclusion. I assumed full and sole responsibility for their fate that looked very bleak. I didn't know how can we get out from this pit, but I resolved to do everything to put things to rights, through thick and thin. One thing seemed sure for me: that place was not a starting spot.

Eva and I lived through extremely difficult times, especially during 1939-1950, and I had been witnessing her superb fortitude and valor, but in those first days after our arrival in Israel: she surpassed herself in her behavior, and restored thereby my courage and resoluteness.

We called Fodor Eva and discussed our problem and my wish to try my fortune in Tel Aviv. They had a four-room apartment in Rehovot, in the compound of the Weizmann Institute of Science, where her husband worked as a senior scientist - and they invited us to live with them until some good arrangement will be found. We accepted their invitation with thanks, and returned the house, together with everything the Jewish Agency gave us - and moved over to Rehovot. Next day I went to Tel Aviv and tried to contact Somogyi Laszlo, who should already had arrived and was going to conduct concerts the next days. We went to the concert with Eva - and it was for us like a blood-transfusion; we attended a concert a long time ago, and music was for both of us the highest intellectual delight. Next morning the four of us met in Tel Aviv, in a coffee-house, where an old friend of Somogyi joined us. The subject of our discussion was - obviously - our problem: a new immigrant, an engineer with 25 years of experience, etc. Somogyi's friend was also of Hungarian origin, an old-timer in Israel, who had a small workshop producing plastic bags. He had an idea: he knew the chief-engineer of the big transformer factory in Israel: ELCO company and he immediately called him and recommended me to his company. He invited me to see him next morning. I went there and it turned out that he knew very well the Laub factory and on this basis he accepted me as an engineer in the ELCO, and gave me a letter addressed to the Jewish Agency, asking them to grant us an apartment in the vicinity of their factory where I was going to be employed as an engineer. I thanked him and assured that I'll do my best. He told me to present myself after arranging apartment and all bureaucratic running around.

I took a deep breath; called Eva telling her the good news, and called Somogyi's friend, thanking for his kind and successful help on our behalf.

Next night a number of intellectuals of Hungarian origin held a reception in honor of Somogyi, whom they tried to cajole into staying with the Israel Philharmonic Orchestra. That evening he mentioned to me that he met a newly arrived Hungarian immigrant, a scientist by the name of Professor Szamosi Geza, who told him that he knew me and wanted to meet me urgently. I knew him too: he had been the General Secretary of the Physicists Association, and we had had official contacts through our Federation. I called him the next morning and on his warm invitation went to see him in his hotel. We embraced warmly, sat down to a coffee and he asked me to tell him my story first. I told him our story concisely and showed him proudly the letter from the ELCO company. Then came his turn: he with his family: wife and two children, fled to Vienna from where the Israeli Embassy brought them to Tel Aviv. He had been Professor of nuclear physics at the University in Budapest. At the Embassy in Vienna they told him that the Israel Atomic Energy Commission wanted to speak with him, he should wait for their call. At the same time, two young nuclear physicists arrived in Tel Aviv through Vienna and they were waiting too for an interview. He was told that they were looking for me, because I disappeared from Kiryat Gat and they didn't know my address. He would now inform his contact man about me - if I was interested to be interviewed. Of course I was! Could I have got a more marvelous opportunity than to join in the most advanced scientific field?

Professor Szamosi was then notified about our interview with Professor Bergman, the Chairman of the Israel Atomic Energy Commission, at his home, in the evening. He received me very warmly, offered coffee, cakes, cigarettes, and started the interview, a sort of friendly conversation. He asked me to relate, in detail, my education, works, highlights of achievements, scientific interests, activities in scientific-technical societies, etc, etc. The interview took about two hours. During the discussion it became clear to me that he was very well informed about my past, he knew even small details. By the end he asked me about my current situation, everything about dwelling, money, relatives, prospects, conception and hope of work, etc. I showed him the letter of acceptance by the ELCO company. He looked me in the eyes and said: "You are not an industrial man - you belong to us: scientists. We embark now in a huge scientific task - come, join us!" And I answered: "It is a great privilege to me to be able to work for you."

Professor Szamosi and I were then asked to come to the office of Professor Bergman for arranging the administrative details. For the next morning I was summoned to an office in the Ministry of Defense. It was an office of the Secret Service. A Hungarian speaking officer received me, politely but coolly. He hoped I understood the reason of a detailed discussion of my past being a nominee for a senior position in the Atomic Energy Commission. He stressed that this was not an interrogation. Starting from my childhood, from my parent's home, he listened attentively to my curriculum and asked many questions. Our discussion lasted two straight days, interrupted by lunch together, and coffee, cakes, cigarettes in the meantime. The atmosphere became friendly. Sometimes he asked questions seemingly unrelated to my history, for instance he asked what was the hobby of one of my colleagues in my Office, and others like that. It was the first time I was subjected to such a discussion, but I slowly realized that by such side-questions he wanted to check his knowledge about me and the straightness of my narration. By the end of the second day, he shook hands with me and wished luck.

Needless to say that I told everything to Eva and the nights, both of us, pondered on the role of luck on our - or any ones - fate; in our current case we recalled the sequence: the poster on Somogyi's concert in Genoa; Somogyi's getting acquainted with Szamosi in the hotel in Tel Aviv; meeting with Szamosi; introduction to Professor Bergman; his invitation to a fantastic job: a series of events where the lack of anyone would make this miracle impossible to happen. We found the reason in luck; we came no nearer to a more intelligent answer than all the people who asked the same question in the course of civilization. We told everything to Robi too: he was a very intelligent boy, he grasped the meaning of everything that was happening around us.

Contracts were offered to Szamosi and me, for five years

employment; Szamosi as full Professor, I as associate Professor, at the Israel Atomic Energy Commission (IAEC), (that had been affiliated to the Hebrew University in Jerusalem), effective March, 1. 1957.

A program of great importance had been decided upon by the Israeli Government, to build two nuclear research reactors; one for doing basic research, and the other for industrial, medical, etc, applications. Delivery contracts had been signed, and organization was to be prepared for their installation and operation. We were assigned to the basic research reactor, of 1 MW power. We signed our employment contract, on one day by the end of February, and started to work on the same afternoon, starting to draw up the organization scheme, as outlined by Professor Bergman, of our Nuclear Research Institute. A number of extra provisions were provided to us, such as: accommodation in a medium hotel with full board (until our final apartment arrangement will be reached); car transport to and back the Weizmann Institute, where we got temporary offices; bank loans for buying apartment and furnishing; etc. A special "ulpan": a Hebrew language course was arranged for us: six-seven new immigrant colleagues. Hard to imagine the difficulties of a new immigrant in Israel who did not know the language, not even the letters. Most people knew Yiddish, some spoke German and English, and that was some help for us. The easiest was for Robi who easily made friends and playing together: he picked up the language. Eva was listening in on the radio and diligently studying the language by using vocabularies and dictionaries - and progressed nicely. Due to the fact that every written material in our work was in English: we could start working, in English, and thus we neglected to properly learn Hebrew.

In the first days, when started working with Szamosi, my only mental preoccupation centered around the question: was I qualified and suited to the novel task. First: we assented that our task was not to design or build a reactor: it had already been designed and was being built by the "American Machine and

Foundry (AMF)" company in the USA. Our task was to assemble the components to be sent by AMF, simultaneously with erection of the concrete parts of the reactor that was being designed by a German company BROSH. Some supplementary design work had to be carried out by us of site-dependent components and assembly. Thus: our task - tall as it was - had three subsequent stages: to properly erect the reactor with all necessary accessories; to bring it to "criticality" (the scientific jargon for the start of the nuclear chain reaction); and to operate the reactor. As regards "qualification": when Fermi, the Italian physicist, together with a few American scientists and engineers, made the first test of controlled chain reaction, in Chicago in 1942 - no one of them had had any specific "nuclear" qualification. Fermi was a genius, a physicist of remarkable talents, who concluded that nuclear chain reaction could be attained under certain conditions; his conclusion based on a series of theories and experiments made earlier by him and by other talented scientists. Their qualifications were scientific and engineering and had a fair amount of inspiration in progressing scientific knowledge.

Specific university education in "nuclear" engineering was then, in 1957, only for the future. The twenty-odd reactors in operation in the world, in 1957, had been designed by a small number of scientists and engineers, very-very talented, but without any particular formal nuclear qualification. As regards the question whether I was suited to the task, briefly described above: I had practiced engineering work for the last twenty-five years, and had been lucky enough to do original, novel, creative engineering work all the time, which proved successful. I had taken up quite a number of challenges - and always succeeded. I took it as an exceptionally great privilege to take up this new challenge in contributing my engineering knowledge and inspiration to build a nuclear research reactor in Israel (Picture 31).

Professor Szamosi fully consented and thus we set about doing our work. One of the first things was to pin-point the exact location of the area of the reactor. Professor Bergman, Professor

Picture 31 – building new reactor

Szamosi, I, and two representatives of ministries involved, went on a caterpillar carrier to check the area in the desert, somewhere between Rehovot and the seashore. An office was set up to deal with infrastructure and the biggest building company in Israel: Solel-Boneh was entrusted with all building activities, according to the design drawings of the BROSCH company. Actually, the reactor building had been designed by the famous American architect: Philip Johnson, gaining an award for his beautiful design: a big tent that nicely adapts itself to the surrounding desert environment. A separate office was charged with dealing of the shipments, storage, and transport to the site of the components manufactured and shipped by AMF.

I took upon myself the difficult work of coordinating all activities of the various offices and contractors. In addition to the general responsibility, a very special and formidable super-responsibility was included in my work, due to the nature of the reactor's swimming pool. A water pool, like a swimming pool, contains the reactor. The few main differences between the reactor's pool and a conventional swimming pool are: a conventional swimming pool is built in a depression in the ground, whereas the reactor's pool walls stand on the floor, to a height of some ten meters. The shape of its layout is quite complicated: a smaller cross-sectional octagonal prism connected to a larger rectangular one, with a total length of approximately 20 m, and a width of approx. 12 m. Due to its many radiation related components, the containing walls of the pool have thickness from 0.8 to 2.80 m (at the base). Moreover: the structure is cast of heavy concrete, and is actually a double-walled container, having all along in the middle a thick, app. 20 mm lead sheet, for a dual purpose: sealing and radiation shielding. In the huge, complex concrete structure hundreds of metal components, small and large, are embedded or protrude in and out, each one necessitating special fixing and sealing before the heavy concrete is poured around them. Once the concrete is poured and solidified - there was no way to move them for relocation or repair. Consequently:

extremely good care had to be taken to check and recheck that every single component was in its proper place before start pouring the concrete. A mistake would mean the whole reactor a junk. It was my duty to care for it that such a mishap should not occur, otherwise causing millions of dollars loss and an immeasurable loss of prestige.

This was a super-challenge for me; I tried to count how often had I already encountered such situation, and the fact that I succeeded every time: increased my self-confidence. All that happened between April and June, when we still stayed at the Hotel Yarkon, and I discussed everything with Eva who even more than earlier, effectively participated in the mental process of solving the problems. I was enthusiastic about my job and was happy in doing it - and she was happy seeing me happy. We were already assigned a nice apartment in the southern part of Tel Aviv, in one of the houses built specifically for new immigrant academicians; we had only to wait for the turning of wheels of bureaucracy. We ordered a few basic pieces of furniture for the new home. The apartment had three-and-a-half rooms, besides all other rooms: kitchen, bath, entrance, and two terraces. We had the wall removed between the living and dining room, and so we got a larger living room. Eva was enthusiastically busying herself with planning our new apartment. This was the third time that we started to build a new home and life from scratch. No words can describe Eva's superb fortitude, courage, and moral strength in those situations. Without one word of complaint, without looking back and weeping over the beautiful things we had had and lost - she looked ahead with resolution and confidence. This was the real basis of our successive rising to our feet again, beyond luck.

The IAEC arranged excursions to a few bigger factories for making us familiar with their production potentials. One of them was the SOLTAM factory, for producing military hardware. Walking through the departments; in the maintenance department I saw an extremely large rotor of an electric machine, obviously a direct current one, with a huge commutator of approximately 300 mm dia x 600 mm. It revived my memory that I had once designed such a huge galvanizing dynamo at our factory, during the war. I asked them to show me the stator of this machine and it turned out that this was one of my babies. The nameplate on the stator housing said: "LAUB Electrical Works, Budapest, Hungary". To their astonishment, I told them who I had been when I personally designed this galvanizing dynamo for the WEISZ Manfred war factory, during the war years. They remembered that sometime in 1944 British naval vessels captured German cargo ships and surplus materials were sold and most probably they bought it at that occasion. They were very satisfied with the machine. Unintentionally I scored a considerable triumph. As the first practical phase of my work, I had to start to learn the designs of the reactor proper plus the structure, and the building housing them. I was shown a big store room where a large number of small and big boxes and cases had been collected that had arrived, and still were arriving, from AMF and BROSCH, containing thousands and thousands of drawings, manuals, instructions, etc. The only way to make myself familiar with the multitude of components and their connections with each-other; the primary sub-assemblies, assemblies, etc, etc. was to study the drawings: the jargon-language of engineering. From my first university year along the twenty-five years of practicing engineering especially creative design work -, my visual memory and ability to design mentally, in my mind: were my valuable assets for my work ahead of me. A large conference room was allotted to my "Coordinating Office", with five-six large desks. I started to open the boxes, unfolding and spread out the drawings, trying to coordinate them: and concluded that it was absolutely impossible, both physically and mentally, to harmonize them. Ten times as much desk surface and room area wouldn't be sufficient to spread out even part of the drawings, and running from one spot to the other - and back - would take a life-time with no result. An idea struck me: to equip a stage-loft arrangement, hanging the large assembly drawings on wooden rods, attached strings on both ends, running them through wheels fixed to the ceiling and hooked them to the desks. Six rows were equipped, hanging on them 20 - 24 assembly drawings. By this arrangement I could lower any big drawing, look at it, coordinate with component-drawings, etc, raise it up again - without the need to unfold and stretch out them and fold back again, etc. It was a great hit.

By the middle of June, 1957, we moved in our own apartment. It was on the (European) second floor, so it was not too difficult for Eva to climb the stairs. The alteration was already finished; the few newly ordered furniture delivered, and were supplemented by second-hand pieces: tables, chairs, etc. Kitchen utensils, tableware, etc, were bought (Picture 32). We had to be very careful because my salary had been overloaded by monthly repayments of the bank loans. Half the price of the apartment was paid in cash, the other half in 18 years installments. We lived a very modest life that only Eva's superb ingenuity made pleasantly acceptable: she became a first-class lady of the house; she cooked, prepared the meals, and baked cakes, pastries better than those in the best confectioneries. We had household help for a few hours a day. The only luxury items in our budget were concerts and books. We gathered slowly a small company, starting with the Michaeli's (Fodor Eva and her husband). Fodor Eva's brother Ali Fodor (Zvi Dor in Hebrew) married Michaeli's sister; an interesting kinship. Then, I found three colleagues from the university years. All of them were "old-timers" relative to us; they came to visit us frequently. We became good friends with Szamosi and his family. All of these people had children, about Robi's age. We were above all worried about Robi's transition from the old to the new situation in the school, but - to our great relief - he succeeded very well; he was very intelligent, self-contained, and inventive.

The Soreq Research Reactor program began to move. The Chief Engineer was at the top of the organization, controlling a series of departments' activities, such as: infrastructure-, building-, component-shipments' receiving, etc.-departments, and the coordinating office of mine, involved only with the reactor

Picture 32 – New apartment in Israel

structure. One copy of every drawing, manual, specification, etc, related to the reactor structure was sent to me; likewise one copy of component-shipment's bill of delivery, receipt-endorsement, and storage location.

BROSCH's drawings of the reactor-structure and building specified exactly each and every reactor component that had to be embedded in the concrete structure, by coordinates of their position and their identification number, given by AMF or by the Infrastructure design office. The principal task of the building contractor was to ensure putting and fixing these components at their specified position before pouring the concrete - for preventing catastrophic consequences. A special control team - independent of the contractor, was entrusted with checking the placement of components, at pre-specified levels of the pouring. My duty was to prepare easily readable drawings and specifications for each pouring-level, specifying the components and their positions, by coordinate dimensions, identification numbers, and their storage locations. At each step in the pouring level sequence, the control-team checked, on the basis of my drawings, that all components had been properly placed.

I devised a method of easily readable and reliable instructions for the checking team. The reactor structure was composed only of plane surfaces, inside and outside; no curved surfaces were designed. I made drawings of each individual plane surface and specified the components to be embedded into it, by coordinate dimensions and identifying numbers, plus their availability and location in the store. These drawings were then used by the checking team at times when pouring reached the pre-specified level. Besides this application, I checked on the drawings, ahead of subsequent levels, whether all necessary components had been received - and if not: I sent a note to the shipment-receiving department for their urging the manufacturer to ship the component still missing. The whole system worked perfectly, without a hitch - and established my reputation at all high-level management connected with the reactor.

In August, 57 we had Robi enrolled a school in a class equivalent to a first year junior high school, although, as a consequence of the turmoil, he didn't attend school between January-June. We hoped only that by his intelligence he will surmount the difficulties. We started a campaign for acquiring a car in order to make Eva's life easier. Cars were very expensive in Israel, because of 100-200 % customs-duty. But there was a law allowing exemption of this customs-duty, partly or totally, for invalids. A physician committee of the Health Ministry, after examinations, issued a permit for 100 % exemption. We ordered an English-Ford "Consul" car, with 4 cylinders, 1600 cc, with an attachment for speed shifts and brake on the steering wheel. The car arrived in March, 58. and all of us, especially Eva, were happy that we could move freely. We made trips almost every Saturday, shorter or longer, to see the country (Picture 33). There was not a single flower exhibition we missed to visit, and coming home from trips: the trunk was full of flowers we picked on the routes. In May we started to go swimming in the sea; we tried the shore from Haifa to Tel Aviv, until we found a nice bay with natural breakwater so that we could swim like in a pool. She loved swimming: it was much easier to swim for her than to walk. By the way: Eva was an excellent navigator for my driving; I could rely on her.

The next task on my agenda, when the reactor was still being built, was to organize and set up an Engineering Department. Deja vu! But this Deja vu referred only to the task to create something novel that had never been done before. The new task, in 1958, was in some respect similar to that in Hungary, in 1950, but in many more aspects not only different, but at a much higher level. At once I realized intuitively that the matter was non-conventional and controversial, and so I resolved that I wanted to go to the root of the matter, to clear up the subject - and not simply collect a few engineers and a few machine-tools and start designing whatever will be needed for the researchers around the reactor.

Setting up an engineering department was the paramount

Picture 33 – weekend trips in new car

goal that had been side-tracked temporarily by the urgency of the reactor's erection. Recapitulating now the primary goal of our future research institute, as we discussed and defined with Professors Bergman and Szamosi, at our few meetings earlier: I started deliberating on the entire problem-complex. Soon we will have a prestigious research reactor, basically an effective tool for providing neutron, gamma, and other radiation to be used for all sorts of research, in nuclear physics, chemistry, etc. for solving problems of various sections of natural sciences, industry, medical sciences, etc.

I stated the fundamental problem as: how can best produce special equipment to research scientists' novel research projects.

For complementing my twenty-five years' industrial design practice, I turned to professional literature - but found very little on the specific subject. Then I took careful, unhurried thoughts on the subject, gathering and balancing many facts and reasons. I could do it simultaneously with the reactor being built.

The Engineering Department to be set up would consist of a design section, a workshop, and a raw-material store. In order of time: the first task was to specify all machine-tools and all other equipment to be ordered. This was a very difficult task, because I had to equip a large workshop for manufacturing unknown products: what the special research equipment will look like, what would be their task they will have to perform, etc. - I could make a guess-work only. One thing was sure: all research equipment we will have to design and produce will have to be of superb quality. Consequently, the machine-tools had to be the highest degree precision ones. Additionally, a large set of hand tools, precision measuring equipment, etc. were ordered. The next item was: buildings, for housing the design-office, the workshops, the raw material store, and the hygienic building. Based on our specifications, an architectural design contractor prepared the designs. We had to fight heavy battles until they consented to my demands that the first priority in each building was functionality, architectural beauty was only second. Workshop main building was roomy, well lighted and ventilated; designed and built as the first phase of the final building. An electric crane served the total area. Separate smaller buildings housed sheet-metal- and welding-building; and at a distance, a shielding-walled building that housed the X-ray testing equipment. At the opposite side of a wide courtyard was located the raw-material store building. Adjacent to the workshop complex but an elevated level was the design-office building, with one large drawing room and a series of single office rooms; with separate rooms for copying drawings and storage.

Simultaneously with all these and a host of design works - I was deliberating on my fundamental problem: the method of best providing research scientists with the highest quality special research equipment. I discussed it with Professor Szamosi, who was enthusiastic about my concept. I discussed it with Eva too, who liked it but was a little pessimistic about its success - not because of its scientific correctness, but because of self-conceit, haughtiness, and arrogance of some, maybe many, scientists, who would erroneously feel themselves impugned. I made a few corrections, and the result was as follows.

I was aware what Machiavelli wrote in 1513, on new systems: "It must be remembered that there is nothing more difficult to plan, more doubtful to success, nor more dangerous to manage, that the creation of a new system, for the initiator has the enmity of all who profit by the preservation of the old institutions and merely luke-warm defenders in those who would gain by the new ones." However, I thought that in our case, the Soreq Nuclear Research Center: there was no "old institution" and nobody to profit "by its preservation" - and I didn't want to "gain by the new ones": I wanted only to best contribute to the success of scientific research at our Institute. Nevertheless, I resolved to check my credo at other similar institutes that I was going to visit soon.

For the organization of the whole Institute it was a heavy set-back when Professor Szamosi gave up his appointment as director, because a higher administrative authority didn't want to adhere to some important points of his contract. He was invited to join the

University of Rome. Both of us were very sorry; we both felt that we together could have achieved beautiful things.

In September, 1958. Robi succeeded to enroll the best junior high school in Tel Aviv, and so all of us looked forward more optimistically to his future. At home we lived quite modestly - but contended. We subscribed to the Israel Philharmonic Orchestra; 11 concerts a year. Both of us loved classical music, and we enjoyed the concerts. We found a few more friends, two of them from my university years.

We corresponded quite regularly with the family members: Mama, Fred's and my brother's in Budapest, the Goda's in New York, Paul's in Sidney (Australia). One day we got the alarming news that my brother suffered a heart-attack, although a mild one, and we were anxiously waiting the news until he recovered.

The Goda's had been writing a few times that they intended to come to visit us - until by the fall of 1959 they really arrived for a ten-day visit (Picture 34). More than ten years went by when we saw each other the last time; all of us were happy when they arrived. We stayed at a nice hotel in Herzeliya, near to the sea-shore. One day they mentioned an idea that since George's marriage and moving out from their apartment: his room stood empty, and they would like to invite Robi, for a year, to live at them, and attend there a school for his last junior-high year. We made great effort to confront this important choice frankly and conscientiously, Robi drawn into the discussion as an equal partner. From Robi's point of view: three years ago he had the very difficult task to continue in school in Israel, not knowing the language, not even the letters, and succeeded without loss of class, and now to repeat it once again, with no knowledge of the English language; it would be too much. And doing this in the last year of junior high: seemed quite hopeless. Against these cons, the pro was defined like this: supposing that he won't be able to get through with his studies - wouldn't it be worth-while to take the chance to learn English during the year's stay, and see New York and America . He would loose a year in his education, but it won't be a

Picture 34 – Sightseeing near Jerusalem

loss in life-experience. After deliberations, we came to the unanimous conclusion that Robi should go and try his luck in the school, because all of us - and especially Robi - thought that his stay will be beneficial for his future: the main motive in our deliberations. Eva and I had mixed feelings: on the one side we wanted to do everything for the sake of Robi's best future, but on the other side we felt woeful living separated for a long year. We were unselfish - and on an August day, in 1960: we put Robi on a flight to New York.

In the last three-four years, there had been no improvement with Eva's leg condition; the problem that remained was that the left foot flagged and when she moved it forward, the tip of the foot got caught in the ground and she lost her balance. We went to the best orthopedic surgeon, who made an operation to alleviate on her condition. It resulted in some improvement.

All work in establishing the Institute had been progressing quite rapidly, especially of the Reactor and my Engineering Department. The Reactor was completed in the spring of 1960, and went critical (the scientific jargon for the time when the chain-reaction starts) in June, 1960. Everybody was happy, especially the chief engineer that such a complex project had successfully been completed without a hitch. My role as coordinator had been the most determining for this success, but nobody came to me to congratulate. It was not the first - or the last occasion when I had to experience that what really counted was not good work - but to belong to a proper group of people or political connections. In Israel, it was not generally customary to appreciate anybody's good work and to express it in some way, because everybody had been convinced that nobody else cold do better. We felt right from the beginning a very peculiar phenomenon, that in Israel, a par excellence immigrant country, where some fifty or more nationalities, all Jews, converged to live together, one group of people, the Hungarians, had been discriminated against, in all respect. People speaking any foreign language - nobody cared or made remarks, but hearing people to speak Hungarian - nobody endured it without some remark: "ige-mige", "jaj Istenem", etc. This peculiar behavior would need a professional analysis.

By November 11, 1960. Fred called us to tell the saddening news that Mama died. She had been hospitalized for a few days and one day she suddenly died. Eva was afflicted and all of us were mourning our dear Mama, who had not only been the mother of the family, but she had been the president and main benefactor of the Hungarian Jewish Orphanage for more than a quarter century.

Eva had been right to some extent when we discussed my credo and she had said that some scientists were self-conceited, irremediably. Luckily, they were the minority; the others made use of the indispensable engineering cooperation. This way, a series of smaller and bigger equipment were produced, many of them novel, and were published in scientific journals.

A success-story: by the end of the school-year 1960-61, Robi finished his high school senior year's studies in New York, with very good grades that allowed him to enter college. As we had learned from the Goda's during the year: Robi went to work in movie-theaters in the evenings, to earn pocket money. For his return journey back home, he arranged for himself an electrician's job on an Israeli ship, so that instead of paying for a ticket - he earned money. He arrived home in July, 1961. and, according to law, he had to join the Defense Forces, where the draft-board would attach him to one of the many detachments. He was very talented in all sorts of technical branch, and thus he preferred the Air Force, in particular doing the service as an electrician - or electronics - technician. I discussed the matter with a few colleagues in the Defense Ministry, and they persuaded me that the only sure way of such an assignment would be for Robi to enroll a special technical school of the Air Force, for a one-year special course in electronics. The three of us deliberated on the alternatives, taking into account the disadvantage of the electronics course venture of one year loss versus the double-advantage of securing an interesting electronics-technician's assignment for the three-year' active service - plus the benefit of gaining an electronics-technician diploma from the special school and the subsequent three years' practice. Our unanimous decision was: the special school, in Haifa, that he enrolled by the end of August, 1961. He could come home every second week-end, or we visited him there. By the end of the school-year, in 1962 he got a diploma, and on that basis he was assigned to the Air Force, as an electronics technician. His unit was stationed in a suburb of Tel Aviv, so he could come home every evening.

By the beginning of 1962, all my expertise has became fully engaged. In the years 1962 and 63 we designed and produced a yearly average of 200 special equipment, on a very wide spectrum of design-man-power requirement from 20-25 hours up to 1200 hours per equipment. It would be beyond the scope of this narrative to list even all the biggest ones, suffice to mention only a few selected highlights of them, realizing novel creative design features as congenial engineering solutions to imaginative research investigations for achieving the hoped for results. All of them proved the correctness of my "credo". I was the principal designer, in various design-teams, of all of this equipment.

One of the irradiation facilities of the IRR-I (Israel Research Reactor No I) was the thermal column, providing thermal neutron fluxes that were utilized for studying nuclear reactions produced by thermal neutrons. Most of the experiments required introduction of electronic equipment into the thermal column. The reactor had to be shut down for the loading and unloading of these apparatus, and at times considerable cooling periods were required to permit removal of the radioactive components. To overcome this difficulty, automatic loading equipment was designed and installed at the thermal column, for permitting introduction and removal of experiments during full power reactor operation. Among the principal functional features of the equipment was a shielded loading chamber which served as an entrance lock between the thermal column and the reactor hall. To prevent escape of radiation into the hall, the equipment entered the thermal column through this loading chamber via two interlocked movable shields. When published: acclaimed by all similar reactors.

My request for a study trip to a few European nuclear research institutes was granted in 1963. I visited Wurenlingen (Switzerland) and Saclay (France). I was interested in studying their main installations, special research equipment, and - last but not least - their method of providing research scientists with special equipment. The Swiss Institute was somewhat bigger than ours, the French was a huge establishment, about ten times as large as ours, but among other departments, a research reactor installation comparable to ours was of my main interest. Both institutes had engineering departments engaged in designing and producing special equipment, thus their task was the same as ours. In the course of my discussions with my counterparts it became clear to me that our viewpoints were almost the same; although I felt that they directed the work of their department on a rather routine way. As it turned out: there had had controversies with scientists some time previously, but now they did the work as they had been asked to do. One important data was given to me, on my request, namely the ratio: design engineers - research scientists, and as I guessed: this ratio number was about 30 % higher at Wurenlingen and 15 % higher at Saclay than at our Institute. I submitted a detailed report on my visit, and, among other things, I stressed the importance of this ratio to be considered at the next budget allocation.

The IRR-I had originally been equipped, among other irradiation facilities, with two pneumatic tube sample irradiation circuits, so-called "rabbit" systems. These were similar to pneumatic tube transfer systems, used before the advent of fax-machines, for transferring documents from one office to another, e.g. in banks and post offices. One of the two systems was a "to - back", and the other a "through" convey line. Each circuit had its own sending and receiving terminal, on either side of the outside wall of the reactor. This arrangement did not meet the increasing requirements; thus, the erection of a comprehensive new facility was necessary.

The pneumatic sample irradiation system was the main tool of the IRR-I. The goal of the system was to put a small quantity of materials very near to the neutron source, the so-called core of the reactor, for irradiation by the neutrons, thereby transforming them to an isotope of that material. An isotope of a material differs from the original material only by its radioactivity that can be detected and measured by a simple hand-held instrument; otherwise the isotope maintains its original physical and chemical properties. Isotopes were needed and used in medicine, agriculture, industry, etc, etc. and research. A simple example could illustrate the phenomenal usefulness of isotopes. Thyroid gland absorbs iodine; the measure of absorbed iodine is an indication of its health-situation. Iodine isotope injected could be measured by a simple hand-held instrument at the neck, within minutes, for diagnosis. Innumerable application of isotopes for diagnostic and therapeutic uses in medicine, and countless other uses in industry, agriculture, etc. necessitated efficient production of a great number of isotopes.

The design, production, and installation of the new, comprehensive pneumatic tube sample irradiation, transport, and dispensing system was not only the biggest work of my department up to that time, but the system was the biggest composite unit of the Institute. Previously, using the irradiation system delivered by AMF, the irradiated materials had been transferred manually from the system's receiving terminal to the counting or processing location. This had been a lengthy operation and the transport container had to be handled a great deal before the irradiated material had reached its destination. In many cases the time involved constituted a great handicap, and short-lived isotopes' production had been severely curtailed. The excellent performance of the new system was achieved by many factors: proper stating the problem-complex; good cooperation with the system's manager: the director of the Reactor; a good deal of inspiration; fine design and production work; checks and rechecks; etc. There were a few elements of the system that met requirements of a patent, e.g. the rabbit, which served as the sample carrier, or the automatic dispensing equipment. The rabbit was a molded polyethylene cylindrical vessel, with the top end open, fitted with a snap-cap, and having replaceable polyethylene riders on each end. A bottle, containing the gas, liquid, or solid sample, was also made of polyethylene and was held in a cup at the open end of the rabbit. The automatic dispensing equipment transferred liquid or gas isotopes from the rabbit automatically, directly to the processing or counting place, by using gas pressure. A rabbit carrying up to 70 gr. of material could travel in the system at speeds of the order of 15 m/sec. Three or four seconds after leaving the reactor core, the rabbit arrived to the automatic dispensing equipment. One second after this, the liquid, gas, or solid sample could be processed or counted at the dispensing equipment. Previously, these operations had to be handled manually and had taken at least 20 seconds. No handling whatsoever of the rabbit was needed, nor transfer of the sample from one kind of carrier to another. Since the operation was completely automatic, only one person was needed for control.

The principal benefit of this system manifested itself by enabling to process a great number of short-lived isotopes that couldn't be done at all by the old manual handling.

We wrote a paper: "A comprehensive pneumatic tube sample irradiation, transport, and dispensing system", and offered it for oral presentation to the 14-th Conference on Remote Systems Technology, held in Pittsburgh. It was accepted and I went and gave a lecture, with slides, on our new rabbit system. It was well received, many questions asked. It gave me a good feeling.

I had related to Eva quite often the progress of this system and she was at all times not only very interested but had some good ideas; but what was more important: she encouraged me when I had problems. She was happier than I was when we finished putting into operation the equipment, which was really a big success: maybe we, who worked on it day by day for a long time, couldn't it properly appraise.

During the years in Israel we felt a small annoyance because of our family name: Balla was a distinctly Hungarian name which transcribed into Hebrew, had a slightly unpleasant connotation; neither was it suited for English or other European usage. Thus, we changed it into a Hebrew name: Baron and I kept my first name Alexander that was given as my Jewish name by birth.

Robi was nearing the end of his military service. A nice girl, who had been his class-mate in the junior high school, and did her military service in the last two years, were steady. One night, the four of us sitting at the dinner table, when suddenly Robi, after a few moments of silence, announced to us that they wanted to marry - and go to the USA for studying in a university. We were a little perplexed, for a long period of time, on three counts. First: their decision to marry. Not that we had anything against the girl - Liora -, on the contrary. And we told them so, that we are happy, and wish them good luck and happiness. But second: I was sorry, I told them, that I was not in a position financially to provide them with money for their stay in the States plus paying tuition fees. Robi's answer was that they didn't intend to ask for financial backing; he already arranged for himself a stipend at the Austin College, in Sherman, Texas. We knew how independent, self-confident, capable, and resolute he had been, but his arrangement with the stipend - it was just wonderful. But on the third count: both of us were down-hearted on the thought that Robi would leave us, go so far away, at the time when we started to live again a happy family life, after so many years of difficulties. But that thought we kept for ourselves, and started to reconcile ourselves to his leaving; hoping that this will be beneficial to his future. In this hope - we gave them our blessing.

At the beginning of 1965, Professor Bergman delegated me to a big study trip, to four European nuclear research institutions, in Norway, Italy, France, and Holland. The study trip had a dual purpose: to get acquainted with their institutes and to inform them about our progress.

The research institute at Kjeller (Norway) was a proficient, well organized and equipped, and somewhat larger than our institute. Their second reactor, JEEP II was being built and at a quite advanced stage at that time. Hearing about our rabbit irradiation system, they expressed their wish for a proposal of mine for a sample irradiation and transport system to irradiate samples in the JEEP II reactor and then transport and deliver them to anyone of three laboratories, away from the reactor's containment building. I worked out my proposal during my stay there, including a novel solution for the transport tubing passing through the containment wall with foolproof safety of preventing containment atmosphere to escape to the outside environment.

The research institute at Ispra (Italy) was a joint establishment of the European Communities. It was located on the shore of the Lago Maggiore, with magnificent scenery. The institute was significantly larger than ours and seemingly with abundant budget allocation. They built a few very large special equipment, although they farmed out a considerable portion of the work to outside factories, contractors. They built a big research equipment, using one beam tube of the reactor, for the so-called "polarized neutron" experiment. Our physics department was interested in doing research with polarized neutrons; so I examined their installation, and on the basis of the information, we designed and built a similar, although more complex equipment.

At Saclay and Fontenau aux Roses (France), two of a number of research institutes of France, I visited only their research reactor departments. They were much interested in our rabbits; what they had been using up to that time was a very simple rabbit, where its lid had to be fastened to the body by a nylon string, complicated to remove after irradiation. The institute at Petten (Holland) was a rather modest one, though some information I gathered there were valuable too.

The summary exchange of experience and information was very valuable for me in my coming work. Still, I felt that we didn't remain in their debt for their information; my counterparts were much interested in what we had done - and how. Subjects common to the five places visited were: 1) contest between researchers and design-engineers: the problem was not new for the engineering departments' heads, still they took it as something inevitable, thus not worth while to fight it. 2) Ratio: design engineering staff versus research scientists: the numbers were some 20-30% higher at their institutes that at our, in spite of the fact that they farmed out some portion of their work to outside factories.

Returning home, I prepared and submitted an extensive report on my trip, listing topics worthy for our adopting them in our future work, especially the considerable discrepancy in the number of engineering vs. researcher staff that needed to be corrected in the coming years' budget allocations.

Robi and Liora married on May, 31. 1965. The wedding ceremony was held in a medium hall, by an army rabbi (both were army veterans), followed by a modest buffet-dinner. We were very happy, for them, for their hopeful bright future. We knew, as every parent knows, that, sooner or later, Robi would marry a girl, and leave us. It was only very difficult for us to let our only son leave our home, and especially to let him leave so far away from us. By the middle of August they took a plane and left, first to New York, and from there to Sherman, Texas. We were corresponding frequently, by letters, audio-tapes with photos: so we knew that they settled down in a nice house at the campus of the college; Robi started learning, and Liora went a few times a week to teach Hebrew; so they managed somehow. We were waiting for their letters impatiently, measured passing time not by days or weeks - but by "letters". Slowly we made up our mind and decided to visit them in the summer of 1966. I had difficulties in obtaining a US visa, because of my communist-party membership in Hungary that I did not want to hide. First, my request was rejected. I asked for an interview by the secretary of the visa department, and explained to him what the circumstances had been in Hungary, and that I had been investigated by the Israeli Secret Service - and cleared for working at the Atomic Energy Commission. He looked at me - and granted me a "waver" and so I got a visa. Eva went ahead and was waiting for me in New York; Robi and Liora drove up to New

York to take us down to Texas. We synchronized our plans: they drove to San Louis and waited for my flight from New York, and then we drove down to Texas, in three-four days. We spent with them a few very happy weeks; they introduced us to the American way of life.

As a consequence of an increase in the number of departments at our Institute, a reorganization was carried out, by establishing four divisions - besides the administration - : research reactor, physics, chemistry, and scientific- and technical-services. I was assigned to head this last division, having seven departments in addition to my ED.

An additional special irradiation facility was designed for carrying out irradiation of relatively small amounts of samples at the highest neutron intensity spot: within the core. Its irradiation station was designed in the form of a fuel element, with pneumatic tubes connecting it to the sending- and receiving-station. Due to the very restricted space within and around the core, and the relatively small amounts of samples (approximately 15 cc): a novel sample carrier was invented: a spherical vessel of molded polyethylene, called the "bullet". The bullet was a thin-walled ball, with an outside dimension of 35 mm dia. About one third of this ball was cut off, and formed into a circular conical opening with its apex inside the ball. The opening was closed by a corresponding conical, arrow-shaped plug. This plug could not be removed after it was once plugged in. Samples could be measured without the need of removal from the bullet, and if, for any reason, the samples had to be removed: the bullet could easily be cut in two halves by some simple device. If, for any reason, the bullet had to be hermetically closed, the plug could easily be heat-welded to the body. This "bullet" carrier had a series of advantages compared with the "rabbit", e.g. the bends of the convey piping could have as small a radius as 100 mm, as against the bend-radius of the rabbit of about 500 mm; no riders were necessary; ideal shape as regards strength of the carrier; practically no possibility of the bullet getting stuck in the convey piping; etc. This bullet carrier was patented in the

USA, France, and Israel.

During the last week of May 1967 the necessary organizational steps were taken for a threatening war situation. The predominant point to defend against missiles or air bombardments was the reactor. The technical director of the reactor: Mr. Alex Hoffman and I were charged to devise some effective shelter for the reactor. We defined as the main danger point: the pool, containing contaminated water and the core with its radioactive materials contents. We worked out a plan to completely cover the entire pool by a reinforced steel plate structure. High profile rail tracks were used as the substructure of steel plate units, that were placed side by side, staggered, across the pool. It was not put to use because of the swift victorious end of the war.

By mid-April, 1968, Mr. Alex Hoffman, the technical director of the Reactor, an excellent engineer, and me, made a study trip to Grenoble (France), one of their finest nuclear research institutes. Among many other subjects, we were interested in their equipment for irradiating liquid-nitrogen cooled samples, for solid state physics experiments. On the basis of their equipment, we designed and built similar equipment, adapted to our reactor. The irradiation loop was inserted in a dummy fuel element, located in the core lattice. The sample to be irradiated was immersed in very pure liquid nitrogen and the radiation-heat was dissipated through a pure liquid nitrogen commercial liquid nitrogen heat-exchanger.

We were booked on a night flight to Paris, when in the afternoon a big demonstration took place in the city, organized by the many thousands of university students in Grenoble. It turned out that our flight was the last one before the next days' general strike in the whole of France. Paris was completely paralyzed; buses, metro, taxis, air-flights, railroads, everything went on strike; we walked the city all the time, experiencing huge demonstrations, revolutionary meeting in the Sorbonne under a big red flag, etc.

- - - - - - -

One day, in September, 1968, we got the sad news that my brother died. The grief over my brother's death made me to relive my youth-years with my brother in our parent's home. He was my senior by eight years, and this difference meant a lot for me, along all the years when I had been four up to eighteen. My brother, with his inbred tenderness, cared for me, as an addition to our parents' care. He had taught me, consciously and unknowingly, by his own exemplary behavior, to understand human life and family love; how to learn the world around us; how to appreciate beauty and harmony; to love music, literature, arts, science; how to live honestly, and how to live in a way that makes life worth living; and - last but not least - he had not only given me guidance, but helped and sponsored my engineering education. I have been in his debt for becoming an engineer. He had given everything whole-heartedly, not expecting thanks. I had not thanked him until I could have done it, and later it was weighing on my conscience up to this day. Now, I want to thank him for everything - before it is too late.

I hope, these few words would represent a memorial of a just, selfless, and self-sacrificing man: my brother.

- - - - - -

A prerogative, all over the world, of scientists working continuously for six years at a university or research institute, is that they can spend the seventh year (sabbatical) at another institute or university. Since I had been working continuously for eleven years (1957-1968): two sabbatical years were due to me. I sent out a few applications to US universities and nuclear research institutes, attached a resume with some 70 papers and reports on my name, for an "exchange scientist" job. The "Brookhaven National Laboratory (BNL)", Upton, Long Island, N.Y. offered me a job, at their Accelerator Laboratory, beginning September, 1. 1969, for one year only, as per the relevant law. I requested the approval of our management, that I received by March, 1969. I sent the forms filled in to BNL, and was looking forward with much expectation and enthusiasm to the next big challenge in the States - and so was Eva too. I handed over my department to one of my young engineers, appointed by the management, and was asked to do some special advisory work to the Israel Aircraft Industries, besides caring for a smooth transfer of progressing works of the ED. About this time, a new director was appointed to our Institute, who - as we learnt - had been maybe a good chemistry researcher, but had not the slightest idea of how to manage a research institute. By chance he was a close friend of one of my obstinate contestants in the research-scientist vs. design-engineer cooperation theory and practice, and my coincidental leaving for a two years sabbatical gave them the impetus to get the upper hand by interfering in every steps of designing and producing in the ED.

About that time the Atomic Energy Commission requested to carry out a big improvement on the reactor: to increase its power to about ten MW and the project had to be completed by the end of July. My successor started to work on the project. By mid-April, the technical director of the Reactor invoked my help because preliminary conceptual designs until then were not promising. The next day was a holiday, the Independence Day. I took the drawings and the list of the required functions to home, and early in the morning sat down at our big dinner table and started studying the conceptual designs. I defined for myself: the problem was to make modifications on the present cooling system of the reactor, for rendering possible an increased heat removal from the core, plus making possible a series of individual or simultaneous flow patterns among the components of the cooling system - as those became necessary during the seven years' operation of the reactor - and all these, over and above, by complying with the restriction that existing concrete structures, such as buildings, walls, etc. must not be altered, not even touched.

Apparently, the problem was a very complex and difficult one - maybe the most difficult so far at the Institute. It seemed to me that only a miracle could help, or rare inspiration was needed, but how could one effectuate inspiration. But the task to solve this difficult problem was not only a great challenge for me, but at the same time: my prestige was at stake. What I did was: I let my imagination roam, freely for some time, but casting a glance at the sketch I made on the components of the cooling system, from time to time. Suddenly, an idea struck me. Using an electrical system as an analogue to the water system in question: would I make wire connections from each of the 10-12 peripheral points to all other points. Certainly not. The solution would be to bring wires from each point to some centrally located point and using there a sort of a selector switch to make connections as needed. I realized then by intuition that this was the right solution in principle. I started to draw on a big sheet of paper a line-synopsis of the existing situation: components of the system to be connected to each other by predetermined "flow-patterns", corresponding to specific functional states of operation: two parts of the reactor, water tower, storage tank, delay tank, heat-exchanger, demineralizer - and the existing pipe connections with valves, etc. Then I draw some ten different "flow-patterns", as specified, by different colors, complementing the existing pipes, valves, etc, with new ones. I realized thereby that two distinct sub-systems should be defined: one for the water supplies from the demineralizers, and the other for all other connections.

I went into ecstasy over my promising solution. I related to Eva the principles of my idea - she was happy for me. Next morning I made photos for photogrammetry, for arranging in space the additional pipes and valves. I worked again feverishly in the night, making separate "flow-sheets" for each flow pattern. I reported in detail to the director of the reactor who approved everything enthusiastically.

The principal design - the first stage of the project accomplished; we discussed the second and third stage: production and installation that were not less difficult, although of another nature. The reactor was already shut down for the modification project; the time up to the deadline was very short - less than three months; my colleague was in a quite precarious position, and I wanted to help him. To place the order for completing design, production, and installation with the ED: was absolutely hopeless. It was a total impasse. My colleague implored me for my help that I promised to give him the next day, together with my conditions. I took upon myself the very risky undertaking under one condition: to officially grant to me the absolute dictatorial power to direct the project that should get supreme priority above every other work, in man-power, machine-tools' capacity, raw-material and accessories acquisitions, money-allocations etc. I got the authorization and I put up my command post in the big office of the Reactor's director (who was on his sabbatical abroad); took the best draftsman in my room, and set to this challenging but extremely risky work. The crucial part of vital importance was in my design the novel solution of a central "selector center", comprising two batteries of stainless-steel valves (of 6 in dia): one of eight and the second of twelve valves. We worked overtime and checked daily the progress. We encountered many difficulties along the installation work, but we succeeded superbly.

It was the biggest and most complex installation completed in the Institute. It was inaugurated by the IAEC, the Management, the scientists, engineers, and workers. Everybody was loud in praises of the installation - only my role was not mentioned. My colleague requested leave to speak and said that without my invention and active direction - the whole installation could not and would not had been accomplished. Applause - with some restrained gnashing of the teeth by a few dilettantes disguised as scientists. Fact was: our improved reactor was the first of its kind in the world.

And I was proud of our success. And so was Eva.

A small leave-taking ceremony was held by the Management referring to my sabbatical year as "assignment of the Institute".

We were making preparations for our two-year stay in the States. We were looking forward to our life there with much expectation and confidence.

NIGHTMARE ENDING TO HAPPINESS - 1969 - 1973

Robi and Liora must have worked pretty nicely during the years 1965-1969: both received their B.Sc.-s. Of course, we knew all along about their progress and life: they even worked aside to earn some money. Since they wanted to continue studying, both applied to the University of Massachusetts, in Amherst, and were accepted. As part of their moving over to the new place, they came to visit our two families, in August, 1969. All of us were happy that we will be quite near to each other when we go for one or two years to Brookhaven. They returned to Amherst somewhat earlier than we started to Brookhaven, but met us at New York when we arrived by the end of August. A car from the BNL was waiting us at the airport and brought us to a cottage assigned to us, located within the premises of BNL. Everything was nicely prepared, we had only to go to bed.

Next morning I went to present myself to the Director of the Accelerator Department and was warmly welcomed. I was shown around and introduced, and the Technical Director came to my room - nicely prepared, with my name on the door, etc. - for explaining what they expected from me to do. Right at the beginning I stressed that I knew nothing about accelerators, as I emphasized it in my resume, but he reassured me that they were fully aware of this; they had a very good team of physicists, experts in accelerators; what they needed was an engineer, an expert in engineering design who can transform research scientists' ideas into hardware. He told me frankly what predicament the BNL was in: some 65 million dollars were allotted for improving and increasing the strength of the accelerator that should be operational by the end of 1970. They had been working on this project for the past two years and everything had been progressing satisfactorily - except one important component, a so-called "pick-up electrode (PUE)". A team of two engineers had worked on it, with no success, so they gave up the appointment. They made two types of PUE-s that I can study in a laboratory-room that will be at my disposal for my work. Then he explained to me the job of these PUE-s, in an extremely confused way. I had to gear up all my imaginary potential for figuring out for myself what those PUE-s have to do, and had to interrupt him many times with questions for clarifications. By the end of his almost two hours' long explanation, the gist that I could figure out for myself was something like this: In a big circular underground tunnel 80 huge, powerful electromagnets were arranged in a polygon along the circumference. Inside the magnets, along the entire circle, an aluminum tubing, with high vacuum inside, was installed for leading a proton beam to near light-speed. It was essential to keep the proton beam at the center line of the vacuum tubing, in spite of the tendency of the beam to deviate from it. The goal of the PUE-s was to detect and measure beam deviations, for enabling to steer it back to its proper line.

He gave me no specifics, no matter how I tried to ask for them, nor did he want to refer to the physicists dealing with the subject. I asked for literature and reports on existing equipment at other accelerators - he didn't know about them. I felt that I was in a quandary; seemingly he didn't know the details - but wanted to remain the leader of the project. However, I couldn't tell him that his explanation was not sufficient for designing the required equipment. When he left, I promised to deliberate on the subject; and I was near to a decision to give up the assignment. On second thought I resolved that I mustn't back down from the challenge which I thought would be my biggest one, in America, since so far I never retreated from the many challenges I encountered - and always succeeded, and so will I now.

I resolved therefore to take up the challenge and solve the problem by recalling first of all my "credo" - and act accordingly.

Besides my personal prestige, I mustn't give up because I was there an exchange scientist from Israel, representing my country, and will be judged as an Israeli and not as Baron Alexander. As per my credo: a problem existed there irrespective whether or not he could explain it to me - or I couldn't understand it at first glance -

so I had to state the problem, since stating a problem properly is the first and most important and indispensable step in the design process. But due to the insufficient information I got, I would have to do some detective work to find out the scientific information missing. I started by checking the prototypes my predecessors had made. One type had been made with printed circuit electrodes on a ceramic cylinder, and the other with thin copper sheet electrodes cut to form and wrapped around a thin-walled glass cylinder. The shape of the pair of electrodes had been formed out of a cylinder of about 130 dia x 160 mm, cut by two diagonal planes, and the corners rounded. Then, I started pondering on the theory of capacitors, on the basis of relevant equations.

Two-three days after I started working there, one day a rather stubby, powerful person came to my room, introducing himself in Hebrew, welcomed me "on board", and explained that he learned that I was from Israel to work there; he was from Israel too, but had become US citizen, and had been working as a physicist at BNL. We started chatting, and marvel of marvels - it turned out that his task had been to permanently control the slight movements of the earth below the heavy magnets of the accelerator and compensate deviations by re-adjusting magnets.

I immediately realized that he was the person who could help me in my predicament. I explained the situation I was in and asked for his help in collecting information material. He was more than ready to help, all the more because he himself was much interested in having better PUE-s than the previous ones, for his own work. We agreed to sit down in a few days, when I would be ready to present my preliminary ideas.

During deliberating on the theory of capacitors, I came to a dual conclusion. First: due to the values of the dielectric constants of various materials: air seemed to me the best, instead of ceramics or glass. But for using air - the electrodes would have to be made out of metal sheets that would need no support material but would have to be self-supporting, integrated. Thus, my preliminary solution was to cut the electrodes out of standard aluminum pipe, fixed together by three-four thin polyethylene rods. When we sat down to discuss the subject, my colleague accepted my ideas with much enthusiasm. But I wanted to check the whole equipment by learning what solutions had been used at the few other accelerators in the world; I wanted to search for reports on the subject from other institutes, e.g. CERN (Switzerland), USSR, or other places. He took upon himself to try to find such documentation. I wrote a report on my preliminary ideas to the Technical Director, who then called me to his office and told me that I need not send reports to him, I should do whatever I deemed necessary; I was authorized to order whatever materials, accessories, etc. I wanted; he sent instructions to the central workshop and the design office to carry out my instructions, on first priority basis: in brief, I was completely free to do whatever I wanted - but the new PUE-s should be ready by June. It was a high-risk proposition - but I wanted to meet this newest challenge and was determined to succeed. I made sketches of the components and asked the workshop to produce them.

Needless to say that I told everything to Eva about this new challenging work and that I felt confident to succeed in it. She was happy, and she was taking delight in our new life style. The cottage was one of some 12 similar houses, located in a beautiful clearing in a huge forest, for the sole purpose to house foreign exchange scientists on sabbatical. Our cottage was situated about 12-15 minutes walking distance from the Accelerator Laboratory. It was rented at a very low price, that included furniture, tableware, bed-clothes, etc. plus cleaning. We found out the first day that the nearest supermarket was at some 10 km distance, and thus buying foodstuff, etc, - we had to buy a car first. The many buildings of the Institute were spread about in the forest that had been a military basis during WWI. To manage our household was much easier than in Israel: the many sorts of foodstuff and all the gadgets helped a lot to Eva. Robi and Liora came to visit us every month at weekends and we visited them the alternate weekends. We often visited the beautiful arboretum on Long Island and the Zoo that

Eva enjoyed very much. We had dinner sometimes at one of the many diners on LI. We visited the Goda's in New York, and they came to have a look at our cottage and the forest around it. We enjoyed also the malls and department stores. All in all we enjoyed life in the States, or more correctly at the BNL, where we lived as in an ivory tower, in maximal security: guards criss-crossing the premises day and night. All employees of BNL had been checked and double-checked; thus we could feel ourselves safe. A ladies' club had been operated by the wives of the exchange scientists or lady scientists, doing cultural, etc. activities. Every month another lady prepared her national food for a dinner, to which all other scientists were invited to participate. A nice cultural center building was situated about the center of the Institute, consisting of an elegant theater-concert hall, lecture halls, cafeteria, restaurant, etc. A H. Moore bronze sculpture, symbolizing the atom, was placed in front of the building. Regular concerts, theater performances. lectures, etc. were staged. Eva was happy with everything; she cared for the household - with the help of the cleaning personnel -, she cooked and baked cookies, etc, she was always active, she even enrolled in a correspondence English course. By the way, we frequented the swimming pool, also within the Institute.

My colleague developed the computer program for the purpose. After all measurements of a set-up completed, I punched the data into cards and handed in the Computer Center. The computer output consisted of 50-60 pages, including graphs showing calibration maps. The maps showed a basic mesh, of 12.7 mm unit, and all the intersection points of PUE-s set-up. One glance at the map sufficed to give direct and precise answer as to the deviation of the beam position indicated by the actual PUE from those of the ideal PUE. A few prototypes of the novel, integrated PUE-s were tested and the first few results already showed that nonlinear deviations were about 1 mm/25 mm, and a resolution of about 0.1 mm/25 mm: results above all expectations: proving the superior quality of the novel PUE-s.

It was a great success, on more than one count. First: it was my personal achievement, proving repeatedly the correctness of my "credo", in all its details. Second: it was an Israeli achievement, because implicitly Israeli research scientists were judged of first as Israelis and only second as individuals. Third: the Management of the Accelerator was much relieved of their heavy predicament because of the danger of not completing the improvement program by the deadline and within the budget allocation. Some 80 PUE-s were produced and installed, as BNL reported proudly in its yearly report. We wrote a paper on it in "The Review of Scientific Instruments".

I also designed a few additional pieces of equipment, among them an integrated PUE with an elliptical cross-section that until then was considered impossible to produce, until my jig-device produced a perfect elliptical aperture PUE that was accepted by acclamation.

Two sabbatical years were approved to me by my home IAEC, but by US law: exchange scientists could get contract only for one year, extendible for two more years. Due to severe budget cuts, BNL was unable to offer me an extension. Instead, the Director of BNL offered me the possibility to continue my sabbatical at the National Accelerator Laboratory, near Batavia, Illinois, being constructed. NAL had been newly established as the joint research institute of 49 US and 1 Canadian university and research institutes, designed as the most powerful accelerator on Earth. BNL proposed to NAL my participation in their work as their contribution, and so I was invited to NAL for an interview.

I discussed this new development with Eva. Although our life at BNL had been very comfortable and pleasant, she was confident that we shall find a similar environment at NAL, not to speak about new and bigger professional challenges for me at an institute in "status nascendi". I presented myself to the Technical Director and gave him my resume. Our meeting was very friendly; he showed me around at a few points of the huge site - 6800 acres -, everything dug up, heavy earth-moving machines working all around, a huge circular trench was being dug and big (about 6 dia x 8 m) concrete pipe-sections lowered in that trench of about 2 km dia; a number of buildings being built, generally feverish activity was in progress everywhere. It reminded me of Soreq at the time we had built our institute; of course at a much smaller scale. As he showed me around: he evidently was very proud of this place, of their work; and I felt: this was the place for me to meet my next challenge. I told him so - and he accepted me on the spot; by September, 1 they will be waiting for me.

I told Eva about my enthusiasm on NAL, my first impression on the place: something extraordinary. She was happy and full of confidence in the new phase. The only regrettable element in our moving to Illinois was the fact that we would be far from Robi-Liora and we won't see each other as often as at Brookhaven.

By the end of August we said good-bye to the people at BNL and to the few friends; packed up our belongings in the car and off we went. We stopped at Buffalo to see the Niagara Falls, and leisurely proceeded to Chicago and Aurora, the nearest bigger city to NAL. We stayed at the Holiday Inn, and I went to NAL the next day. Was warmly received, introduced to the Head of the Engineering Department - and we already had to run for the weekly "Ring" (the circular accelerator beam) meeting. There, I was introduced to the Director of NAL: Professor Robert Wilson, who welcomed me and introduced to the meeting. One by one the scientists, engineers, and technicians reported on the progress, problems, difficulties, etc. from the previous week's work. In five minutes I knew that he (Professor Wilson) was not only the director of NAL, but a prominent leader: he knew about every detail, he appreciated progress and arranged help where needed; assigned tasks and demanded clear and true reports. Two types of work were going on: one type assigned to contractors, e.g. the concrete ring of the accelerator, buildings, etc. and production of equipment, components, etc. of the very many sections of the institute, by NAL workers and contractors. He knew what he wanted and knew how to attain his goal. He was a leader with style.

I was assigned to the Engineering Department (ED), and a room was allotted to me. The ED's Head gave me complete freedom to look around and get familiar with the entire laboratory and the very many works in progress - and select a task for myself to my liking. Besides, he asked me to tell him any remark, comment, opinion, or proposal on anything I think could and should be improved, and advise him on the subject I would be most interested to participate. I designed some 20-25 smaller attachments and equipment, when a bigger project turned up: an alignment-device for the ring's magnets that had to be very accurately aligned respective to each other by a certain angle, defined by the number of magnets on the periphery of the polygon. Alignment was made by using laser beam, reflected by a mirror on the adjacent magnet. An extremely high precision was needed, since along the most part of the circumference of the ring (about 6.4 km), hundreds of magnets (about 8 m lengths) had to be aligned to form an extremely accurate polygon. The next bigger project was to calculate and design a sizable magnet of about 150 kW strength. It was the first time when I confronted such a problem. A computer program had already been worked out for the main details of the calculation, still a lot of additional details had to be solved separately.

After about one month's stay at the Holiday Inn in Aurora, we found a very nice, two-room apartment, on the ground floor of a three-storied building, one of three similar buildings within an apartment complex, situated on a large green field with beautiful trees, extending to the far Fox river. A swimming pool was located in the center of the three buildings on the sides of a triangle. Our apartment on the ground floor had an open verandah to the field and the swimming pool, so Eva could directly walk the thirty-odd meters to the pool and swim there happily. Our apartment-complex was the only exception in the small and exclusive place of North Aurora, with less than 700 residents, all of them living in villas along its four-five roads. The place was about 10 km distance from the NAL. Both of us were happy with the arrangement; I had lunch at the Laboratory and returned home in the evening, when either we had dinner at home or went out for dinner to one of the many places in the neighboring cities. We were invited to the Jewish community at Aurora and went regularly to the Friday evening prayers in their synagogue. Weekends we spent driving to arboretums, zoos, scenery spots, etc. or went on sightseeing trips in Illinois and the surrounding states. We made friends with nice people, both from the Jewish community and colleagues from the NAL. All in all we lived there very happily.

Since my first day at the NAL, my enthusiasm grew from day to day. NAL already was at the top of the world's scientific interest. After much conflict at political level in the US Congress, the idea to build the world's strongest accelerator had been approved in 1964 and a budget allocated of 250 million dollars. Its strength had been initially set at 200 BEV (billion electron volts), compared with the world's most energetic Russian's 70 BEV. The target date had been set for 1972, and when I came to NAL by September, 1970, they were well ahead in their progress. Professor Wilson, who had fought for this project, had been appointed as director - and that decision had ensured the success of the establishment. Its location had been decided to be at Batavia-Weston. Weston had been at that time a small town-development project completed and a few houses already occupied. Professor Wilson bought out the entire Weston - lock, stock, and barrel, compensated the few people, and within days they could start working in the homes with all its infrastructure ready for use, gaining thereby much time and money. He put his individual stamp on everything: scientific program, construction, employment policy, etc. - and all these with an unprecedented style. Houses were color-coded, new structures, buildings were designed not simply to be functionally perfect, but with architectural beauty. One example: the new high voltage electricity transmission lines were designed using original new elegant conical pylons - instead of the conventional, drab steel-structures - with the cross-bars by arched rods. Or: the 2 km diameter concrete tunnel, that housed the ring of magnets, was embedded in earth, only protruding upwards as a mound of earth, resembling a levee. Inside this mound was a green pasture, where Wilson had brought a herd of buffaloes: a symbol of old America, contrasting the accelerator, the symbol of the new America. Wilson was a high energy physicist and one of the world's principal experts in designing accelerators. He had been one of the physicists who worked on the atomic bomb during WWII. He testified frequently before Congress that physics is a cultural activity, and remarked: "They are similar, poetry and physics, because they both try to say a very great deal about the world in a much abbreviated, rigorous manner. An elegant physical equation has such symmetry and simplicity that you can't help but regard it as being beautiful, perhaps having some other significance." An example: "$E = M \times c \times c$". The NAL accelerator had been designed to operate routinely at 200 BEV, and occasionally at near 500 BEV. The big event in the accelerator is to hurdle protons, one of the basic particles of every atom, at huge energy - 500 BEV - to atoms, to take it apart to see what is there and what holds it together so tightly.

Had my contract with BNL been extended for a second year, I would not have received the opportunity to join NAL and experience the wonderful ecstatic feeling of working in this highly cultured scientific community. Day-by-day I told Eva about my increasing joy in my work, and she was happy too.

As a consequence of NAL's novelty of concept, the method and organization of work had to be original too. Except construction works, that had been farmed out and had only to be supervised, the actual design and production of the many hundreds of components, equipment, instruments, etc. were made by hundreds of special teams dealing with individual problems, controlled and synchronized by supervisory teams. Additionally to design and production, partial experimentation were going on for checking their suitability for the task, and every time some novel result ensued - it was immediately transferred to all other related design work. So, the work was a permanent design - development redesign activity.

Another aspect of this novel type of work was that more often than not, conventional calculation methods were not adequate to solve problems, thus first appropriate calculation and checking procedures had to be devised. As an example: one of my few tens of design tasks was a pressure vessel to be covered by a convex lens-shaped plate, with minimal wall thickness at the center. Mathematics calculation models were not reliable enough, thus I made three test cover plates and checked them by a series of experiments using strain-gauges. Since more and more problems arose along the design-development-redesign sequence on the one side, and the good successes of my designs on the other: my boss, the Technical Director, assigned to me two more engineers and the necessary draftsmen, and allotted two more rooms in the house I had my office. Big equipment, composed of two or more parts, were designed simultaneously, for speeding up the process.

I inquired about pick-up electrodes they intended to use in the big accelerator. A Japanese physicist was the head of a team dealing with the subject, and he told me that they earlier designed a PUE without ceramic holder body. He didn't say that they invented it, neither gave me any indication how they arrived to that solution. When I showed him my solution I arrived at in BNL, he said nothing. I could only presume that he got information from physicists from BNL - but I didn't press the matter further.

One day a letter from the NAL management was placed on my desk, informing me that my salary was raised "on merit". This was an unusual action, because exchange scientists worked on contracts that defined the reward-sum for the duration of the contract (one year). Apparently this raise was an exceptional appreciation of my work contribution.

One more symptom of NAL's civilized style.

And I was proud of my success and their appreciation.

Robi and Liora progressed nicely in their Ph.D. work. Our contact was not as frequent as in the previous year when we had lived at BNL, but we spoke often on the phone and Robi visited us now and then when he made trips to professional meetings. Liora was expectant: all of us were happy. At weekends we made trips to Chicago and around Illinois, Wisconsin, etc. We were happy; the bad memories from the past had slowly subsided, albeit not passed away completely. My work made me enthusiastic; the whole atmosphere in the Laboratory was vibrant, no week passed without some extraordinary success of one of the many teams. I drove every morning to the Laboratory, full of expectation in the progress of my work; reflecting on how fortunate I was by attaining being a member of such a wonderful scientific-engineering endeavor.

Once or twice, when driving from home through the beautiful countryside to the Laboratory, a dark thought swept over my mind: what price will we have to pay for all the happiness that fell to our lot (Picture 35). I tried to put these foreboding out of my mind; but I was afraid.

During the winter, Eva put bird-seed into the feeding table hanging on a tree branch, a few meters from our verandah. Besides birds, one squirrel came every morning, and made acrobatic spectacles for reaching the seed from above, hanging on the tree branch. They were Eva's friends, as were birds, e.g. cardinals that came to pick seeds.

Separate buildings were designed and erected for housing equipment of specific experiments. Great care was brought to bear upon the architect-constructors designing such buildings for optimal functionality and concomitant architectural beauty. For a special neutrino experiment, proton beam from the accelerator ring was diverted along a long straight vacuum channel, ending in a large experimental set-up, to be located in a separate building. It was a square concrete structure, of about 20 m side-length and of some 8 m height; the side walls slightly inclined, resembling a pyramid. The experimental equipment needed another few meters head space at the center of the building. A geodesic dome was designed for this purpose, with exquisite features, by an

Picture 35 – Near Chicago

architectural design office. Units of the geodesic dome were equilateral triangles, of about 2 m sides, of a novel, unique honeycomb structure. These triangular plates were made out of soft-drink- and beer-cans, tightly placed side-by-side. That was the time when the movement of environment protection started. One of many items polluting the environment was the cold-drink- and beer-cans, thrown away by the millions every day. Somebody at the Laboratory came forward with the idea to use these thrown-away cans as structural material, by cutting out the two end-plates and glue tightly placed cylinders between two sheets, forming thereby a sort of honeycomb structure. A further improvement was to use for the two side plates Plexiglas sheets instead of e.g. steel plates, making thereby the honeycomb structure lighter and translucent. By using 10 mm thick Plexiglas triangles, the open-ended cans were glued with epoxy between two Plexiglas plates, making a very strong and light-weight building element. Patent was applied for, and a big architect design office carried out a computerized design of the geodesic dome. When the completed design had been delivered, my boss came to me and asked me to check the technical reliability of the design.

This was the first time that I heard about that special honeycomb design and was very much impressed by the geodesic dome structure. I jumped on the task, which - I thought - would give me an excellent opportunity to refresh my memory in descriptive geometry, applied for the special and very complicated geometric configuration of the dome. We had no contact with the architect-design office, we didn't get computations and data of the design; all we got were workshop drawings of the components plus assembly drawings. At first glance, everything looked right, and it would have been reasonable to make a series of computations-checks and approve the design. But I was more ambitious and thus I decided to do a complete design process, starting from the zero point. Were it not for my good command of descriptive geometry - I couldn't have solved the design problems of the very complicated geodesic dome. I worked on the subject with much enthusiasm and as I progressed in the design, partial details proved their results acceptable. Then, accidentally, one morning I hardly could reach my car at the parking place because of high wind. And this event lighted a red alarm signal in my mind: the need to check the geodesic dome for strong wind condition that was well known in the Chicago area: the "windy city". I wanted to compute the forces that would load the dome; I looked for data on the subject in text-books and all available technical literature, but found very scanty details. I went around the universities, asking for data and theory, and it took much work until I gathered some knowledge in the subject, including meteorological data from the preceding twenty years. Based on these references, I made extremely difficult computations on this quite unconventional problem, and came to the conclusion that the dome could not stand high wind conditions, even below peak occurrences, and would topple over, causing extreme damage to the expensive research equipment inside the building. I reported my findings to my boss, who was much relieved about not accepting without check the design by the architect firm. I was not informed how the matter was settled by our Laboratory and the architect firm, but I was asked somewhat later to amend the design.

It was a big success in the series of tens of my design works of a very wide variety: huge electro magnets, tiny electro-magnetic control equipment, laser measuring set-ups, etc.: engineering subjects of such variety that was very uncommon in engineering practice in the US, where specialization was the accepted method. I was delighted with my work.

On March 3 1971, a boy was born of Liora-Robi: Gil, our grandson. Both were doing well; we flow over to visit them (Picture 36). All of us were very happy; everything went well; health, work progress; Robi had good success with his Ph.D. project, and so had Liora too.

I earned and got approval for two sabbatical years from my home Institute (the IAEC), that was due to expire by September, 1971. I was spending my second sabbatical at NAL, from

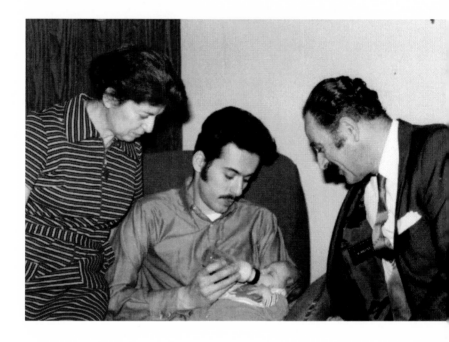

Picture 36 – A grandson is born

September 1970 until 1971. A very fine manifestation of my boss and the Management of NAL in appreciating my achievements was when they offered me to continue working in the coming year too, in the third sabbatical permitted by US law. I told them that I considered it a great privilege to me to continue participating in building NAL - but I need approval for a third year from my home Institute. They immediately sent an official request to the IAEC, and I informed them too, and they approved the request. Thus, instead of two - I was going to spend three sabbatical years, by the end of which, as per US law, I will have to leave the States. My boss informed me that NAL would very much like to have me on their staff permanently and for this purpose the Management officially requested the Secretary of State to pass an act enabling me to continue working for NAL. I asked him to convey my thanks to Professor Wilson.

I was happy - and a little proud. Eva and Robi were happy too. Two events during the latest period of my work at NAL: their offer to continue my sabbatical year, and their raise of my salary for the second time gave me ground to believe that they appreciated my achievements.

By January 1972 the geodesic dome was completed and assembled. The triangular elements were painted light blue, red, yellow, and so lighting inside the building was almost ceremonial. This building was another example of the artistic trend at NAL. The geodesic dome became an official "landmark" in Illinois.

By March, Eva felt general indisposition, and the doctor diagnosed unspecified allergy. We went to "the" specialist-Professor, who was a Jew, visiting frequently in Israel as a consultant expert. Learning that we were from Israel, he was very attentive, and Eva got preferential treatment. A series of tests was made, taking a few weeks, but no conclusive result was reached, and she felt better.

One day in May, when I returned home, she complained about severe pains around the lower ribs, on the left side, when walking. We immediately drove to the closest hospital's emergency room, where she was told that one rib became cracked, which happens often; they put on a strong but flexible bandage and reassured us that it will be over in a few days. But the pain remained, so I called the doctor who treated her earlier, and we went immediately to his office. After examination he told us that she had to be hospitalized for further examination and treatment. I brought her next morning to the hospital the doctor recommended, where she underwent examinations for days, but her condition became worse, she felt weakness, couldn't walk. The doctor told us that she had calcium deficiency and needed x-ray irradiation. I became very anxious and worried, and contacted friends from the synagogue, inquiring about the best hospital and doctor in Aurora. I went to see the doctor they recommended, and next morning transferred her by an ambulance to the other hospital.

Early next morning the doctor called me at home and told me the terrible news. They removed a small piece of bone and diagnosed that one part of her bone structure had already been destroyed by cancer. More details we will have to discuss in the afternoon, when more information will be available by additional examinations. He strongly advised me to go to my office and work, notwithstanding the very grim situation.

The blow was indescribable, I was unable to think, hardly could bring myself to a state to worry about Eva and not myself. I called Robi, told him the bare news and asked him to take the next flight and come over - what he did. First we went to see the doctor, who told us frankly that the situation was very serious, but they already started strong x-ray irradiation treatment to halt the process. In a few days more details will be available, especially as regards the treatment she will need. They will tell Eva that she had some bone ailment, due to calcium deficiency.

What and how we felt was indescribable. It took some time until we dared to enter Eva's room. We told her that Robi was on his way to Chicago to attend a conference, and asked her what examinations had been made and what was the result. She felt better than a few days earlier, had no pains, and apparently she was not in bad mood, her spirit was quite high. They took her away for further tests, so we told her to visit again next morning.

We went home, sat down, downcast, couldn't think or speak. One thought was on my mind: why. Why she had to pay the terrible price and not me? I felt that I failed her by not guarding her better; I felt that I was guilty. But we had to deal with her now; we started to speak about what should be done. The doctor told us that her illness needed a long treatment; they still didn't know exactly: what sort of or what combination. And how could we help her? We, Eva and me, will have to leave the States by the end of August, except we gain an extension, as requested by NAL, but that was only a hope, highly unlikely - and we thought it very risky to start a lengthy medical treatment that would have to be interrupted if and when we have to leave. Besides, the two of us were alone there in Aurora, we couldn't hope to get any sort of help that surely will be needed during the coming months - whereas in Tel Aviv we would be at home, were familiar with the procedures and possibilities of medical treatment, including hospitalization, and had a number of friends and help if needed. We tried hard to consider all pros and cons, and concluded that it would be better to have treatment at home - provided that in Tel Aviv they could assure the same or even better treatment for her ailment than was available in the States. Next morning we told her doctor our considerations; he agreed, and on my request he wrote a few words on her disease, because I wanted to contact on phone the head of the Radiation Department of the Beilinson Hospital, who was also the doctor at our Institute at Soreq and he knew me well. I phoned him, explained the situation, and asked him to give me his most straightforward opinion and friendly advice whether she would get at least the same quality treatment at his hospital than she could get in the States. He reassured me and told me even that the head of the oncology department was a US Professor. This information strengthened the option to take her home. But first of all we had to discuss the matter with Eva, whom the doctor didn't inform about the real situation that she was suffering from cancer;

she was only told that she was ill due to severe calcium deficiency, the treatment of which will be a lengthy one.

Then, together with Robi, we went to see Eva. She felt much better than the previous day, she was in good spirits, told us what treatment she got, and was satisfied with everything in the hospital; she was alone in her room, service was excellent. We started to discuss the future steps by asking her what she thought about a lengthy medical treatment, most probably partly at home and partly in the hospital. Apparently, she pondered over the matter, because without hesitation told us that she would prefer to go home and not wait until our residence permit expires, and get medical attention at home. We reached a common consent, which we thought and hoped was the right decision. It was an excruciating concern to choose one alternative and propose it to Eva; how could I know which one was better; how could I take the responsibility for her life: this was my anxiety that never left me.

She did not lament, was in apparently good spirit, as it was befitting to her wonderful mental strength and unsurpassable disposition. She accepted the diagnosis; showed no sign of suspecting the real illness - or at least controlled herself. She took interest in everything, listened to classical music, watched TV, etc. I didn't know how I could manage to show myself composed when visiting her and were planning our life after returning home. I lived in a trance, absorbed in gloomy thoughts, about the mystery of life and blind, cruel destiny.

Robi returned home; we had to wait some time while she got treatment. In the meantime I had to wind up my work at NAL, where my boss and the colleagues were sorry for me personally and for my leaving NAL. I had to make arrangements at home in Tel Aviv for our return. After a few days the doctor told us that she was now in a good enough condition that allowed the long flight from Chicago to New York and continuing to Tel Aviv. Robi came down again for helping us for our return trip. Actually, he had to arrange everything, shipping all our belongings, etc. He did an excellent job.

An ambulance took us to the airport in Chicago. The Goda's met us in New York, then we took an El-Al flight to Tel Aviv. She was given a couch for the night flight. An ambulance was waiting for her, which I arranged in advance, and we went straight to the Beilinson Hospital, where my doctor-friend was waiting for her as I asked him by phone. After a consultative examination, based on the medical report from the Aurora Hospital, she was put to bed in a room for three. The date was: July, 20. 1972.

Did we choose the right option by bringing her home: I didn't know; there was no possibility to check, and I felt the terrible responsibility, made more difficult by my anxiety and unbearable foreboding. And in that condition I had to pretend to give not more than some normal care for her and speak about the arrangements made at our home for waiting her return. In retrospect: I don't know how I did it: fact is that I cannot remember almost anything what happened in Israel and around the world during those times.

I reported back at Soreq, and a few good friends of mine cared for me, arranged everything for me. I didn't want to return to the Engineering Department, mainly because, as I learned, during my absence, my previously competent department had been ruined by incompetence and turned into a tinker-shop.

By a lucky coincidence, the Government decided to embark on the prestigious long-range program to go nuclear for electricity production and sea-water desalination and gave the go-ahead to the IAEC, where a new department was set up at their Headquarter for this project: "Power and Water Department". The appointed head of this department was an excellent engineer from the Dimona Research Center. I didn't know him, but he had information about me and invited me for an interview. No much persuasion was needed to bring me over to this prestigious work, and I moved over to the Headquarter, in Ramat Aviv. This change helped me practically for giving me more time to go visit Eva, sometimes twice a day.

With my new assignment, I was promoted to "full Professorship". Eva was happy and proud of me. She was getting treatment, as I learned: weekly cortisone injections. She felt well, could walk around, ate well, was in good spirits, interested in everything, chatted with visitors, and made plans for her return home. After a while, her beautiful hair started falling out, as the doctor explained, as a consequence of the cortisone treatment, but assured us that it will grow up after the treatment.

My new appointment was quite comfortable at the beginning; my main occupation was to collect information materials, as much as possible, by direct communications and by the help of scientific consuls at Israeli Embassies abroad. It suited me by allowing to visit Eva very often, and prepare our home for her return. Our apartment was in shambles after three years of sublease. Besides, at that period I was in a permanent depression, I couldn't resign myself to that terrible tragedy of my dearest Eva, and to the fact that I couldn't help her.

By September, she was released from the hospital, and we had to back once a week for injections. First, a blood test was made every time, and on that basis quantity and assortment of the medication was decided upon. We bought a car, compact but big enough to put in the trunk a wheelchair. She never uttered a single word of complaint, on the contrary, she apparently was cheerful, but I couldn't believe that she, with her superb intelligence, wouldn't know what her ailment had been so both of us pretended that she was recuperating from the arthritis and calcium deficiency. We employed a nursing-woman, from morning till night. She could move around, busied herself with reading, listening to music, nursing her flowers, and inquiring about my new work. Weekends we drove around the country, bringing with us sandwiches, made picnics with friends; she loved the countryside, forests, flowers, animals.

By year's end, Robi, Liora, and Gil came to visit her. She was very happy, prepared Robi's favorite meals, cakes, and cookies; and a few times we went for a stroll on the sea-shore, Eva and Gil in their wheelchairs. We (Robi and me) went to see the Professor in the hospital, asking information about her prospect. He told us that we could consider a considerable success that the process was stopped. For how long and what future she could hope for - he declined to answer. When they left home and said good-bye to her, I slipped out the room, weeping, as so often I did, hidden away.

We lived such a hide-and-seek life. She was strong and self-reliant; I was deeply depressed that I tried to hide as much as I could. I have today almost no recollection of things happening in the world during that year.

By the 14-th of August, she felt unwell, some blotches appeared around her hip, itching. We went to the hospital, where, after consultation with two-three doctors, it was decided that until this rash heels, the regular weekly injections must be interrupted. In the meantime, she got some. By September, 3, she felt very weak, was vomiting. In the hospital they gave her infusions and injections. After ten days the doctors preferred her going home, in order to prevent some additional infection. Vomiting persisted and she felt very weak.

Saturday, the 17-th of September, two lady-friends from Budapest, came to visit her. She felt somewhat better, we chatted softly, and she asked me to turn on the record-player and put on the Verdi Requiem. While listening, she said: "were there be no Verdi music - it wouldn't be worth to live." Not much knowledge of psychology was needed to grasp the reason of her remark. We were stunned, and listened in silence. I couldn't bear it and went out on the pretext to bring a medicine the doctor ordered for the night. The two ladies told me later that when they wanted to leave, Eva told them to stay a little longer and listen to her story, how we two met in 1937, in Budapest, in the cafe Japan. Dear God, she must had, consciously or unconsciously, taken farewell of us.

During the night September 17-18, she vomited periodically and had pains at the back of the head. Early next morning, September, 18, Sunday, we went back to the hospital. She got infusion and injections; was very weak, drank a little tea, and fell asleep. Next morning I saw her at 7:30; was asleep and a tear-drop hung at the corner of her right eye. Did she have pains and wept because of it, or did she grieve over her coming death - it was a sight unbearable, that has been staying with me and will last to my last breath. I returned at noon, but she was already removed into a separate room, alone, connected to a respiration-machine. She was in a coma. The doctor couldn't tell me anything. Was waiting. I called Robi to inform him. Stayed there on a bench in the corridor; they didn't let me stay in her room, only now and then could I see her when somebody from the staff entered the room and gave her something. Fodor Eva came to see her and said sadly how beautiful she was. During the night I called Robi again, only to tell him that everything remained unchanged. I stayed there, sitting and walking up and down, during the next day, until in the afternoon they sent me home. At 9:30 pm the phone rang: they called me back to the hospital. The doctor made me sit down and told me that she died, at 9:30 pm, without regaining consciousness, without pain. It was on September, 20, 1973.

I sat there, a body, devoid of soul. They made me to drink something; they spoke to me; I heard their voices, but I couldn't comprehend. After a while, the doctor asked me whether I would allow an autopsy. When my question whether this would help other patients recovery was answered affirmatively: I consented.

When I got home, I called Robi telling him that we became orphaned. Fodor Ali, the brother of Fodor Eva, came to my help. I wrote in the obituary: " . . . and mourns for her everybody who loved her because they knew her."

We buried her on September, 23, 1973.

I lived in a nether world. Sat "Shiva" (the ritual mourning week) at home. Friends came to visit me. I lived as an automaton. But deep inside, within me, a search of my heart went on.

- - - - - - - - -

We lived together for thirty-five years, in heavenly harmony, loved each other affectionately, had the same ideals, culture, judgment, manner, taste - but hers were superior to mine in everything. Her integrity, virtue, and moral strength were unsurpassable, they triumphed many times along the dangerous periods in the past. In spite of frightfully pernicious human evil, she persisted in her love for humanness, animals, and flowers. Both of us were professionals, the practice of which she had to give up due to her illness of polio. I became an engineer thanks to my late brother's ingenious upbringing of me, and his unselfish sponsoring of my engineering education. Maybe I had some talent for engineering that, supplemented by professional education, would make me an average engineer, possibly a creative design engineer. But along my long career, what helped me to succeed was Eva's ingenious gift and aspiration to inspire me when I faltered in the inspirational phases of work, and strengthened and sustained my efforts during the sometimes long and arduous perspirational periods. Without her help and support I wouldn't be able to perform as much work as I did. Her help and encouragement was a blessing, but in my insufficiency, I didn't realize how blessed was her help - I just accepted it as something ordinary, normal. When I became aware of how incomparably precious was her help - it was too late. I could never forgive myself for my ingratitude. I consider myself a charlatan: her name should had been put, along with mine, on all my works, papers. I felt - and feel till today - guilty because of my sinful neglect. I visited her graveside very frequently, begging her forgiveness. I want to make up for what I missed to do, but beating my breast won't be enough. As I knew her: she will forgive me. I wish: these of my few, insufficient but sincere, words should represent a Taj Mahal like memorial for my mythological "Muse", my unforgettable "Little-Girl"-wife: Eva.

- - - - - - - - - - -

CONTINUING LIFE ON MY OWN - 1973 – 1990

The previous one and a half year had been a very sad period of my life, but after her death, I became totally depressed. I went to work every day, but I wasn't of much use; I couldn't do any serious work. On October 6, 1973, the Yom Kippur War broke out, and I was called back to Soreq, temporarily, for consultancy in protection of the Reactor. Fortunately, there was no need for it, because the war ended with our forces in Egypt, 100 km from Cairo.

At the thirtieth day of her death, a tombstone was erected at her grave. I sought safety in flight and went to spend a month with Robi (Picture 37). Returning home, I was received in the office with the news that our Government decided to order and erect a nuclear power plant, and so we had to use every effort in implementing this plan.

The "Israel Electric Corporation" (IEC) had been solely responsible for electricity generation and distribution to the whole country, done by 6-7 power plants, about 500 MW each, plus a number of small gas turbine driven emergency generators, and a national power transmission grid. Israel had no energy resources, and all power plants had been fueled with oil, imported from various overseas countries.

A substantial difference exists between fossil (oil or coal) and nuclear fueling of electricity generating power plants. In fossil fueling, heat is generated by chemical energy, by burning the fuel that heats up a cooling medium - water - that produces steam for turning the turbine and generating electricity. In nuclear fueling: heat is generated by nuclear energy, by the chain-reaction of certain "fissionable" material, mainly uranium (U), when huge amounts of heat is generated, that produces steam for turning the turbine and generating electricity. Difference in the fueling process: fossil fuel has to be fed continuously, whereas nuclear fueling is periodical, generally once a year. Another, maybe the most essential, difference is the quantities of the two types of fuel:

Picture 37 – with grandson

since the heat energy content, by weight, of uranium is approximately two million times that of oil: large quantities of oil have to be shipped constantly to Israel vs. 20-30 tons of nuclear fuel per year. As a drawback: nuclear fuel, in the form of fuel elements, that has to be loaded into the nuclear reactor, has a quite long production process: 1) the uranium ore (U3O8) has to be concentrated (yellowcake); 2) the natural content of the uranium isotope: U235, the solely usable, fissionable material, is only 0.71 % of the total uranium, but for the purpose of use as fuel in light-water reactors: this U235 content has to be enriched to 2-3 %; and 3) this enriched uranium will have to be fabricated into fuel elements that will then be loaded, yearly, into the reactor as fuel.

These were the main reasons for going nuclear, to lessen our dependence on oil import, the exorbitant price increases, a possible oil embargo, etc. The "Israel Atomic Energy Commission" (IAEC), already operating two nuclear research reactors, had the experience in the various steps of nuclear fuel procurement, transport, handling, etc. Consequently, the IAEC was entrusted with the task to deal with all steps of fuel management of the future nuclear power plants, such as: procurement of raw material, production of nuclear fuel assemblies, transports, storage, etc. Besides, the IAEC was responsible for all safety aspects of nuclear activities, thus it had been decided that these two bodies should be jointly responsible for erecting and operating the future nuclear power plants.

This decision of a "joint" responsibility was a bad mistake that made much trouble, right from the beginning of our work. Generally, there is no such thing as a "joint" responsibility and accountability, not even in small undertakings and even less in a venture with an initial investment in the order of magnitude of one billion dollars or more.

As the first step, we set up a joint coordinating- and supervisory committee. Unfortunately, our department (Power and Water) of the IAEC had been set up only a year earlier, and we were only four-five people at that time, two-three of them young engineers, fresh from the University. My boss, Mr. Adar Joseph, was an excellent engineer, one of the builders of the IRR-II reactor, and myself, coming from the IRR-I reactor, had experience and knowledge in how to deal with "nuclear" technical problems. Nevertheless: we had to learn a lot for enabling us to properly deal with the problems of nuclear power plants. Our first task was to issue an "Invitation to Bid" of one or two nuclear power plants, to be erected in Israel. Such an Invitation was a very serious matter to prepare, because actually, all requirements had to be specified in it. As a result of my boss' contacts with the "International Atomic Energy Agency" (IAEA), in Vienna: we got some 5-6 Invitations, issued by various countries to various suppliers that we could use as preliminary examples. But real help came when we received a few actual Bids, issued by the leading USA producers - of course containing only technical data - prices and other commercial conditions erased.

Studying thoroughly these materials, we started collecting data of our requirements and organizing them into our Invitation. This was not only an extremely demanding technical task, but additionally very wide-ranging safety aspects had to be "build in". Willy-nilly: the choice fell on me to write the Invitation. This was again a challenge - and a heavy one. I took it on; partly because I knew that there was no one, near or far, who could have done it properly - and partly because it was a heavy work load that would forcefully disengage me somewhat from my depression. Thus, I started working on it with a vengeance, consulting now and then with my boss, who became happier day by day seeing my accurate, scrupulous work. We discussed the matter a few times in the Coordinating Committee, where the IEC people constantly made difficulties. Nevertheless, the "Invitation" was issued, after some 8-9 months' preparation, and was sent to: Westinghouse-, General-Electric-, and Babcock and Wilcox- Companies in the USA.

In the meantime, mainly during waiting for the Bids from the suppliers we were in close contact with both the IAEA - by my boss, and the suppliers and operators of such reactors in the States

- by me. One of the most useful sources of information was for me the "Tennessee Valley Authority" that had at that time 7 nuclear plants in operation, some 8 plants in construction, and a few more plants in design stages. I spent a few days at their central office in Chattanooga (Tennessee), became friendly with the planning director and got very valuable informations regarding ordering, erecting, and operating nuclear plants. During our discussions, my intuition taught me that however complicated was a nuclear power plant, especially its efficient and safe operation process - the real, essential, and challenging task was the so-called "fuel management", dealing with every and all aspects of the "fuel cycle".

Three distinct - although connected - phases constitute a nuclear power plant's program: 1) ordering and erecting the actual plant; 2) operating and maintaining the plant for its life-span of 30 years; and 3) managing the "fuel cycle", for the approximately 30 years of the plant's operational life.

According to the two distinct functions of erecting and operating nuclear power plants, my boss and I divided between ourselves the fields of activity and responsibility: his was going to be erection, operation and maintenance, and safety - and mine the fuel management. I asked for this division, in spite - or because - of the fuel management was a more difficult, a continuous activity, and involving continuous monetary evaluations and comparisons - in contrast to reactor erection. Although the decision for going nuclear had been made on a series of considerations, one of the importance of which had been the comparative unit cost-figures of the generated electricity. Thus, computation of unit cost was for us of paramount importance, basically for comparing unit electricity costs of competing reactor types, and, in addition, for comparing unit costs of fossil and nuclear plants.

Here I was again confronting a new challenge - and I chose the more difficult sphere: fuel management - comprising both technical and monetary aspects. I only guessed that the task I chose was the most complex, the most difficult, and - at the same time -

the most glorious work I ever confronted and accomplished.

I started to work in this new field with gusto. I recalled my university year's method of studying: to go over all available reference materials, learn as many concepts as possible, and then devise my own opinion. Before long, I had a broad concept.

The most fundamental approach to cost calculation of electric power, in general, irrespective of the type of power plant: oil, coal, gas, or nuclear, is based on the requirement that, after appropriate corrections for the "time-value of money", the sum of all cash incomes must equal the sum of all cash outflows. It is of importance therefore to know the amounts of money paid out and received, and their corresponding dates, together with the rules for considering and manipulating payments and receipts occurring at various dates: the engineering economy computations.

The total levelized unit electricity cost, expressed in mills/kWh units, is composed of the following main components:

1) capital cost;
2) operating and maintenance cost; and
3) fueling cost.

The theoretical basis of all such computations is the "engineering economy". Engineering economy is basically concerned with money. Money has earning power, because it works over a period of time; the entire concept of the earning power of money can therefore be viewed as the time value of money.   But, as it turned out: no one of these people, including myself, had clear picture on the subject. I contacted the responsible people of the IEC, banking experts, people of Ministry of Finance, etc. - everybody knew something, but not enough. Then I turned to literature, studied textbooks, etc. It was an arduous task - but I succeeded. The best sources were internal data books of big US companies: AT&T, etc. I wrote a 50 page compendium on the subject, for people engaged in the project.

As I was working on the levelized unit fueling cost computer program, I understood and comprehended that engineering economy is not a discipline separate from engineering of whatever sort: it is an integral part of it and should be used to judge the real value of all engineering work.

One, maybe the most important ingredient of the engineering economy computations of our nuclear energy program was the proper use of the three economic factors: discount- (PW-ing), escalation-(or de-escalation) of prices of materials, services, etc, and inflation-factors. Proper use of these factors was even less understood by the people who had the duty to deal with the whole program than the concept of engineering economy. I wrote a few papers on the subject.

I also started working on a computerized "fuel management" program, for a specific nuclear power plant, for its entire operational life (30 years). We hired an expert in this field from the Tel Aviv University, as a consultant, and started the project. I worked out the "print-out" of the required computer program, done by hand, on big sheets, with the help of a desk calculator, an HP 97 programmable model, with printout.

In the meantime I lived a sad, solitary life. Friends and colleagues tried to incite me to change my life; sometimes they invited me to dinners, etc. Once, one of my colleagues, an elderly engineer, from Transylvania, one of those Jews rescued by Mr. Kastner, in the Bergen-Belsen group, invited me to a dinner at his family circle, at the end of the Yom Kippur fast, in 1974. By the end of the dinner, a few friends of my colleague's family arrived: a lady with his son; a girl, and a gentleman. It turned out that the lady was also from Transylvania (Kolozsvar), and also from the Kastner's group; her son: Paul (Asher, in Hebrew) was an engineer, working with Bank Leumi, and was going to be married with the girl present, the coming week; the gentleman was the brother of the lady, resident of Mexico City, who came to attend the wedding of his cousin. Within two weeks or so I was again invited to my colleague's home, to join his circle of friends, who had visited alternately and quite regularly at each other's home. It was a quite interesting company: the lady from the previous dinner: Judith

Herman; two cousins by the same name: Dr. Schwartz William: one a physician and the other a lawyer; another Dr. of economies, working with EL-AL; the owner of a travel office; an industrialist; a businessman in paints; and a few others, together with their wives. Almost all of them were from Kolozsvar (Transylvania), old-time Zionists. During the conversation, and later from my colleague's relating, I learned that Judith's late husband, Herman Louis, had been a lawyer, who died, some ten years earlier, with cancer, and she worked as a directress of the "Duty-Free Shop", at the Hilton hotel in Tel Aviv, and who brought up, by herself, her only son to become an engineer. She had an only brother who emigrated, in good time, in 1938, to South-America, and who had a shoe factory in Mexico City, and was very active in Jewish circles there. She had two brothers-in-law in Israel, but she had been headstrong and consistently refused any help, and worked hard to bring up her son to become an engineer. She was happy that her son married, but broken down remaining alone at home.

We both felt unhappy, lonely, and desolate. I felt sympathy with her distress, and as we spoke about our fate, we found hope in helping each other in our foreseeable future years to easier overcome our sadness and loneliness by joining together in marriage. I was then 66, she was 56 (Picture 38). We had renovated my apartment, combined our furniture, completely remodeled the kitchen; one room was fitted up as my study, with books on two walls up to the ceiling, one big writing desk, etc.

We married on January, 21. 1975, and started our life with much confidence. She continued working at her previous place, alternately in the morning and evening hours. I drove her to work in the mornings and at home in the nights. Her two brothers-in-law lived in Haifa: Dr. Herman Rudolf, a physician, and Mr. Herman Zvi, a director of the ZIM Shipping Company; whom we visited quite often; they were lovable people.

Sometime in the fall of the same year, we made a trip, first to visit Robi and family in Amherst (Massachusetts), and then to Mexico City, to visit her brother and family. Israeli law and

Picture 38 – with Judith

practice had been very stringent on retirement from civil service at the age of 65. The Managing Director of our IAEC sent a request to the Civil Service Commissioner, asking an exceptional extension of my employment, based on my boss' recommendation on my indispensable expertise in carrying out the Government's nuclear program. This request was approved, for two more years.

Evaluating the Bids, each one separately and in comparison with each other, was a very difficult, and at the same time, an extremely fascinating work. The prevailing points in our evaluations were: (1) the safety aspects, and (2) the levelized unit energy cost, in mills/kWh, if each reactor type, to be compared with each other and with fossil fueled power plant's unit costs.

Along my work in analyzing the unit energy costs' computations by the bidders, I collected a huge amount of reference material on the subject: data, methods of computation, etc. The main task was: how to control, and master those thousands of data, how to remember them, and how to pick out the relevant ones, at will and at the moments when they were needed. I took a delight in my capability to succeed in this very sophisticated analysis work.

The problems were complex, and it was not enough to find a solution to any one of the topics; of paramount importance was to find the proper counterbalance of the many, sometimes contradictory effects. Besides the very many literary information material: textbooks, periodicals, reports, etc, I tried to obtain and collect direct, personal informations, by attending conferences, meetings, etc. of the nuclear societies. During the years of 1973-1985, I participated in 15-16 such conferences, mainly in the USA (Atlanta, Boston, Dallas, Kansas City, Los Angeles, Pittsburgh, San Diego, San Francisco), and in Paris (France), Rio de Janeiro (Brazil), and in a few more places. Besides, I visited a few nuclear power plants in the USA, discussing as much as was possible of the very many problems. But I had to learn that there were no common answers or solutions; every power plant had its own peculiar problems to be taken into account, in addition to the basic considerations.

In addition to my eagerness to meet professional people in the nuclear power field, I was more than happy every time when I traveled to the US, because I used every occasion of a conference or consultation with the bidders, to make a side-jump to visit Robi, Liora, and Gil - and stay with them two-three weeks. These visits provided me real enjoyment; comforting me for our living so far away in distant homes. With Gil we became good friends: I became his "favorite" Grandpa - and he my "favorite" Grandson. As an example of his favoritism: as a small boy of 3-4, he did me the honor to read out a tale at bed-time. A few times on my trips, Judith accompanied me too.

As we progressed in our negotiations with the bidders, we intended to order one 600 MW plant from Westinghouse, with an option of another in two more years. Unfortunately, during the long time in our negotiations, difficulties arose, due primarily to the enforcement of the "Non Proliferation Treaty" (NPT), that prohibited the USA to give export permit to US suppliers to provide us nuclear power plants, because Israel was not a signatory of this treaty. The case dragged on and on, and we had to give up the hope to conclude the deal with Westinghouse. We made attempts to negotiate with German suppliers.

My big computer program of fuel management plus unit cost computation had been almost finished, when the expert from the TA University, who had been hired for preparing the program, went on his sabbatical year to the US, and due to the stop in the negotiations: further budget was stopped for the expert too. Incidentally, during the past two-three years, a group of experts of the IAEA in Vienna, prepared a somewhat simpler computer program for unit cost calculation, and my boss got a copy, by personal contact. I studied this program and wrote a memo on my comments, containing some 15 points that I considered in need of modifications, together with my proposals for the corrections. My boss sent a letter to his contact-man and proposed to consider our comments for the final program. They accepted our proposals, except one point, dealing with a definition, that they found "not sufficiently scientific".

At the highest level, a few more attempts were made to attain our goal, a nuclear power plant. Newer models were offered by a few suppliers. The trend was then: smaller unit powers, of 200-300 MW. The more diverse were the prospective plants, the more grew the need to have a computing model for enabling us to compute the levelized unit energy costs, individually for each one of the units and for comparison purposes.

I worked out my new, special model, called "MICROMAX", that was developed for the single-purpose aim to compute front-end levelized unit fueling cost; an explicit model, capable of showing the effects of various economic parameters, or those parameters that directly affect the fueling cost. As a result, a very simple model, stripped to its essentials, but capable of correctness and accuracy, adequate to fueling cost forecast applications was developed.

My ecstatic work on this novel MICROMAX computational system resulted in a quite voluminous book, issued by the IAEC. I had to resign myself with heavy heart to the fact that I myself and our department couldn't use my beautiful and efficient computational system - to provide its beneficial effects to the Israeli economy, at that time - because we had to suspend our work in the nuclear option.

In 1980, I was compelled to retire from my regular job; but I was given contracts, from year to year, as "consultant", and thus I continued working in my job (Picture 39).

From about 1977, we spent our vacations every year somewhere in Switzerland: Bad Ragaz, Davos, Engelberg, Interlaken, Wengen, and a few more places. Engelberg was our favorite place, a very beautiful resort town, with no through traffic - called: the end of the world - with only rail connection to Luzern, maybe the most beautiful city in the whole Switzerland. I suffered from a mild bronchitis, for which I got medication all year round, but my doctor found every time that the best medication was a

Picture 39 – At retirement

vacation in Switzerland.

During all the years from 1975, I attended regularly the nuclear conferences in the States, sometimes twice in a year - and every time spent a few weeks with Robi and the family. These visits were the highlights of my life. Robi was already away from our home since 1965; letters, conversations on phone, etc. had been very poor substitutions for the personal contacts between me and my only son, whom I loved immeasurably.

At one of my visits, in January, 1985, two very unpleasant events happened. I wanted to order tri-focal or progressive glasses, and went for an examination to the Ophthalmology clinics in Los Angeles where they found an advanced state of glaucoma in both eyes. Prescribed strong eye-drops and advised me to go to the eye-clinic when I return home. Two or three days after that, one night I awoke to strong chest pains that lasted a few minutes, but recurred after a while. I awoke Robi, telling him about the recurrent pains and my suspicion that a heart-attack was happening. He called an ambulance and I was transferred to the nearest hospital. They diagnosed a heart-attack and I was put in the intensive-care department and connected to an array of monitors, infusions, etc. Luckily, it was only a mild case; I stayed in the hospital for ten days, but I was allowed to fly home only after thirty days. Judith flew over immediately and stayed with me. After one month, we returned home, and I continued at my work, at a somewhat leisurely pace.

Another annoying illness started to attack me: a benign tumor of the prostate gland. There was no medication; one had to wait until an operation could be performed.

Hard as it was, I had to take into account in my work program that time was running out: I was in my late seventies. Translating this fact to my work I used my novel MICROMAX computation system; every single step was presented and explained, and the HP 97's printouts attached; checks were calculated; etc. - thus these reports were rather textbooks than simple computations.

I enjoyed this newly found field of work: I lived and worked in the "future", visualizing and solving the upcoming problems of the probable future situations. My boss went on his sabbatical to the US, and an engineer who was appointed to be in his stead during his absence, had no knowledge and interest whatsoever in our subject, and thereby obstructed our trials to keep alive our endeavor. Unfortunately, our boss fell ill, with cancer during his stay in the States, and when he returned he was operated on, but he could not regain his health, and after some time, he died.

Due to the concurrent reasons: my almost completed comprehensive, big computer program had to be put aside, the big reels put in a drawer to collect dust.

As a consultant, I didn't have to work in the office; part of the time I worked at home. Judith had to retire too, in 1985; and we lived a comfortable "retirees" life. We walked every day, most often at the Tel Aviv sea-shore promenade.

Then, one fateful day, our tranquil life was shattered. In the early morning, Judith went to the bathroom. After some time of stillness, I was aroused and went to see what happened. She lay on the floor, eyes closed, still, motionless. Trembling, I tried to revive her, then rushed to our next-door neighbor, a woman-doctor, who came running, examined her - and told me the terrible fact that she suffered a fatal massive coronary thrombosis. The neighbor called an ambulance that arrived in a few minutes and the doctor only confirmed the fact. They took her - and I stood there, numbed, I couldn't think, unable to act, trembled, wanted only to shout: why? Why again? What was it: Nemesis? My neighbor called Judith's son: Asher, who came; then we called Robi and her brother in Mexico City. It was December, 30. 1989.

They arrived, and we buried her.

I knew only one thing; my life came to an end.

GIVING UP MY LAST HOME - 1990 – 1995

Two days after the burial, my health condition became acute and an operation had to be performed urgently. Fortunately, Robi, who came for the funeral, for a week or so, stayed with me, and arranged everything connected with my coming hospitalization. This situation taught me a subject lesson on being alone, facing hospitalization and operation, etc, and especially all these in a state of depression. Robi extended his stay and helped me in confronting my dilemma: how to arrange my future life. I realized then, how foolishly we lived, not considering and planning some solution for our future at the advancing age. Now, I had to decide, urgently, what to do with myself. There were two alternatives: to stay in my apartment alone, or to enter in a sort of an old-age home.

Six families lived in our house, but we had almost no social contacts with them. In the close neighborhood there were schools, banks, apartment houses, supermarkets, etc. - but not one single restaurant or coffee-house. Thus, it would have been quite difficult to live alone, to run my own household; and what if I fall ill? The other alternative, to enter an old-age home: I had not the slightest idea what the life in such an institution was like.

And we had to decide within a few days; I was going to be hospitalized in a few days and Robi could not extend his stay too long. Then, the second or third evening, among the consolatory guests, a lawyer friend of Judith mentioned that he arranged, a few days earlier, for a client to enter the best apartment-hotel for elderly people, the Mediterranean Towers. This was a twin, 12 storied, six-star hotel, with special equipment and arrangement for retired, elderly people. Next morning, we went there, in Bat-Yam, south of Tel Aviv, directly on the sea-shore, elegant, with big lobbies, dining rooms, a swimming pool, a series of play- and work-rooms, a mini market, coffee-house, balconies, etc, etc. One-, two-, and three-room apartments were available, with kitchenette, bath-room, balcony, health-clinic with 24 hours a day physician and nurses, etc. The price was accordingly very high, but it looked like a place where everything would be provided as needed for an aged single person.

We went away and feverishly inquired about other similar homes, but found that there were only very few of them, all occupied. We found out about three-four new such establishments under construction.

We spent the night evaluating my financial situation, using "engineering economy" principle, except one, a very decisive, aspect: what would happen when, beside the programmable incomes and outlays, some extraordinary, instant, payment would have to be made, e.g. the foreseeable eye-operation, or something like this. As a result: we decided my entering the Med. Towers, mainly because I was pessimistic and frightened to live alone, dealing with the daily chores of the household, domestic-maid, etc. It was a very difficult dilemma, beside all other aspects, because I knew in advance that irrespective which alternative I choose - I will feel later that the other choice would have been better.

On January, 10, 1990, I entered the hospital, and the morning of January, 12, I was operated on. Something went wrong - I never learned: what - but by the evening hours I lost consciousness and was operated on a second time, by the Professor-director of the department. For a few days I was in a quite bad condition, and improvement came slowly. Robi extended his stay and he was at my bedside all day long. In spite of this, he arranged everything for my moving in the Med Towers after my hospitalization: he ordered a writing desk with shelves, a separate book shelve; had transported in my temporary one-room apartment everything: clothes, kitchen-wares, TV- and music-apparatus, assorted books; in one word: everything necessary for me when I enter that temporary apartment. We bought a two-room apartment in the second Tower then under construction, and intended to move over furniture and all other things when I could enter the new building, sometime in the fall. I cannot comprehend to this day: how Robi did it; it was beyond all imaginable performance, conception of every one of need in my future unfamiliar life, quick and ingenious planning and performance, and many more similar features. I have been very-very proud of him.

On January, 29, I was released from the hospital, and entered the Med. Towers. Robi had to return home, after staying with me for a whole month. Improvement was slow and I had to go for further treatments several times; and my mood was at a low ebb, depressed. I had to undergo to another glaucoma operation in the other eye, which didn't contribute to my moral. Reading had to be reduced to a minimum; my main consolation was music, and daily walks on the beautiful, long sea-side promenade.

This year of 1990 was the most difficult one in my whole life; worse than the few burdensome years of my past. I had to wind up my apartment. This was the third time I had to abandon my home; the previous two times I was compelled to do so - and promptly; now I had a whole year to destroy, take apart, piece by piece, what had been gathered and assembled during thirty-three years, with much care and work. At the two previous occasions, we had hope for the future - now there was only aimlessness. To select and decide what to do with every single piece - was a task so horrendous that much stronger people than myself - and at my depressed state - would had done it with much difficulty. Paintings, books, photos, my publications, etc, etc. in one word: everything had its token of remembrance that I myself had to tear to bids. I went to my home many times during the year; a few times I just couldn't do anything and returned to the Towers empty-handed. Robi helped me when they were here on a visit. By year's end Robi came again to help to sell the apartment.

It was a very sad, sorrowful period; I don't know how I could endure it. I found consolation in the good news that Gil my favorite Grandson enrolled in the California State University at Fullerton and moved to his own separate house, together with two friends, near to the University. He succeeded in his studies and got his BA in May 1994.

On October 1, 1990, I moved in the new twin building. During the year I changed my mind and instead of the originally contracted two-room apartment: I took a one-room apartment, with shower and kitchenette. One corner is my bed-room; another my study: writing-desk and PC; the third: TV, video, and radio; and the fourth: my dining corner. I do not entertain guests, so I don't need more room. One wall is a window to the south, with a wide view to the sea-shore.

Our Mediterranean Towers apartment hotel is really adequate to a six-star hotel; but in addition, it provides a series of services needed for elderly and aged people, such as: twenty-four hours' medical service (nurses and physicians); psychiatric service; apartment cleaning; coffee-houses; restaurants; swimming-pool; daily lectures and entertainment; maintenance; etc, etc. Visitors are just delighted with everything - but living day-in day-out with approximately 360 people, at least 80 % of them women; many of them could hardly walk, some in wheelchairs; some senile or at early stages of Alzheimer's disease; eyes of many of them focused to infinity, etc, was very depressing indeed.

Robi came to visit me every year; a few times Gil came too. The two week periods of their visits have been the only happy times in my life since 1990. The intervals between successive visits have been smoothed over by expectation periods of the forthcoming visits, and remembrance periods of their completed visits. All along since my stay in the Towers, Robi calls me regularly once a week; these have been my best medicaments and remedy that has kept me alive.

In the meantime, cataracts had developed in both eyes that had to be removed by operation, at half year's interval.

Beginning of 1992, I was asked by my IAEC to do some special consultancy work: they would bring the problem and material to my place and take my written work, so that I wouldn't need to go to the office in Ramat Aviv. I accepted the offer; the subject was translating German safety regulations to English language, and evaluating and comparing its philosophy with the US regulations. It was not an easy task, but I enjoyed it. I completed this work in 1993: by the end of sixty years of my engineering career.

This occasion caused me to deliberate on my life and work during those sixty years, and gave me a strong stimulation to write this assortment of memories.

Sixty years of devoted creative engineering vocation represents a long series of mental endeavor, carried out always in the forefront of progress in engineering, covered the subjects from "descriptive geometry" up to "engineering economy" - the memories of which are a cherished treasure, but at the same time a quite heavy burden. Reliving my Past, by assorting and composing by importance, has given me a Present with meaning, and putting off the inevitable mysterious Future-End. I fear not the END, I am worried only about a state of disability. May God save me from incapacity and disability, and grant me a quiet, painless, and tranquil transition.

Questioning myself now: was it worth all the effort I made during the sixty years; did I contribute in the smallest measure above the average share; would I do it over again?

Answers to these questions by my professional self are definite "yes". But to the universal question, what was life generally good for: I, as one of all the many creatures of this Earth, would answer by quoting two lines of a great Hungarian poet, who allegorically asked what all this entire life is good for, and answered by the parable:

"Why does the grass grow when it withers off,
And why does it withers off when it grows anew?"
- - - - - - - - - -

August, 1 1995.

EPILOGUE - 2007

By Robi Baron

Though he was 86 when he finished the year of writing his memoirs', that was far from the end of his life (Picture 39). For he lived another decade in which there were also a few more "rainbows". At the retirement home he moved into, he was the focus of attention of the 100 or so lonely, single (mostly Hungarian speaking) women who outnumbered the men living there, 10 to 1. My Father had always been a very interesting, attractive and well dressed gentleman. With a lot of hair, and erect posture, he looked 10+ years younger than his actual age and remained an excellent conversationalist. He frequently volunteered to offer a public discussion on some musical history topic, his one and only favorite hobby, classical music.

When he met a wonderful lady, with a big smile on her gentle, pretty face, Anna Weiss Heller, things changed for the better. They became a couple for all practical purposes for the remaining 10 years of their lives (Picture 40). He did not have a chance to write about her, which is unfortunate. She was 4 months younger than him and they made a wonderful couple well into their 90s. In her youth Anna was a Rumanian National tennis champion, who became a dance and yoga teacher. Having lost her husband to the Nazis, she and her children were "bought" from the Nazis and rescued by Dr. Kestner on his famous (or infamous) train of Hungarian Jews and then sent to Israel at the end of the war. Having raised 2 daughters by herself in Israel, she was well known by 3 generations of Israelis who learned dance and movement in her modest Tel Aviv studio. As a coincidence, Fodor Evi (mentioned in the book as the teenager who was hidden in the family's bomb shelter during the war and acted as our first "hosts" in Israel was on the same Kestner train and also took lessons later from Anna in Israel). She continued her career well into her

Picture 40 – with Anna

eighties and only stopped when younger people felt she was taking away their livelihood. Anna was also a master at self-healing. I watched her more than once lie down on her bed after feeling that her heartbeat was racing and becoming irregular and watched in amazement as she "regulated" her heart rate back to normal in only minutes through intense breathing exercises and mind control.

During my Father's 80s and into his early 90s his health was excellent for the most part. Anna was also in excellent health until her last year of life, and passed away in November 2004, few months before my Father. At that time I was concerned that he will not survive long after losing his third life partner and in fact he passed away only 4 month later. He was completely lucid to his very last days and I am sure knew well what was happening. During his last 2 weeks here on earth, he was in and out of the hospital with respiratory problems. He only lost consciousness a few hours before his passing away in March 2005 just one month short of his 96th birthday. His "wish" was granted – he did not have to suffer from being incapacitated and passed away peacefully and without much pain. I had tickets to go visit him on my annual trip right around his birthday of April 8 and I missed seeing him alive for the last time. May he rest in peace…

The amazing facts about his mind are worth noting here. After his passing, Gil and I had the sad task of going through his belongings and deciding what to keep and what to give away. The only things we found written by him were related to the many technical project write-ups about his work in Israel. The most amazing part of the discovery was the fact that he never had a written diary during his entire life. He told me many times that he never wanted to rely on a piece of paper to tell him what to do and when to do it, as if he lost or could not keep the paper, he would not know what to do. This was a result of the many times in his life he had to escape with only the clothes on his back, those events conditioned him to commit everything important only to memory, so as not to lose it.

Whatever the cause was, I know his memory was exceptional for events, dates and details. Otherwise, how could he remember so well the dates, the names and other details about all that's written down in these memoirs, recalling events in details from his age 6 to 86. The way I noticed his aging can be illustrated by the way he would remember details most people completely forget. As an avid lover of classical music, he would frequent concerts and was proud of remembering the details afterwards. Whenever he would hear a favorite classical compositions, he would close his eyes and tell us about a live performance he attended together with my Mother decades earlier and tell us the name of the conductor and other details about the performance. Until his age 90 he could come up with those details in about 30 seconds, later the same information took him 5-10 minutes. During his last 2-3 years, he would complain that it may take him a day or two to come up with the same information. I told him that most people consider it absolutely amazing that he could recall those details at all.

Those of us who knew him personally were fortunate and deeply cherish those memories. Its also worthwhile to note that he wrote this book in the English language, which he only learned in his forties and outside the 3 years he spent in the United States on his Sabbatical, he never lived in an English speaking country. My hope is that these memoirs will enlighten the reader about how one can restart a life following drastic turns and misfortunes. May his spirit soar and his memory live forever.

I live on Cape Cod, Massachusetts getting ready to retire from a career in Information Systems. Gil, his only grandson (whom Alex always referred-to as his favorite grandson) lives in Los Angeles and is an animator in the movie and advertising industry. Gil is the only remaining carrier of his genes and I remind Gil from time-to-time that he has so many of Alex's characteristics, especially an intense focus on his work to the detriment of his personal life. I know it too well, as I had very little knowledge of my father prior to emigrating to Israel at age 13. He was always a good provider, but had little time for me while I was growing up. In his later years, he did say how much he regretted not spending more time with me and getting to know me better. But I did get to know him quite well as an adult and am personally blessed by his memoirs – for they show me the man that he was.

The irony of history was well stated by my favorite aunt, who frequently lamented in her later years that the 4 close-knit families who enjoyed each others company, took care of each other ended-up on four separate continents after 1956. Not only did the 4 siblings ever again had a chance to be together (only 2 at a time on a few occasions) before their passing, but my Mom never saw her brothers again. I know that I missed growing up together with my 4 cousins and I imagine my parents missed having the close supportive family near them for the rest of their lives.

Of the four remaining Laub cousins, I live in America, one cousin lives in Hungary and a brother and sister live in Australia. The four of us got together from the 3 corners of the globe for the 1st Laub family reunion in 50 years in 2006, on the 50th anniversary of the Hungarian Revolution. We are now planning to meet at least every 5 years as long as we can travel these great distances.

The irony of 20th Century European history is that wars not only destroy cities and alter borders of states, they significantly change families, even for the ones where none perish in the turmoil.